S0-CRD-504

LIVING CLASS IN
URBAN INDIA

LIVING CLASS IN URBAN INDIA

SARA DICKEY

RUTGERS UNIVERSITY PRESS

New Brunswick, New Jersey, and London

Library of Congress Cataloging-in-Publication Data

Names: Dickey, Sara, author.
Title: Living class in urban India / Sara Dickey.
Description: New Brunswick, New Jersey : Rutgers University Press, [2016] | Includes
  bibliographical references and index.
Identifiers: LCCN 2015041071 | ISBN 9780813583921 (hardcover : alk. paper) | ISBN
  9780813583914 (pbk. : alk. paper) ISBN 9780813583938 (ebook : epub) | ISBN 9780813583945
  (ebook : Web PDF)
Subjects: LCSH: Social classes—India—Madurai—Longitudinal studies. | Social
  stratification—India—Madurai—Longitudinal studies. | Madurai (India)—Social
  conditions. | Madurai (India)—Economic conditions.
Classification: LCC HN690.M325 D53   2016 | DDC 306.30954/82—dc23
LC record available at http://lccn.loc.gov/2015041071

A British Cataloging-in-Publication record for this book is available from the British
Library.

Copyright © 2016 by Sara Dickey
All rights reserved
No part of this book may be reproduced or utilized in any form or by any means, electronic
or mechanical, or by any information storage and retrieval system, without written
permission from the publisher. Please contact Rutgers University Press, 106 Somerset Street,
New Brunswick, NJ 08901. The only exception to this prohibition is "fair use" as defined by
U.S. copyright law.

Visit our website: http://rutgerspress.rutgers.edu

Manufactured in the United States of America

To three guides,
Freddy Bailey, N. R. Chendur, V. Natarajan,
and to my father, Ward E. Dickey, a model as well

Contents

Acknowledgments

In the early years of writing this book, I assumed that I would open these acknowledgments with a standard warning about the large number of people I needed to invoke from over the years of research. Instead, I begin with a story of lost research materials. As my sixteen-year-old son recently reminded me, I have been working on this project almost as long as he has been alive. It was meant to have been finished years earlier.

In 2001 I had the most remarkable, satisfying, and gratifying set of interviews I have ever taken part in, and the pleasure in them was echoed by other participants. (This is not how interviewers and interviewees always feel about the experience.) The interviews were meant to form the core of a book that would be built around four respondents and their families. (Three of those individuals remain in the "narrative portraits" of chapter 3.) After I finished the fieldwork, however, the recordings of ten of the Tamil-language interviews were lost.

The interviews were amazing. For the first time in over fifteen years of fieldwork, I worked with a research associate, a young and savvy man from the region, bilingual in Tamil and English, sardonic and insightful, and our questions and positions worked off each other beautifully. Because this was 2001, the interviews were recorded on cassette tapes rather than in digital files. Because of time pressures, I didn't take many notes about them, as I usually would have; I knew I had the taped recordings. (I do have reams of hand-written notes from the time, but mostly they are about doing intensive fieldwork with an unhappy two-year-old. They wrestle with strategies for keeping him content and healthy—neither of which I managed completely.) My associate was going to transcribe the interviews after we finished them; I would leave him with copies of the tapes. The day before I left Madurai, however, I went to make tape-to-tape recordings on the only machine I knew of, in a nearby office. The machine was broken. Given the illness of my son and the related stress of departure preparations, I did not think to do what I should have done: take the tapes to the United States, copy them there, and send the copies back. But neither did I have any prior reason to doubt the soundness of what I did do: give the tapes to my associate to copy, transcribe, and return to me with the transcriptions. The tapes never reappeared. I waited for years, by then having no luck in reaching my research associate; at some point I began hoping they would appear in a delayed post, and then finally I gave up. During the first years, I held off work on the book because the material in the interviews was central to it; and once I accepted that the tapes were gone, I could not face return-ing to the "empty" book. Other small projects filled the research gap in 2004 and 2005, and it was not until 2008 and 2009 that I finally returned to begin fieldwork devoted directly to this book.

I feel the disappearance of those tapes and the record of those inter-views as a corporeal loss. I also regret the loss of my relationship with the man to whom I entrusted them—and who may have tried to return them to me—who remains someone I respect a great deal. But the vigor and the energy and the excitement of the interviews haunts me even now. What does it mean to have this sense about a lost moment of fieldwork? Sometimes, I still dream that they will appear in a battered box, covered with stitched muslin and sealed with red wax.

On the other hand, "this" book has become whatever it has become in part because of those extra years. The text is stronger, given the proj-ect's focus on long-term change, for having covered a longer stretch of time. Both the Indian economy and my friends' and other informants' lives have changed in significant ways over these years, and this book now reflects those shifts and developments. The analysis has improved as well. In any case, I do now have many people and institutions to thank for their help.

This research has been generously funded by a National Endowment for the Humanities Research Fellowship, two American Institute of Indian Studies Senior Fellowships, and several Bowdoin College Leave Supplement and Faculty Research Awards. I am fortunate to live in a country, and work at an institution, where such funding is available.

Parts of Anjali's story in chapters 3 and 7 have appeared in Dickey (2010); chapter 4 is a revised and expanded version of Dickey (2013); and chapter 7 is a revised version of Dickey (2012). I thank *Modern Asian Studies* and *Contributions to Indian Sociology* for allowing me to use that material here.

I have been blessed to have had many readers for the manuscript. Those who have read and discussed portions of the chapters in various forms include E. Annamalai, Arjun Appadurai, Barney Bate, Frank Cody, Melanie Dean, Deb DeGraff, Assa Doron, Rajinder Dudrah, Punnie Edgerton, Joellen Fisherkeller, Celeste Goodridge, Robin Jeffrey, Jim Lindholm, Diane Mines, Lisa Mitchell, Costas Nakassis, Kalpana Ram, David Rudner, Tulasi Srinivas, Ravi Sriramachandran, Selvaraj Velayudham, and Amanda Weidman. Their suggestions and critiques have been invaluable in shaping this work. My most thorough and steadfast readers have been Susan Bell, Nancy Riley, and my mother, Fritz Dickey, and I am deeply grateful to them. My mother, who used to say she was not a reader, has read every word of the chapter drafts, and added perceptive comments and a fresh perspective. (She also encouraged me to finish.) Susan's and Nancy's stamps are all over this work. Two anonymous readers provided exceptionally thoughtful and helpful reviews, which have shaped the final manuscript in highly productive ways. I am also grateful to David Washbrook for a kind and generous reading of an early version of what is now the second half of chapter 2. And, ever since he served as a reader for my first book, Chris Fuller has complicated my understanding of the class–caste relationship in the most fruitful ways, and provided a model of scholarship to which I aspire.

I have also benefited greatly from being part of two writing workshops, a Travel Writing course taught by Susan Conley at the Telling Room in 2010, and a Stonecoast Writers' Conference workshop on memoir led by Ann Hood in 2014. While I attended both for work on other forms of writing, the feedback from leaders and participants alike has had a notable impact on the writing for this book. None of them are fans of discursive footnotes!

In India, I have had help from scholars and community activists that propelled me in my thinking and understanding. I am grateful for formative discussions with Dr. R. P. Nair of SCILET in American College, Dr. Venkatratnam of the Sociology Department at Madurai Kamaraj University, Belinda Bennett, Dr. Taj, and Dr. C. Rajeswari. I will always remember the delightful conversation in Koshy's in Bangalore with Dr. Anand Inbanathan, of the Institute for Social and Economic Change. J. Rajasekaran and Dr. V. A. Vidya have provided numerous forms of assistance with research in the field, and I am awed by their talents. A. Dinakar went above and beyond to help me at different times in different ways.

Many other people have assisted with the research in both India and the United States. V. Kirushnasamy, N. Prakash, and G. Sara transcribed Tamil-language interviews in the 1990s and 2000s. Elango, Arun Ram Kumar, V. Velraj, R. Revathi, R. Rohini, and V. A. Vidya have provided first translations of some interviews, or helped me untangle translation knots. Employees at the CMCentre in Madurai have also contributed these types of assistance. Sarah Brant, Lauren Weiss, and Sarah Wilke transcribed some of the English-language interviews from my 1991–1992 project on domestic workers, portions of which appear in this book. Christine Olmsted, of Before and After Photo, made prints and scans of old photos and slides on a moment's notice, one of which is now in the book thanks to her quick and beautiful work. My good friends Dharni

Vasudevan, Rachel Sturman, and Jayanthi Selinger have given invaluable support at key moments. Sudhakar Selwyn, whom I was lucky to meet in 2011, has taught me things about Madurai I would never have learned otherwise. He, his wife, Chrishanthi, and their children have been gracious hosts in Chennai. Danica Loucks, sleuth extraordinaire, was a wonder at the end of this process (she's always a wonder), helping with the fine details of formatting, bibliography, proofreading, and generally excellent advice. And I am deeply grateful to the library staff in numerous institutions who have helped to procure the many offsite sources I depend on. At Bowdoin, this includes especially Guy Saldanha and Jaime Jones, who are unfailingly resourceful and gracious.

For many wonderful conversations and a great deal of laughter over the years, I thank dear friends Kathleen Adams, Joellen Fisherkeller, Ernestine McHugh, and Carla Petievich.

I also wish to recognize the many teachers who have inspired me with their "aha!" ideas and pedagogical excellence over the years, most especially (and in chronological order) Steve Harrell, Val Daniel, John Atkins, V. Arokianathan, Carol Eastman, Freddy Bailey, Guenther Roth, and Michael Shapiro.

Thanks to Marlie Wasserman, who generously helped me understand publishing many years ago, and with whom I have been honored to work now.

All my life I will be grateful to those people in India who have taken in my families and me: starting in 1985, V. Natarajan and N. Gomati, and V. Arumukattay and M. Velu; in 1986, V. A. Vidya and J. Rajasekaran, and N. R. Chendur, Malathi Chendur, and Saradambal; in 1991, S. Thangam and G. Srinivasan; in 1999, Arun Rajaselvan and A. Nirmala, G. Gobi and G. Gandhimathi, Babu and Hasina, Premila Paul, and R. P. Nair and Shanta Nair; in 2004, Bhanumathy Vasudevan and A. S. Vasudevan; in 2009, Suneetha Saggurti. I have always been touched that my current family unit, a somewhat unlikely family in India—two middle-aged women and a boy—have been treated precisely as what we are: family. While there are "rules" about what normative families look like in South India, many people don't live in one, and the standards for constituting real families are ultimately based on mutual responsibilities rather than necessarily on fitting those rules. The ways that people "really" behave, often contrary to social rules, are also a theme in this book.

My American family—parents, siblings, spouse, son, and all the affines—have been exceptional in their support of this research, and some of them have been present during my fieldwork as well. In September and October 1999, my parents spent a memorable month in Madurai, Chennai, and Bangalore with my infant son and me (their second visit during a fieldwork trip), helping us to settle and begin this project. The following March, my sister Stephanie and my mother came to help me prepare to leave, and then traveled partway home with us. My mother returned in 2008 to attend the marriage of my friend Anjali's brother (my parents too have known Anjali since her childhood). Stephanie helped solve technical problems with photographs, Matthew visited once many years ago and has returned on his own, and I look forward to Jennifer and Susan joining us in Madurai someday. All have read parts of these chapters, willingly. And my parents-in-law Honour and Starr Edgerton were the best. I am blessed.

Punnie and Daniel. What can I say? You have supported, endured, applauded, and suffered the course of this project. You have kept me rooted and made me laugh, often uproariously. In immense and immeasurable ways, you have made this work possible. I am so grateful for all my family.

Notes on Transliteration
and Pronunciation

For Tamil words, I use a somewhat simplified transliteration system sufficient to indicate the pronunciation of words, and thus the terms themselves (since no Tamil homonyms are used), for those familiar with Tamil diacritics in roman script. (I do not use diacritics to differentiate Tamil letters with identical or near-identical sounds.) Other readers may wish to use the pronunciation guide below.

For Hindi/Sanskrit words, I use standard transliterated spellings in English literature, usually without diacritics (such as *bhakti, darshan*) except for those words that are central to a portion of the analysis and therefore appear frequently (for example, *dān*).

For names of places, castes, deities, and people, I avoid diacritics and use one of the standard transliterations likely to be readily pronounce-able for readers unfamiliar with Tamil, Hindi, or Sanskrit.

For readers unfamiliar with Tamil transliteration conventions, I offer this informal pronunciation guide to the letters that appear in Tamil words in this text.

Vowels:

a ("uh")
ā ("ah")
e ("eh")
ē ("ey" as in hey)
i ("i" as in bin)
ī ("ee")
o ("o" as in or)
ō ("oh")
u ("oo" as in book)
ū ("oo" as in toot)
ai ("ai" as in aisle)

Consonants:

Several consonants have both retroflex (back-of-the-palate) and dental (front-of-the-palate) forms. These consonants are in the dental form if they are unmarked (i.e., if they have no diacritic), and in the retroflex form if marked with a period-like diacritic underneath the letter (ḷ, ṇ, ṭ).

In addition, many consonants are pronounced differently depending on whether they occur at the beginning of a word, are doubled in the middle of a word, or occur singly in the middle of a word. "K," for example, is pronounced in a way familiar to English readers if it appears at the beginning or if it is doubled ("kk") in the middle of the word. If it appears as a single consonant in the middle, however, it is pronounced "g" or "h." (In phonological terms, these are unvoiced vs. voiced consonants.) Consonants that follow this rule are pronounced as below, with the initial or double consonant sound listed first and the single mid-word consonant sound listed second.

k ("k" / "g" or "h")
p ("p" / "b")
t ("t" / "th" as in the)
ṭ ("ṭ" / "ḍ")

Other consonants:

c is pronounced "s" or "ch" when it falls at the beginning of a word
   or is doubled, "s" when surrounded by vowels, and "j" following n
   (i.e., nc = "nj")
ḷ is pronounced either like the retroflex ḷ, or a back-of-the-mouth
   "standard" English r, or somewhere in between, depending on the
   speaker
ṅ ("ng" as in sing)
ṣ ("sh" as in wash)

Finally, certain consonants (d, j, s) indicate a "loan word" borrowed from another Indian language, and are pronounced in a way familiar to English speakers.

LIVING CLASS IN URBAN INDIA

1 Introduction

Our lives are shaped by class structures, but we live those classes as a daily process. How do these processes play out in urban India? What does it feel like to live in a class, to aspire to one, or to fear falling from one? And what immediate and long-term differences do these everyday experiences make? In this book I aim to make the lives and views of people in different class positions understandable, while exploring how class relations themselves produce inequality. To begin this exploration, I open with a conversation I had with a friend in 2011, a conversation that later drew me to reflect on my three decades of studying class in South India.

Early in 2011, I was visiting my friend Lakshmi in Hosur, a city hundreds of miles from where we had first met twenty-five years earlier. She had moved from her home in the South Indian city of Madurai when her husband found a job as a lathe operator in one of Hosur's many factories. Later Lakshmi herself had become a forewoman in a tire factory. I hadn't seen her for two years—before that, it had been over a decade—and this was my first chance ever to spend more than a single day in her small home.

We stayed up late that first evening, talking as we tried to keep ourselves awake for a 2:00 A.M. firewalking ritual at the nearby temple. The temple's main deity, Karumariamman, is a fierce mother goddess. Decades earlier, Lakshmi and I had often visited the large temple to Meenakshi at the center of Madurai, but Meenakshi is a somewhat gentler goddess, and I had never attended a festival for a deity as ferocious as Karumariamman. Lakshmi's sons were going to walk the fire that night. Lakshmi herself had walked it for the three previous years, always carrying out a month of austerities beforehand. These austerities allowed Lakshmi to become possessed by the powerful goddess and then cross the embers safely in a show of her devotion. But recently, the caretaker at the temple—a Brahman woman like Lakshmi, and a mentor of sorts— had cautioned her that possession was unsuitable for high-caste people, who typically value controlled and moderate behavior. To let a deity inhabit her body meant she was temporarily not in control of herself. So Lakshmi, chastened, reluctantly gave up the ritual, but she still permitted her two teenage sons to walk the fire. While she and I chatted in the bedroom that night, the boys rested on the floor next to their father in the front room. I lay on a cot on the household's only mattress while Lakshmi lay next to it on the bare floor. Like her sons, Lakshmi had carried out the month's austerities to demonstrate her continuing devotion, and mats and mattresses were two of the things that Karumariamman required her to avoid (other taboos included pillows, shoes, and heavy meals).

As we talked, Lakshmi began reminiscing about the first time we met. We both remembered it vividly—but from different angles. Lakshmi recalled that, when she was fifteen years old and I, then twenty-five, had just moved into her neighborhood, she began to see me walk down the street every day to buy a newspaper and carry it home. No one else on the crowded lane did that; the newspapers people read were the ones kept in tea stalls, so my newspaper purchases stood out. And then one day, after she and her neighbors had observed me making this daily roundtrip for some time, I stopped and asked if I could take a photo of the *kōlam* that decorated their threshold.

This is where my memory of that day kicks in. I had moved into the neighborhood two weeks earlier. New to Madurai, still tentative about

Photo 1. Walking down the lane, possibly holding a newspaper, 1986. Photo credit: Ted Adams.

my Tamil language skills, I was too shy to speak to the people who watched me as I walked down the crowded lane (apparently, though I don't recall it this way, to buy a newspaper). Children would run up and ask my name, but the adults at most would smile briefly as they continued what they were doing—pumping water, heading out with a stainless steel container to buy fresh milk, squatting over a butane stove to prepare snacks for sale, or returning from the market with a cloth bag full of vegetables. I had finally worked up my nerve to broach this distance, deciding to ask to photograph the beautifully colored kōlams in front of people's homes. Kōlams are the daily work of women, created morning and evening by sprinkling rice powder in geometric and figural designs on the threshold between house and street. It was then December, during the Tamil month of Margali, when kōlam patterns are especially elaborate. Some of the most complex designs on that street were put down in front of Lakshmi's housing compound. That evening, Lakshmi was combing her hair outside the low thatched-roof entryway, standing with her neighbors Anjali and Kumar, two children who were still in their school uniform skirt and shorts. A couple of women clustered around the pump near the door, waiting for the evening flow of drinking water. Camera in hand, I approached the group and asked if I could take a picture of their kōlam. The younger children burst into grins, grabbed everyone within arm's reach, and crowded behind the kōlam. "Yes!" they chorused. I took several photos, and then Anjali and Kumar's mother— who had heard the commotion through her window—invited me into her home.

At last I was in. The five one-room homes in that compound became the center of my gradually expanding social networks in Madurai, and they have provided some of the most abiding relationships of my life. This was my "arrival story," that moment dear to the heart of many culture-crossing anthropologists. But though I had in a sense "arrived" on that day, my interpretations of what I saw there would take years to develop. And even as my knowledge grew, class identities and categories in Madurai would be in flux as well.

I had chosen to live in this neighborhood in 1985 because I thought its residents were poor and working class. I had come to Madurai to study what made Tamil movies so popular among the poorer residents of the city, and I "knew" that such people were the main audiences for commercial films because of what I had read in graduate school. After a month of staying in a guest room and exploring the city, I had selected this neighborhood to begin my research in. It was in the bustling center of the city, equally convenient to the large Meenakshi Temple and the City Bus Stand; and, crucially, the landlord of a three-story building on the street was willing to rent an apartment to a foreigner. And what made me think that most residents were poor or working class? I used signs from everyday life that seemed obvious to me: housing, clothing, and other material goods that are visible in public. These physical goods are only part of class, but they seemed sufficient indicators at the time. And to some extent they were, if only I had known how to read them properly.

What I saw when I entered those first homes on that day appeared to support my interpretation of these families' class standings. Anjali and Kumar's father was a bicycle rickshaw driver. He had already gone back to work that evening, but his wife was home and their seven children were all back from school. Inside, the narrow room was dark, with just one window overlooking the street. The family's only solid furniture comprised a narrow metal bureau and one folding chair, and I was made to sit in the chair. Neighbors crowded in. Rapid-fire questions began in Tamil: "What's your name?" "Do you have children?" "You eat only bread, right? No rice?" "How much is your rent?" Looking around, I could see how sparse this family's belongings were. Clothes were strung over lines of rope, a few pots were stacked in the corner next to a wood-burning cooking pit, combs and talcum powder stood on a shelf with a tiny mirror, and lithographs of Hindu deities hung on the walls. I saw several upended reed mats that I knew would be unrolled at night when everyone slept side by side on the floor.

After I and a few of the adult neighbors—but no one in the family—drank coffee in Anjali and Kumar's home, the children escorted me to the other houses in the compound. All were thatched one-room dwellings. The back wall of Anjali and Kumar's home formed part of the next one-room house, where a temple priest and his wife and their two daughters lived. From there, the compound opened onto a blindingly bright court-yard. Arrayed around the courtyard were three more homes and a separate bathing area and latrine. Lakshmi's was the third house on my introductory circuit. Lakshmi's father, an accountant who had recently lost his job when the company failed, was at home, as were her mother and four younger siblings. Her father was courteous and reserved, pulling on a white shirt over his undershirt and *veshti* as I came in. (A veshti is a man's unstitched lower garment that wraps around the waist and hangs to the ankles.) Her mother, whose bright nylon sari caught my eye, was warmly enthusiastic, inviting me to eat though it meant sending a child out to buy Britannia biscuits. Small images of their favorite deities were kept in a shrine area on the far wall, but otherwise the house was even more sparsely furnished than the others.

I thought these families were poor. They had homes just large enough to provide space for everyone to sleep on the floor, and they all shared a common latrine, used cheap cooking fuel, wore inexpensive clothing, and owned few other material goods. Although I already knew that these families were not by any means among the poorest residents of Madurai, my own understanding of material class markers—which were mostly shaped by my enculturation in the United States—suggested poverty, or nearly so. Later, though, when I learned more about these family members' occupations and educations and tastes and attitudes, I came to think of them as working class (in Anjali and Kumar's case) or even lower middle class (in Lakshmi's)—still, however, in the terms I had grown up with.

And as my increasing understanding of Madurai's class indicators led me to recognize that these families were not poor by their own standards, I also learned that the categories of "working class" and "middle class" were foreign to most people in Madurai at the time. Soon my assessments were also informed by a growing understanding of *local* ways of distinguishing class. The people in that compound, like almost everyone else in the neighborhood, called themselves *illātavaṅka*, "people who don't have," and in everyday conversation—whether talking about politics, movies, or vegetables—they frequently contrasted themselves with *periyavaṅka* and *paṇakkāraṅka*, "big people" and "moneyed people." Such terms formed part of the idiom of daily talk, and they reflected the dichotomous class terms with which most people thought about their society as well as their everyday lives. There were people who have and people who don't, with no middle ground.

Over time, these categories would change as the structure of the regional and national economies changed. In 1985, though I was only vaguely aware of it then, India's economy was slowly becoming "liberalized," moving from a planned economy to a more market-oriented one. That process—which eventually, among its many other impacts, opened the economy to imported goods and enabled local manufacturers to produce a wider variety of consumer goods as well—was formally instituted in 1991. The social and economic changes that liberalization has wrought have complicated Madurai residents' ideas about class. Whereas, for example, almost no one on the lane thought in terms of a "middle class" in 1985, within a decade or so the middle class would become a widely recognized category in Madurai, and an increasingly important one for everyone from policy-makers, manufacturers, and retailers to filmmakers. This new middle class was defined in many ways, including by education, occupation, and increasingly English-language ability, but perhaps most visibly by the use of consumer goods. It was also defined behaviorally, using the language of moderation, control, and self-discipline that was once primarily associated with caste differences but now has become adopted for class markers.

When I visited Lakshmi in 2011, having watched and documented these changing class identities from 1985 on, I would certainly have identified Lakshmi and her husband as middle class by the local criteria of the time. They and their two children now lived in a three-room home furnished with a metal cot, television, gas stove, and a bureau filled with clothing. Their older son, a high school graduate, was working nearby in Bangalore's Electronic City, and their younger son was studying for his electrical and electronic engineering degree. Thus I was mildly surprised to hear Lakshmi still refer to her *contemporary* family as "people who don't have," illātavaṅka, even as she was clearly proud of their movement into the middle class. There was no sense of contradiction for her in holding these two identities. It made me more conscious of something I had been sensing: that people could see themselves as "being without" (relative to people with more wealth, more goods, and more power) while also seeing themselves as "middle people," naṭuttaramānavaṅka (because of certain objective indicators that they possessed).

I was also surprised to hear Lakshmi say, as we talked about the old days, that her family had been "poor" (ēḷai) back when I first met them. I had long ago moved from viewing her family of origin as poor to seeing them as lower middle class. What she told me now was that "in those days we were hungry." What I had initially taken as signs of poverty were not so; but I had missed something that *was* a local sign of poverty. Even though Lakshmi did not remember the Britannia biscuits as I did, I had recognized the material cost of their hospitality in those days, yet still I hadn't realized that her family had too little to eat. Class identities are performed, continually, by individuals, and despite their hunger, Lakshmi's family was working hard to perform as not-poor people. In this they were aided by their high caste status, which provided them a familiarity with behaviors such as controlled comportment (like the type that would be enjoined on Lakshmi by the temple caretaker in Hosur years later) that had moved from being caste-related to class-related behaviors.

Lakshmi's family did not stay poor. Those same signs that I eventually recognized as middle-class indicators (primarily education) enabled the family to prosper and move out of poverty. Here is part of that story. When I left Madurai in 1987 after my first fieldwork stay, I gave Lakshmi's parents all the money I had remaining. It was a way of recognizing their expansive hospitality, and of marking our responsibility to each other. The sum, two thousand rupees, was roughly what her father's annual income would have been when he was employed. Her parents invested the money—though, as I describe in chapter 7, in a different way than I might have anticipated—and their investment yielded a new job for Lakshmi's father as the manager of a small bus company. His higher income eventually allowed them to move to a larger home in another neighborhood, buy consumer goods such as a bedframe and some chairs, and save up a bit of gold for their second daughter's wedding. On the other hand, their neighbors, Anjali's parents, stayed in their home until their deaths two decades later, with few more material goods than they had had in 1985. Anjali's parents did, however, educate all seven children through high school, a rare accomplishment on a rickshaw driver's income, and Anjali herself went to college, built a business around technologies and expertise that were enabled by a liberalized economy, and married into a solidly middle-class family.

In sum, Lakshmi's and my stories of my arrival and of her life since that day illustrate both how my relationships to people and my understandings of meaning-making in their lives have changed, and how the changing economic environment they live and labor in has shifted the terms within which those meanings are made. These are stories of encounters, returns, reflection, and social change. João Biehl has written that long-term ethnography "open[s] a critical space for examining *what happens in the meantime*" (2009, 17–18; emphasis in original). I understand this idea in a number of ways. This ethnography engages what has happened in friends' and informants' lives over the past two to three decades. It tracks the changes and developments reflected in what I learned in each stay and have continued to learn after I leave, as well as in informants' retrospective accounts over these years. Through such nodes over time I work to make everyday experience visible in a period in which extensive changes have occurred in the economy and in the lives of the people I write about. Marriage preferences, kinship obligations, consumption and debt practices, class and caste identities, and philanthropy are only some of the changing aspects of those lives that I discuss in the chapters that follow. This work reveals the interactions of material and ideational aspects of class relations in order to focus on the experiences of class in everyday life and their long-term impacts.

The research specifically for this book took place over a combined total of two years of fieldwork during seven stays between 1999 and 2015. That research was itself preceded by several earlier periods of fieldwork, including fifteen months in 1985–1987 (when I first met Lakshmi), two briefer visits in 1989 and 1990, and one year in 1991–1992. It is based primarily on interviews, conversations, and observations, as well as on research in newspaper archives and with statistical data. Over my years in Madurai, I have aimed to interview people across lines of caste, class, gender, religion, occupation, educational attainment, rural and urban origins, and age. Much of this work has been carried out with people I have known for twenty to thirty years, and over this time I have had the chance to watch their lives change—and for us to come to know each other differently as my life has changed as well.

The Setting: Place and Imagining

I move now to the place and period that form the context for this long-term ethnography. Madurai has been the setting for most of my fieldwork since 1985, and the research for this book has taken place in the time after economic liberalization was instituted in 1991.

Madurai and the Imaginings of Modernity

Madurai is a vibrant city, one of the oldest inhabited cities of India and now a commercial and religious center of over a million residents. Most of the city's population is Hindu, but many Christians and Muslims live in the city as well. Most residents speak Tamil as their first language.

The central area where I first lived is a mix of residential, commercial, educational, and ritual spaces. Houses are densely packed, separated by a maze of narrow lanes. In 1985, walking within two blocks of the lane I first lived on, I would have traveled past two mosques, a Catholic church, small shrines to Murugan and Ganesh, tea stalls and small restaurants serving vegetarian and nonvegetarian food, sweets shops, numerous hotels, schools, shaded vegetable markets in narrow lanes, and a long band of small gold and silver stores. Two blocks further in various directions would have taken me to several temples, a Protestant church, a taxi stand, the main bus and rail stations, and a variety of book, clothing, and vehicle parts stores. In those days, I would likely have been passed by bicycles and bicycle rickshaws, hand-pulled or bullock-led carts, city buses, and possibly an autorickshaw or motorbike, but no cars except for the occasional police vehicle or taxi. Thirty years later, all those vehicles compete for road space with a high volume of automobiles, motorcycles, and scooters, and the creation of parking space has become a major preoccupation. Today the main crossroads near Lakshmi and Anjali's lane hold massive glitzy jewelry stores and high-end clothing shops, and a few years ago the compound in which they grew up was replaced by solid two-story middle-class homes.

Indeed, most of the downtown housing appears to be occupied by middle-class people today. The poorest neighborhoods are outside of the city center. Often the poor must shift their residences as their homes are deemed "encroachments" and razed by city officials, or as "empty" government land (purampōkku, on which people are by custom allowed to build) is claimed for government projects or sold to private developers. While some wealthy residents lived, and still live, in the crowded downtown area, the city's most luxurious residences are also located far from the center. Increasingly they are built on the outskirts as agricultural land is taken over by housing developments and small industrial or IT parks. Where I used to pass Saurashtrian weavers' backstrap looms in the dirt streets at the very edge of town (as I walked from the end of the bus route to my lessons with an esteemed Tamil professor), there is now a major arterial. The area has become an upper-middle-class subdivision, and today is flanked by many more subdivisions, extending far out into what had been scrubland and agricultural fields.

The plan of the ancient city is still visible in the downtown area, where four concentric roads encircle the large temple complex of the Hindu goddess Meenakshi. Legal limits on building height have meant that the central commercial area remains dominated by the temple's tall towers. The Meenakshi Temple provides a destination for many pilgrims and tourists from India and abroad. Goods and services provided to temple visitors comprise a significant portion of Madurai's economy (Dutt, Noble, and Hasan 1994, 100), making the Meenakshi Temple—like all major temples—an economic as well as a religious center. Madurai also serves as a market center for the surrounding agricultural region and for other trade, and as the administrative center for the district. Its hand-loomed silk and cotton textiles have been renowned for centuries (Roy 1997), and now textile mills—first built in the 1890s (Baker 1984, 339)—and small vehicle manufacturing provide light industry as well. Granite, rubber, and chemical plants are situated in or near the city. Madurai lacks, however, the heavy industry found in other South Indian cities such as Coimbatore or Tiruppur. Nor has it so far developed much of an infrastructure for the major information technology firms found in Bangalore, Hyderabad, and Chennai, though Special Economic Zones are being developed for this purpose. It is generally seen as more conservative and less modern than these other cities, whose urban infrastructures, job opportunities, entertainment, fashions, and diverse populations make them more cosmopolitan and sophisticated.

As A. R. Venkatachalapathy recounts, this contrast between the venerable and the modern has a long history:

> The ancient Tamil classics, the Sangam literature, paint dazzling pictures of Madurai. Many towns, through the ages, have vied with Madurai for pride of place as the Tamils' city, with varying degrees of un-success, and now lie in the byways of historical cartography.
>
> Not until the genesis of Chennai, in the mid-seventeenth century, was Madurai's pre-eminence challenged. Chennai was an entirely new kind of city—quite unlike the ceremonial, unitary city that was

Madurai—a colonial city, a presidency town, the centripetal vortex of a colonial political economy. By the nineteenth century, Chennai became the real *pattinam*, the City, for the Tamil people. (2006, 59)

The modern contrast to Madurai is still represented by Chennai, and now, in local imaginations, by Coimbatore and Bangalore as well.

In India Madurai is deemed a "Second Tier" (or Tier II) city, a government classification based on population, but equally a tag that reflects the view of such cities in the national imaginary. While Madurai retains its (increasingly less celebrated) pride of place as the center of Tamil culture and language, the great majority of the residents I know see it as distinctly not-modern. Outsiders frequently refer to this city of over a million people as a "town"—or even, "like a village." Still, Madurai's residents view their city as more "advanced" than its surrounding villages, and I expect that most (but not all) residents would like to be viewed as modern people. As we will see, the city's location on local scales of modernity helps to shape the operative signs of class distinction used there.

Thus, as in many places, in India "the modernity-tradition distinction" has "marked certain cities and urban cultures as outside the realm of the modern (and the urban)" (Robinson 2006, 9). But despite the sidelining that appears to marginalize this city away from metropolitan "centers," it is also like all other cities everywhere—it is, to use Jennifer Robinson's (2006) term, an "ordinary city," one that can teach us a good deal about the political economy of cities worldwide.

Economic Liberalization

For the first four decades following Independence in 1947, India's economy was driven by state planning aimed at economic development and the reduction of rural poverty. The urban middle class remained "relatively invisible" in official rhetoric and visual images until the 1980s (Fernandes 2000a, 613), when the political heirs of Jawaharlal Nehru, first prime minister, began to advocate new images of modernity and to shift the economy toward the interests of the middle class. In the early 1980s, Nehru's daughter Indira Gandhi (who served as prime minister 1966–1977 and 1980–1984) moved tentatively toward deregulation by removing some constraints on private industry and foreign investment. Her son Rajiv Gandhi, who followed her as prime minister in 1984, began loosening import restrictions and further reducing state control of manufacturing and industry. As Leela Fernandes notes, "if the tenets of Nehruvian development could be captured by symbols of dams and mass based factories, the markers of [Rajiv] Gandhi's India shifted to the possibility of commodities that would tap into the tastes and consumption practices of the urban middle classes" (2000a, 614; see also Lukose 2009, 8).

These reforms were broadened and accelerated in 1991, when the coalition government of P. V. Narasimha Rao came into power. Faced with an imminent economic crisis brought on by massive internal debt, significant inflation, and an immediate shortfall of foreign exchange reserves (see, e.g., Joshi and Little 1996, 14–15), Prime Minister Narasimha Rao and Finance Minister Manmohan Singh launched an economic stabilization and structural adjustment program paired with extensive deregulation and liberalization of the economy. Loosened import restrictions allowed a wider range of consumer goods to circulate, and changes in banking policies made loans and thus durable capital investments far more available to middle-class people. Opening the economy to foreign investment and foreign corporations also created new types of private-sector employment in India, including prestigious managerial and information technology positions as well as lower-level service positions. Public-sector salaries have grown substantially since the mid-1990s, while personal income tax rates have been reduced. Simultaneously, income disparity has grown between the rich and the poor (see, e.g., Motiram and Sarma 2011; Pal and Ghosh 2007).

Class Relations and Resources

Lakshmi's recounting reveals a deep consciousness of class and its performance. It encourages us to consider the many ways in which class shapes both everyday lives and long-term life chances in southern India. Class conditions, for example, the dignity and respect that people claim and are accorded in their extended families, neighborhoods, schools, and jobs, and on the streets; the material ease with which they move through the city, the spaces they are allowed to enter, the physical comfort of their homes, and the frequency with which they eat; their health and the care they can access; the status-producing value of the knowledge and goods they can acquire and the rituals they perform; the occupations they help their children prepare to take on; and the marriage alliances they negotiate for those children. While class is not the only determinant of opportunities or influence, it is a highly significant one. Class indeed "determines what people must do, what they have the freedom to do, what they cannot do. It structures the realm of choice. . . . Defining that choice matrix reveals a structure of freedoms, capacities, and compulsions: i.e., the class structure" (Herring and Agarwala 2006, 325).

A person's place within this "structure" is dynamic rather than static, however. Similarly, there is little stasis in the daily living of class. Class is produced and reproduced every day. Sherry Ortner writes that "we may think of class as something people are or have or possess, or as a place in which people find themselves or are assigned, but we may also think of it as a project, as something that is always being made or kept or defended, feared or desired" (2003, 13–14).[1] In addition, E. P. Thompson cautioned decades ago that "we must remember that class is a relationship, and not a thing" (1963, 11). Thus I take class to be not only a determining structure but also a process that produces and is generated in the *interactions* of individuals' and groups' resources, as well as through the *relationships* themselves. As Ronald Herring and Rina Agarwala also note, "at the micro level, where all of us live, are the day-to-day practices through which classes define and reproduce themselves" (2006, 347). Or, phrased from a slightly different perspective, it is the daily interactions of individuals that buttress (or change) the categories that underlie and legitimate class relations.

In the following chapter I will return to culturally specific ideas about class; for the remainder of this one, I discuss analytical concepts that apply across societies. To set up an understanding of how class distinctions are created and carried out, I introduce ideas about the resources of class. Furthermore, because my work focuses on how people create class distinctions relationally, and why both the distinctions and the relationships matter, I focus on the immaterial as well as the material aspects of class, since everyday well-being and long-term life chances are both critical to understanding the power of class in Madurai.

A Relational Approach to Class

I approach class analytically by focusing on the class identities and relations that people establish with each other as individuals and as groups, drawing on local cultural categories and rooted in local economic institutions, while keeping always in mind the forces and institutions of transnational capitalism within which these processes take place. Specific class systems, in other words, are continuously produced through the interactions of individuals and groups. Those interactions—which take place face-to-face, through discourse, and through the agencies of political and legal structures—are highly informed by preexisting assumptions (or, knowledge) about categories of people. These local class categories possess their own distributive logic (logic, that is, about who possesses and deserves access to which resources, how much access, how many of the resources, and which resources are most valued). The idea that certain people "deserve" more or fewer resources than others is important; the class categories current in Madurai, which I discuss in the next chapter, are imbued with moral qualities. This makes them highly effective in producing inequality because they rationalize how different types of people live and are treated (cf. Harriss 2009; Mosse 2010, 1156–1157; also see Donner and De Neve 2011, 6, 8). It also means that the occasional broadening or dissolution of categories can be a powerful act.

I arrived at what has recently been termed a relational approach to class for two reasons. The first is the decided emphasis that Madurai residents place on class relations when commenting on their world. When I began my first fieldwork on Tamil film watching and politics in Madurai in 1985, I became interested in class (rather than the forms of identity I had expected to be most important) precisely by having neighbors, film-watching companions, fan club members, and movie directors refocus my attention. When my neighbors spoke of "people like us," they almost always meant illātavaṅka rather than people with shared religious or caste identities or party affiliation. When filmmakers divided their audiences into categories, it was usually "mass" versus "class" (using a different meaning of class than I do here).

The second reason I am drawn to a relational approach is my observations over the years of the powerful role that class relations themselves play in the creation and continuation of inequality. This role is all the more significant for being largely unrecognized or at least unarticulated. Rather than simply viewing class relations as determined by inequity, I focus on the ways in which class relations—and the moralized categories on which they are based—make possible a system of inequality.

The ranked categorization of people is fundamental to any system of inequality.[2] Charles Tilly's work, which has been foundational in the relational approach to inequality in anthropology, helps to explain why. Tilly argues, "In a relational view, inequality emerges from asymmetrical social interactions in which advantages accumulate on one side or the other, fortified by construction of social categories that justify and sustain unequal advantage. . . . Categories, in such a view, do not consist of mental constructs, but of socially negotiated boundaries and changing relations across those boundaries. Most large-scale systems of inequality involve incompletely connected, inconsistent, contested, changing, yet powerful differences among clusters and categories of persons" (2001, 362–363). Boundaries mark inclusion and exclusion, belonging and not-belonging, and the categories they distinguish play a large role in determining individuals' and groups' access to class resources. Inequities in access to resources and in treatment are often justified (or contested) in moral terms. Ultimately, this process rationalizes and naturalizes inequality.

(One corollary of the relational approach, to my mind, is that class is to some extent culturally specific, because categories, their boundaries, their defining distinctions, and their moral valuation are culturally specific. It is not simply that class groupings are defined differently, but that entry into them is somewhat differently determined.)

Anthropologists using a relational approach to class have focused largely on poverty.[3] In South Asia, for example, Maia Green has argued forcefully that "poverty is a social relation, not an absolute condition" (2006, 1115). David Mosse, who has been at the forefront of developing Tilly's ideas, argues for a "'relational' approach to poverty" that "rejects the individualism of neo-liberal rational choice models by emphasizing the effect of social categorization and identity in reproducing inequality and making exploitation socially viable" (2010, 1157). He points out that we cannot understand any one element of the system (for him, poverty), without comprehending those other elements to which it stands in relation (in his case, wealth), since "the existence and working of the one can only ever be understood by tracing its connection to the other" (Mosse 2010, 1159).

I expand this approach to examine the relational production of multiple class positions. The insights of the relational approach to poverty apply equally to people of all classes. If it is the case that "people are poor because of others" (Wood 2003, 456), it is equally arguable that the middle class and the wealthy are what they are because of the poor (and because of each other as well as themselves, to whatever fine gradations we wish to pursue this). Everyone creates class, participating in a system of categorical inequality that advantages some and disadvantages others. To understand the full workings of class at the local level, we require the perspectives of people from many vantage points in that system.

This study, then, is unusual in its analysis of the perspectives of social actors from across the class spectrum. As I explore the sources and force of class inequality in my work, I strive to make people in all class positions—those most advantaged and those most disadvantaged, friends and brief acquaintances alike—understandable on their own terms. For me, the most acute challenge in representing a system holistically has been recognizing and representing inequality without demonizing the perspectives of those with power and privilege.

I have chosen to present each person's point of view on its own terms for two reasons. First, I argue that we cannot grasp the roots of unequal social relations without understanding the attitudes, assumptions, beliefs, and ideologies that motivate them. Second, I believe I owe each informant who willingly shares her story or his views—which are necessarily positioned, as all of ours are—the same respect and recognition in my presentation of those views. I wrestle with this decision at times, particularly when I interview informants whose actions

I judge by my own morals to be unethical, and I am certain that my ethics sometimes color my portrayals despite my general intention to avoid this. But ultimately, I land on the side of equal consideration as a moral choice, at least within the limits of the kinds of narratives I have been told over the years. (Which is to say, I have never learned anything about an informant through an interview that was so morally, ethically, or legally egregious that it tested my limits for non-judgmental representation. For a considered argument about the value of conversing with and representing sympathetically those whose ethics and politics diverge from the anthropologist's, see Ginsburg 1993.) The overall gist of my analysis nonetheless demonstrates the differences in privilege and power accorded to and claimed by differently positioned individuals and groups.

In sum, to grasp any part of the class system fully, we must possess a balanced picture of the whole. Such pictures have been rare in the anthropological and sociological literature,[4] but they reveal a great deal about the workings of the systems we interrogate.

The Importance of the Subjective, Immaterial, and Intangible in Studying Class

Reckoning the impact of such social relations means, for me, focusing less on the material and objective aspects of class that are more typical in studies of class (and in commonsense Western understandings of it), and more on the subjective experience of class and its intangible effects. Before proceeding, my own definitions of these terms are in order. By "material" we usually mean goods that are visible and tangible, and economic resources that might not be precisely so (such as bank funds) but that can be used to acquire those goods. I include these goods, as well as some bodily practices, in my meaning of the material. "Objective" in my use refers to those attributes and impacts of class that can be empirically observed and/or measured—such as housing, types of food and calories consumed, health outcomes, savings, and education.

My work in Madurai has led me instead to foreground the *subjective*, *immaterial*, and *intangible* aspects of class, with an eye to what these mean for (a) the experience of everyday life, and (b) the long-term production and consequences of class inequality. By "subjective" I mean the ways that people experience and perceive class, and the emotions that class life engenders. By "intangible" or "immaterial" I mean those things that shape, contribute to, or represent class but are not material goods (including interactions, discourses, and intangible resources). Thus while these categories of the subjective and the intangible, and of the objective and the material, often overlap, they are not identical.

Focusing on the subjective and immaterial sides of class is fruitful for a number of reasons. For one, the critical power of material life cannot fully be grasped without comprehending immaterial aspects of class. Furthermore, it is those immaterial aspects that often feel most salient and powerful in people's lives in a class system. We should at least consider Michael Jackson's argument that regardless of the circumstances of daily life, it is the *"experience* of being in control" that matters more consciously than objectively being in control of wealth, power, or "the fate of one's fellow human beings" (1998, 22; emphasis in original; see also Chambers 1992). What people experience in everyday life—the challenges and victories they face in daily activities and interactions, and their feelings about themselves, their neighbors, and their lives—reveals not only the immediate concerns and pleasures of their lives, but also the daily impacts of class process. These experiences have a great deal to do with well-being, and in Madurai much of the sense of having or lacking control is tied to class relations. While "objective social structures" would shape class even in the absence of these subjective features, to acknowledge the contingency of subjective experiences is not to suggest that they are unimportant, as Andrew Sayer also argues: these subjective experiences remain "of central importance to the quality of our lives and what we care about. . . . Whereas [structural features of class] are experienced as changes happening *to* people, identity-sensitive processes such as class contempt are both felt and enacted by individuals" (2005b, 169–170).

The subjective experience of class also exposes, and is tied to, the moral nature of class. Sayer observes that "people experience class in relation to others partly via moral and immoral sentiments or emotions such as benevolence, respect, compassion, pride and envy, contempt and shame" (2007, 3). I pay attention in particular to the ways in which the construction of class difference involves the drawing of moral boundaries between and around categories of people (Lamont 1992; Liechty 2003). The material and symbolic elements of class are endowed with moral significance, and the boundary-making of class in India is very often a moral project (see, e.g., Dickey 2012; Radhakrishnan 2011a; Srivastava 2015; van Wessel 2004). As a small set of scholars have recently argued, it is precisely the moralizing attitudes and assumptions underlying class distinctions that make the system of inequality possible. Again, we cannot understand how class persists without comprehending the taken-for-granted concepts employed by people in all positions of a class system. When such assumptions are applied to categories of people and enacted relationally, they permit and enable the "hoarding" of resources within specific groups and hinder access to them for others (Mosse 2010;

Tilly 1998, 2001) by naturalizing the characters of different types of people and the unequal distribution of resources among them.

Subjective aspects of class are also important because they themselves contribute to an individual's and a family's long-term socioeconomic chances, that is, the more "objective" aspects of class (cf. Donner and De Neve 2011, 6–8). How people feel about themselves as persons of a certain class and how others treat them based on perceptions of class shapes not only the experience of everyday life but also the chances of gaining those goods that determine class standing (Castleman 2011). An intangible good such as honor or respect can affect, for example, access to credit and the terms of repayment, the ability to join a cooperative savings organization or commodities-purchasing group, or marriage prospects for children. Thus I argue strongly that the discursive elements of class are far from ephemeral; rather, the discursive helps to produce the unequal distribution of resources that makes up class inequality (see also Ortner 2003, 11). Those interactive effects are demonstrated throughout the course of this book.

One of the conceptual tools I employ to explore the interactions of the material and objective with the immaterial and subjective in class relations is the concept of "capital" that Pierre Bourdieu developed in his analysis of class as an "economy of practice." The "practice" that produces class refers to embodied activities that Bourdieu calls "the ordinary relation to the world" (1990a, 78). The everydayness and taken-for-grantedness of practice is key to my analysis. Of all the major social theorists, Bourdieu has most explicitly and systematically highlighted the interaction of economic, cultural, social, and symbolic resources in the production of class. While he was largely uninterested in "the immediate experience of the individual and his own interpretations of the social world" (Throop and Murphy 2002, 189) and in the moral nature of distinctions (Lamont 1992, 5), his concepts of capital can nonetheless be employed toward examining such topics—in this case, to understand why people behave and judge each other as they do.

While, as Sayer notes, we must remember that forms of capital are also sometimes ends in themselves—or "internal goods" (Sayer 2005b, 111–112)—I focus primarily on how they are used instrumentally to make statements about one's own class and others', and how they thereby shape class processes and relations. I do so not merely because the values of capital provide powerful insight into the quality of lives in this class system, or into the ways that individuals and households use assets to shape their class, but especially because they provide insight into how relationships shape inequality.

The uses of capital do not capture all of the most significant subjective impacts of class, however. I will also pay attention to one idea that was both implicitly and explicitly key to my informants' everyday behaviors and experiences, that of dignity. The pursuit of dignity, which results from the regard of others, is central to Madurai residents' subjective lives. For reasons I discuss below, I examine dignity primarily as a goal in and of itself—rather than a utilitarian tool, as capital often is—though we will see that at times it too can shape material aspects of a person's class situation. In the reminder of this chapter, I discuss the concept of capital and its forms, and then introduce the idea of dignity and its role in everyday life.

Economies and Capital

To think about why it is helpful to discuss intangible as well as tangible goods in terms of an *economy*, begin with this description of economies: "Economies are systems whereby scarce resources are allocated among competing parties. In particular, they are systems of allocation that have an interactive or aggregative dimension. What individual agents do gives rise to aggregate patterns that feed back in turn into the things that determine what individual agents do" (Brennan and Pettit 2004, 2). Geoffrey Brennan and Philip Pettit's description succinctly evokes characteristics that are key to understanding how an economy of practice works—and why we can think in terms of the logic of an economy at all. It highlights the distribution of resources within economies, the interactions of different types of resources, the cumulative nature of capital, and the recursive character of economies (in particular, the interaction of process and structure). Viewing *class* as an economy of practices encourages us to recognize that class is measured, interpreted, and produced in a number of interrelated realms: in other words, individuals' and families' class positions and identities have material, social, and cultural sources and attributes. And, crucially, examining the practices in an economy of class helps us attend to "the strategic actions through which the borders and contours of classes are maintained" (Fernandes and Heller 2006, 513).

This economy contains multiple forms of capital. I view capital as something (a good, an asset, a resource) that a person, family, household, or group possesses or has (potential) control over, and that can be accumulated, invested, and parlayed into additional capital (and often, significantly, into a different *form* of capital). Critical features of this concept of capital include the possibility that one form of capital can be converted into another; that some kinds of capital are more liquid and/or more fungible than others; that future return on any capital investment is uncertain, though assets vary a great deal in terms of how reliable or predictable they are in yielding returns; and that any form of capital can be either inherited or acquired.

Over the course of his career, Bourdieu discussed an array of forms of capital (and some of his definitions varied over time). I find four of these forms most relevant to both the subjective and the objective impacts of class in Madurai: economic, cultural, social, and symbolic. Here I provide a brief overview of these four forms. While my definitions often draw directly from Bourdieu, I also depart from his treatment of capital in significant ways.[5]

Economic capital includes monetary and material property: cash, economic assets, property, and other material goods with monetary value. Bourdieu states that economic capital "is immediately and directly convertible into money" (1986, 243). Some kinds of property are more difficult to liquefy than others, but Bourdieu's point nonetheless holds if we think in terms of being able to *assign a monetary value* to economic capital.

Cultural capital, in some ways the widest ranging of the forms of capital, comprises dispositions, credentials, and other conventionalized signs of class distinction. These include, for example, competences, comportment, tastes, skills, identities, ideologies, and educational attainments. Cultural capital exists, Bourdieu argues, in three states: "in the *embodied* state, i.e., in the form of long-lasting dispositions of the mind and body; in the *objectified* state, in the form of cultural goods (pictures, books, dictionaries, instruments, machines, etc.)," as well as in the knowledge of how to use and appreciate these goods; and "in the *institutionalized* state," primarily in the form of educational qualifications, which Bourdieu characterizes as "certificate[s] of cultural competence" (1986, 243, 248; emphases in original). Cultural capital takes time to absorb and inculcate. While cultural capital can be either inherited or acquired, one of its differences from most types of economic capital is that it cannot be passed on quickly from one person to another. It is absorbed over time from family, community, and often formal education (all of which contribute to what Bourdieu calls habitus, "the system of durable and transposable *dispositions* through which we perceive, judge and act in the world" [Wacquant 2008, 267]). As Satish Deshpande explains, "an identity or skill cannot simply be handed over from person to person (as other economic assets can), but has to be learnt afresh" (2003, 141). Cultural capital provides one of the most pervasive and consistent means that people use to classify and categorize themselves and others, and it is the form of capital that I examine most extensively in later chapters.

Social capital consists of social connections, the networks they make up, and the resources they potentially afford. Social capital has the least reliable and predictable outcomes of all the forms of capital. Alan Smart captures this well: "obligation is always potential. . . . Thus, you do not really know how much you have until you try to use it" (1993, 393). Alejandro Portes notes similarly that "transactions involving social capital tend to be characterized by unspecified obligations, uncertain time horizons, and the possible violation of reciprocity expectations" (1998, 4).

Symbolic capital, in my usage, is the respect, honor, or prestige that accrues to an individual or group for reasons not directly related to any of these other types of capital. In Madurai, this form of capital is often alluded to, for example, when a family discusses the "reputation" of another family with whom it is considering a marriage alliance. Reputation is based largely on integrity; its connection to material wealth and occupation is disavowed. (Some analysts may argue that membership in certain castes can confer symbolic capital [see, e.g., Jeffrey 2001; Kapadia 1996]—when the castes are seen as particularly honorable—but while this is occasionally the case, caste identity is more frequently viewed and used as a form of cultural capital [while caste identity also makes access to economic resources and social connections either more or less likely, as I discuss in chapter 2].)

In my view, these different forms of capital derive to some extent from one another, but none is fully derivative from, or reducible to, any other (see, e.g., Säävälä 2001, 303). Bourdieu most famously argues that economic capital is "at the root of [the] effects" of "all the other types of capital," but that this is true "only in the last analysis," and that other forms of capital are "never entirely reducible" to the economic (1986, 252). And indeed, we might see the economic as "at the root" of class in India, in that class is often referred to as or referentially reduced to "money" (paṇam in Tamil); but this is only a synecdochic representation of class, in which the much more complicated whole is referred to by a single feature.

Capital can carry positive or negative value, or both simultaneously. Sometimes the value varies according to the social position of the persons assigning it. (While, as I discuss below, the value of economic capital is fairly consistent within a society, the value given to cultural and other forms of capital in Madurai can vary by class, as well as by gender, caste, religion, and other categories of identity.) Bourdieu locates all forms of capital on a linear spectrum of negative to positive valuation (see, e.g., Bourdieu 1984), where the only positively valued capital is that deemed "legitimate" by dominant members of society. I depart from this view, finding the concept of capital to be more useful when it is understood as providing either positive or negative value within *a relevant social group*.[6] Simultaneously, it may also carry a different specific value determined by others outside that group. Any particular bit of capital can have positive value within one social group and negative value in another.[7]

Thus consumer goods, language use, or tastes that are disparaged by middle- and upper-class residents of Madurai may nonetheless accrue *positive* cultural capital to poorer residents of the city *among* those residents' most relevant social community. One example that I have observed for decades is membership in a Tamil film star's fan club, which is almost uniformly a male activity. Being a member of such a club is largely disparaged in Madurai—indeed, frequent film-going in general and intense fandom in particular are excoriated as "cinema madness." Nonetheless, within a specific neighborhood and its social networks, fan club membership can serve as positive cultural capital, as I use the term (but not as Bourdieu does). It can provide distinction because of the member's association with the star—particularly if that star is identified with the struggles of the poor—and because of the access to material goods (usually as charitable donations to needy residents) and even political favors (see Dickey 2001). Membership in a fan club thus may generate cultural and social capital that produces social distinction, separating the fan from the rest of the lower class, giving him an indirect access to wealth and glamour that he would otherwise not possess, and symbolically narrowing the distance between him and the wealthy.

Here then we have another difference between cultural and economic capital: while the value of economic capital is fairly consistent throughout a society (and even transnationally, since many kinds of economic capital have fixed values on world markets), the value of a particular instance of cultural capital is much more variable across classes.

I am interested in how people create distinctions among themselves, how they attempt to show that they belong to certain groups, and how they align themselves with certain others and distance themselves from yet others. What David Palumbo-Liu says of cultural capital is actually true of all forms of capital: it is used to "position the self in particular relation to others" (1997, 5). The utilization of all forms of capital in concert helps to produce class relations and is a key component in the performance and production of class identities.

Dignity

Independent of the experience of material comfort or deprivation, one of the most immediate daily concerns for many people is how they will be treated by the others they encounter. Will they be seen as someone who counts, someone worthy of recognition, someone who has done and will do what it takes to qualify as a full social being? While capital is often used and interpreted instrumentally, there are also less instrumental goals of class practice, goals that serve as ends in themselves rather than as means to an end. One of these is dignity.

"Dignity" in my usage is an acquired or contingent dignity (Meyer 2002, 197; Schaber 2011, 152)—something that results from other people's accord, and is neither intrinsic nor self-bestowed. It is thus *not* the essential human dignity discussed in much contemporary human rights literature (see, e.g., Kaufmann et al. 2011; Kretzmer and Klein 2002).[8] It is much more closely related to the intangible qualities of esteem, regard, and recognition that have recently been taken up by a small number of economists, political scientists, and political sociologists (see Brennan and Pettit 2004; Castleman 2011; Offer 2006; Sayer 2005a, 2005b, 2007; Varshney 2000). I should note that despite the growing currency of these other terms, I retain "dignity" as my concept of analysis because while these other qualities help to create dignity (and therefore precede it), it is dignity itself that consistently captures my informants' attention. As I will discuss in chapter 4, social recognition in particular (or apprehension, as I sometimes describe it) makes the recipient into someone who counts, and it is therefore the resulting subjective experience of dignity—the closest English term to what Madurai residents describe—on which I focus.

Dignity, however, is rarely foregrounded in any class analysis (cf. Castleman 2011 and Sayer 2007), though it has made important appearances in now-classic studies of class, such as Thompson's (1963) history of the English working class and Richard Sennett and Jonathan Cobb's (1972) analysis of the American working class, as well as in a limited number of more recent class studies (see chapter 4). Yet, as Thompson and Sennett and Cobb have insisted, what is true of immaterial capital is also true of the immaterial effects of class: they matter.

Discussions of dignity do appear in South Asian scholarship, but almost always in studies of caste, and usually in regard to the lowest ranked castes, as I discuss in chapter 4. Yet dignity is an issue that, as I will demonstrate, is vital for people across all classes—not just the lowest of them—since it serves as a register of an always precarious counting in the social body. Moreover, the criteria for gaining dignity are to some degree different for class than they are for caste. Finally, in Madurai, the primary way of articulating the desire for dignity in everyday discourse and behavior has to do with class more than with any other form of identity. As I argue in chapter 4, dignity depends on feeling recognized as of worth by other people—as someone who deserves to be recognized—and material and cultural capital are the key goods that make one worthy of regard.

Dignity is not a form of capital, but the two are intertwined: not only does capital accumulation produce dignity, the accord of dignity may directly or indirectly result in the acquisition of capital.[9] Thus it, like esteem (Brennan and Pettit 2004, 3), *can* be instrumental.[10] But it is also a nonutilitarian good, and the most poignant discussions of dignity that I heard in Madurai invoked it in this way. Thus whereas my interest in capital lies primarily in its extrinsic value—even though forms of capital can also have value in and of themselves—conversely, it is dignity's intrinsic value that is most important to my analysis. Dignity is most crucially an end in itself, a good in itself, not simply a type of capital that can be invested and converted to something else.[11]

I am drawn to the intrinsic value of dignity because it so frequently underlies my informants' discussions of, and behaviors in, their daily lives; the struggle for dignity is one of many Madurai residents' most compelling concerns. This struggle is clearly relational: it emerges in residents' talk about their interactions with others, and in behaviors that aim to elicit regard from others. Although I discuss dignity most directly in chapters 4 and 9, it underscores all of the topics that appear in this book. Finding a way to count in the social body, and to have that standing reflected back through cordial regard, is a striking issue for people in all class positions. Yet this topic is rarely raised in contemporary studies of class, despite its critical impact on behavior and well-being. As Brennan and Pettit argue, "It is almost as if there were a conspiracy [among social scientists] not to register or document the fact that we are, and always have been, an honour-hungry species" (2004, 1). Because the experience of class is not entirely about instrumentality, we must also attend to the intangible, intrinsic goods of class if we are to apprehend the quality of everyday life in a class society.

In this book, then, I focus on two fundamental features of the practice and experience of class. I examine capital primarily as an instrument (though its deployment may not be conscious or even intentional) and dignity primarily as an end in itself. The resources of capital help to produce—interpret, negotiate, perform—class identity and relations; in other words, I view forms of capital as *determinants of* class. Dignity and indignity, on the other hand, are primarily *determined by* class. Both resources and dignity affect well-being. Some analysts will object to my approach, particularly those who desire quantitative measurements of class and its aggregate effects. Even those who are comfortable with qualitative studies of how symbolic assets affect material resources and long-term circumstances may counter that a quality as subjective as dignity cannot be understood to affect objective indicators of life chances; or they may simply find my discussion of dignity too divorced from class outcomes. I understand these points of view, and in my own work I rely on others' analyses of the structural features of class. (A small set of scholars, as noted above, do see dignity as influencing material outcomes of class; but even this is not my primary interest in dignity, despite the significance of that approach.) I am after, rather, what Madurai residents communicate—through discourse and behavior—as mattering most to their daily experience of living a life shaped by class, and the long-term consequences of those experiences and of the relationships from which they result.

What Follows

The schematic version of the book's structure is this: In this chapter and the next I introduce places, concepts, and analytical approaches. Chapter 3 introduces individual people, their lives, and my interactions with them. Chapters 4 through 7 then alternate between focusing on class boundary-making (consumption; the middle class) and the long-term impacts of intersecting forms of capital (debt; marriage). The final two chapters turn to the intentional breaking of boundaries and defiance of classifications.

A more detailed overview of the remaining chapters is as follows: In chapter 2 I continue to introduce conceptual elements of class that are necessary for making sense of the accounts that follow. These include past and present concepts related to class and status in southern India; contemporary class categories in Madurai; and intersections of class and caste.

Chapter 3 presents narrative portraits of four Madurai residents. These portraits expose class-based contrasts in all residents' lives, and provide concrete examples to illustrate the abstract concepts from the first two chapters and to inform the topical chapters that follow.

Chapter 4 begins to examine ways in which individuals demonstrate their own class and evaluate others', focusing on two quotidian topics: the need to present oneself as "decent," a concept that incorporates neatness and cleanliness in clothing and grooming; and the use of cell phones as a fetishized signifier of class standing. Consumption of these goods and practices is aimed in part at making the person visible to a highly judgmental audience, and I focus on the drive for recognition that shapes those interactions. These topics return us to the issue of dignity. I ask what it means to "count" in society, and why dignity and counting are deeply important to people.

Chapter 5 explores another topic rarely foregrounded in studies of class in India (outside of work on poverty): the symbolic and economic significance of loans and debt. The poor—and even many members of the middle class—have difficulty procuring non-usurious loans. Debt is not only impoverishing but also stigmatizing for those who have access only to high-interest loans. Meanwhile, the moneylenders who provide these loans are vilified in political and popular rhetoric. For the better-off members of the middle class, however, debt (or "credit") has moved from a source of shame to a source of prestige, and it enables them to acquire large and prestigious consumer goods that increase their social and economic distance from less well-off residents. I consider the substantial objective and subjective impacts of moralizing about (some) debt and (some) debtors and creditors.

Chapter 6 moves from considerations of particular kinds of class capital to the performance of a specific class identity, that of the middle class. It develops themes presented in previous chapters—decency, regard, performance, the judgmental audience—to examine the ways in which self-conscious class identities are enacted by the middle class, and the means by which class boundaries are drawn and defended. It considers especially the continuous need to reproduce class identity and the fragility of that identity, and explores how judgments and discrimination affect everyday life with poignant and long-lasting impact.

In chapter 7 I explore a dramatic event used to display and enact class: marriage. After discussing marriage arrangements, wedding ceremonies, and dowry transactions, I demonstrate the class processes involved by exploring marriages made in Lakshmi's and Anjali's families. Lakshmi's and her four siblings' marriages illustrate the complex real-life choices made around marriage and dowry, the power of public display in negotiating class standing, and the strong tendency for marriage to reproduce a family's current class position in a child's long-term situation. Anjali's marriage, on the other hand, demonstrates the complexity of attempting to utilize marriage for class mobility.

In chapter 8 I continue the focus on display by examining a public wedding feast. The chapter moves from the anxiety of boundary-drawing to attempts to create ties across classes. Utilizing the symbolic importance of feeding and eating—acts that can either include or exclude others in powerful ways—I examine the giving and receiving of gifts of food. Three sets of participants in the feast (including sponsors and guests) construct three contradictory representations of the event's meaning, while also creating an image of sameness across class lines through an idiom of shared hunger and hardship. Their narratives reveal the potency of the discourse of hunger in binding people across lines of class.

The concluding chapter focuses on Murugan, a videographer who must decide whether to replace his father in the hereditary position of *cāmiyāṭi*, the "god dancer," for his lineage's fierce ancestral deity. Murugan's anxious concern about combining his "modern" middle-class identity with a "village" lower-caste religious practice—one that signifies lower-class practice as well—and his eventual resolution of conflicting class indicators provides an example of how people contend with multiple forms of inequality and challenge existing definitions of class attributes.

I hope that this book's exploration of the large and small moments of living will satisfy those readers who are interested in how others like or unlike them experience their lives—how those others feel about their lives, and how it feels (however partially) to *be* in those lives. This book is also written to demonstrate how the quality of everyday life, and other intangible aspects of class, affect everyday well-being and contribute to the long-term impacts and inequalities of class and class relations. These distinct aims are not entirely separate; to my mind, they coexist comfortably.

2   *What Is Class in Madurai?*

In this chapter I move from the more or less universal features and workings of class to a more specific focus on class in Madurai and the Tamil region. The first two sections of the chapter provide different types of historical background: a quick introduction to the study of class in India over the past century, and a brief history of political economy in the Tamil region and of Tamil Nadu's economic and development programs. The rest of the chapter takes up topics tied to local understandings of class: past and present concepts related to class and status in the region; contemporary class categories in Madurai; intersections of class and caste; and local concepts and sources of power. While the final sections of chapter 1 focused on etic concepts of class—an external way of understanding—most of this chapter examines emic concepts, that is, local ways of characterizing, comprehending, and talking about class. Taken together, these two vantage points—the distanced and the in-the-thick—can provide a powerful understanding of class in Madurai.

Analyzing Class in India (The Short History of a Century's Scholarship)

Class is not the form of identity or inequality most commonly associated with India. Much of the study of social life in South Asia has focused on caste and religion, two realms that fascinated both colonial and later scholars of the region (Dirks 2001; Inden 2000). Although the focus of scholarship has changed over time, the legacy of that early scrutiny has been to define caste and Hinduism as the "core symbols" of India (Dirks 2001, 3), a legacy that continues to shape our knowledge and assumptions.[1]

Nevertheless, class in India has been studied for over a century.[2] Literature on class in India often parallels wider scholarly trends, developments in academic institutions, and economic and political shifts inside and outside of India. Economic events such as the Depression and liberalization, developments in postsecondary educational institutions and policies in India, the rise and decline of Marxian social science, Western left-wing politics in the 1960s and 1970s, university programs in North America (including area studies programs, which in the United States are tied among other things to State Department "critical language" fellowships), and changing definitions and measurements of class in social sciences and cultural studies, have all had an impact.[3] A definitive history of class scholarship in South Asia has yet to be written, but here I provide a very brief overview, in broadest strokes, of the English-language South Asianist class scholarship that precedes, contextualizes, and often informs my work.[4]

Studies of class-related issues in the first half of the twentieth century were relatively limited and focused largely on labor conditions and movements. Research on class accelerated in the 1950s, beginning with the first studies of particular classes or occupational groups, which were almost invariably identified using Western categories (such as "industrialists," the "bourgeoisie," or the "working class").

The real surge in class analysis began late in the 1950s, with a distinct shift toward agricultural labor and rural sites. This trend, which would continue through the early 1980s, reflected not only the demographics of the country's workforce and population but also the common image of India as an agrarian nation or village society (see Nair 2005, 1–7). Much of this scholarship drew from Marxist perspectives. A strand of this work known as the "mode of production debate" flourished in the late 1960s and 1970s. The vigorous debate was largely "couched in the terms that: 'If the mode of production is correctly specified then its laws of development will be understood and 'correct' lines of political action determined" (Harriss 1991, 17).[5] By the 1980s a number of authors working in India—both Marxists and their critics—had taken up a sub-theme of the debate, critiquing the teleological certainties of Marxist theory while modifying that theory and its class categories in accordance with Indian class development. They were among the first to argue that class systems are in part the products of local cultural and historical factors.

The field of class analysis in South Asia was altered significantly during the 1980s by the appearance of Subaltern Studies, a formal series of essay compilations first published in 1982, launched by a collective composed primarily of Indian historians. Starting from a position that emphasized "histories from below," and combining intellectual work with politics in a way much more standard in India than in North America or some of Europe, early Subaltern Studies work applied a Marxist perspective even as it distrusted and critiqued the developmental paradigms of classical Marxist theory. Within several years, however, contributing authors had largely moved away from a strictly materialist approach to more culturalist and discursive analyses of subordination and dominance (an intellectual approach taking hold in other academies and disciplines of that time as well).[6]

As materialist approaches diminished, attention also turned to the intersection of class with other hierarchies. From the mid-1980s, a diverse set of studies on gender (or women) and class began to appear, paralleling the development of feminist scholarship elsewhere. A smaller number of works focused on the mutual imbrication of caste and class, and others on the interaction of religion and ethnicity with class.

In the 1990s, economic liberalization changed not only the Indian economy but also the scholarship of class. This shift resulted not merely from the altered class landscape of economic formations and practices, but also from a fascination with the material products of, and identities produced by, liberal economies (see Dickey 2012). Much of the post-liberalization research has focused on the cultural meanings and symbolic values of consumption, and on the middle class. Research since the early 1990s has also taken a decided "urban turn" (Prakash 2002). In addition, it has made a critical shift toward the study of informal labor, which makes up the great (and steadily increasing) majority of Indian labor.

My own work reflects most of the contemporary trends in class analysis: the focus on the urban, on consumption and performance, on intersections of class with other inequalities, and on the nonmaterial aspects of class. In addition, I join a small number of scholars in emphasizing the processual nature of class, the intersections of subjective / discursive with material features, the moral components of class, and a relational approach to class analysis. What further distinguishes my study from most past and present work is the exploration of indigenous concepts of "class" and a balanced consideration of the perspectives of actors of all classes.

A Very Brief History of Regional Political Economy and State Welfare Policies

All social configurations are, of course, the result of long historical processes. While economic liberalization has captured the attention of many who have become interested in India's new "classes" over the past two or three decades, Madurai's socioeconomic situation is in reality the outcome of centuries, even millennia, of developments in political economy. A brief consideration of those processes, and of certain key measures of status over that time, allows us to understand more thoroughly the contemporary situation.

Madurai has been part of a monetary and trade economy for at least one thousand years (Washbrook 2006, 5; 2010, 268). And indeed, for the past six centuries or so, the elements of economic production in the surrounding area have been remarkably consistent, at least when stated in the abstract: trade, temples, agriculture and agricultural markets (especially cotton production), weaving, mining, and banking. By the late sixteenth century, Madurai—then a provincial capital with at least 50,000 residents—was a central node in the "overland arteries" of trade between the coast and inland areas, with "an essentially courtly and administrative character" (Subrahmanyam 1990, 23, 85). The city was a renowned temple center, supporting the financial, investment, and borrowing activities common to South Indian temples (Mukund 1999a; Subrahmanyam 1990, 87–88). Settled agriculture also gained a firm hold in the Madurai region at this time (Subrahmanyam 1990, 21).

Market economies and merchant capitalism predated British colonialism (Bayly 1983; Haynes 1991; Ludden 1985; Rudner 1994; Washbrook 2010). By 1800, the region was well incorporated into a market exchange economy that was part of "a worldwide capitalist social system" (Ludden 1985, 214). Madurai's economy and society were also influenced by changes in the occupational sectors available there. British civil service and educational institutions created a variety of new occupational positions that centered largely in towns and cities such as Madurai, by then a district headquarters (Bayly 1983, 195; Haynes 1991, 49; Ludden 1985, 121–122). Textile mills provided industrial employment in Madurai from the 1890s onward (Baker 1984, 339), even as largely family-based handloom textile production continued to flourish (Baker 1984, 393–414; Chandavarkar 1998, 46–47; Roy 1997, 440–441, 447–448). The heaviest rural–urban migration in the South began in the 1940s, when the government initiated welfare services and began monitoring wages and job conditions in major towns (Baker 1984, 417), drawing large numbers of the rural poor in search of employment. Thereafter, the most significant catalyst to the local economy was arguably the "massive expansion of groundwater irrigation" (Harriss 1982, 32), which coincided with other forms of agricultural intensification.

The impacts of these economic shifts on relations of production were varied and sometimes diffuse in Tamil Nadu. (During precolonial and colonial periods, caste, for example, was associated with control over land and thus over production and labor in the "wet zones" of the Tamil region, but not so in "dry zones," such as around Madurai [see Kumar 1983, 233–234; Ludden 1985, 84–94; Washbrook 1989, 204–205, 217].) Nonetheless, the effects of increasing agricultural productivity, changing forms of commercial enterprise, the greater role of a market economy, adoption of British-style educational systems, and growing wage employment contributed directly to the class distinctions found in Madurai today, as well as to the manner in which they are expressed.

Since India's Independence in 1947, the region's political economy has also been shaped by the policies of state and national governments.

Tamil Nadu today ranks high on most "human development indicators" among Indian states. Social welfare programs and policies—including food distribution programs (such as the Public Distribution System and noon meals programs in schools), early childcare centers, and health care projects such as antenatal and disability benefits—are heavily subsidized, are generally implemented more thoroughly than in most other states, and have improved material conditions of many residents' lives over recent decades (Harriss-White 2004; Heyer 2012; Vivek 2014). Children have almost universal access to a primary school within 1 km of their residence (although while school enrollment is high, retention is not) (Ehouman et al. 2002). There are, however, significant disparities in access to these benefits according to district and often by gender and caste, and access is frequently routed through systems of patronage (see Harriss-White 2004; Price 1996b; Vijayabaskar et al. 2004; Vivek 2014, 4). Thus, while these programs have enhanced the quality of life for many people in Tamil Nadu, their unequal distribution has itself shaped class differences in Madurai.

Conceptual Antecedents: *Mariyātai* and *Antastu*

To begin the exploration of local understandings of class, I start with the closely connected concepts that preceded and contributed to them. Understanding these concepts is critical to anchoring class analysis carefully in emic concepts, a process that must begin with local understandings of hierarchy and inequality.

Social standing, authority, and power have for centuries been tied to a mix of material factors and intangible or symbolic elements. David Ludden has identified four types of "symbolic assets" or "social networks" that have produced dominance and subservience in southernmost India for over a millennium. In his view, these are "kinship, religion, state, and market interactions" (1985, 9), or more precisely, "caste status, temple honors, official titles, and cash" (1985, 94). Versions of all these assets have continued to play a role in status production into the present. In the late precolonial and colonial period, these resources could include the strictness of a caste's or sub-caste's social codes and the care with which they were followed, and a family's marriage alliances (Dirks 1987, 239); an individual's charity or generosity (*tānam, tarumam, vaḷḷanmai*), or valor in battle (*vīram*) (Blackburn 1978); and (for banking communities) an individual's trustworthiness (Rudner 1994). During these periods, as noted above, "market assets" also became increasingly important (Ludden 1985, 214). The combinations that we see today of material and immaterial features of class, and of different forms of capital in producing class, are thus continuous with a long history of status production.

The two concepts related to social standing that have been examined most closely in the historical and anthropological literature—qualities that were constituted through the assets just described—are *mariyātai* and *antastu*.[7] Mariyātai, usually translated as honor or respect, can be both possessed and given by humans and divinities (Daniel 1984, 64n. 4). It was a significant component of merit or standing in precolonial and colonial eras (see Dirks 1987; Price 1996a, 15, 135–136; 1996b, 360; Rudner 1994, 138ff.), when for elites it was primarily linked with the right to receive "honors" (mariyātai) in particular temples, often in exchange for religious gifting (see Appadurai and Breckenridge 1976, 196–198). Thus, as Pamela Price points out, mariyātai in this period was a relative rather than an absolute quality, determined by one's favor with or closeness to the deity compared to other community members (1996a, 135). It was relative proximity, not the possession of an absolute quantity of any quality or substance, that determined level of honors. Distinctions of mariyātai—who was accorded what level or type of honors in the temple—drew boundaries of inclusion and exclusion (Mines 2005, 92; Price 1996a, 135), as they still do today.

Another precolonial element of elite social standing was antastu (Price 1996a, 135), which Nicholas Dirks defines as "status or dignity, [referring] particularly to a royal model for what would constitute dignity" (1987, 239). Price cites glosses for antastu that include "degree of dignity, rank, position" and "prestige" (1996a, 135). Antastu, unlike mariyātai, was tied to wealth rather than ritual, especially to wealth gained through "proximity to royalty" via kinship (Dirks 1987, 239) or gained through formal attachment to the civil state (Price 1996a, 131). It also differed from mariyātai in being absolute rather than relative (Price 1996a, 135; 1996b, 362). As Price notes, "the distinctions of mariyatai were vulnerable, taking place in a shifting political universe. The model for antastu expressed a fixed hierarchy, describing the storeys of a building, 'being one above the other'" (1996a, 135).

By the colonial period, mariyātai and antastu together generated the "complex conception of status" (Dirks 1987, 242). The former was highly symbolic, the latter highly material. But the cultivation of mariyātai required material resources, and the acquisition of antastu required social ties. (In the colonial period as well, then, "status" was produced through a combination of social, symbolic, and material assets.) Both Dirks (1987) and Price (1996a) indicate that these terms maintained these meanings at least through the end of the colonial era.

While the two concepts seem to have retained similar meanings even in some parts of postcolonial South India (see Holmström 1972, 772; Price 1996a, 135; 2006, 308), I have found that their usage differs in contemporary Madurai. Antastu retains the sense of a ranked hierarchy, or (metaphorically) a ladder or a series of steps, but in my experience it is rarely referred to in everyday speech. Mariyātai still denotes temple honors, but it is also much more widely used in the general sense of "respect" or "deference," as in showing respect or disrespect to another through one's behavior. Madurai residents engage in lively conversations about which people deserve or are accorded mariyātai these days, and such conversations make it clear that mariyātai has usurped antastu's determinants. As I discuss in chapter 4, gaining mariyātai in everyday interactions is a significant concern for Madurai residents, and the mariyātai they receive depends a great deal on their perceived class. Respondents frequently bemoaned the fact that mariyātai is less rooted in proper behavior than it is in "money." They nostalgically located the "old" qualities befitting mariyātai in spaces that were temporally, spatially, or culturally distant from them. For example, they often claimed that these old values were followed in villages but not in the city. (Four decades earlier, Mark Holmström's informants had made a similar nostalgic displacement in lamenting the contemporary shift of mariyātai from those who behaved honorably to those who were "rich and powerful" [1972, 772].) As I will discuss in the following chapter, mariyātai is also closely tied to dignity.

The material in these last two sections demonstrates interwoven points. South Indians have increasingly become part of a market economy over recent centuries, and today wage labor dominates in urban areas. Simultaneously, the significance of material assets in determining social standing has increased. Recently, as I discuss below, ethnographic evidence shows that "money" is believed to be more important in determining status today than it was in the past.

Class in Madurai

Making sense of "class" in Madurai is complicated, not least because there is no close gloss for the term in either Tamil or Indian English. Tamil has no lexical equivalent: although a near-literal translation can be constructed by combining a word for "division" (such as *pirivu* or *nilai*) with a modifier such as "social" or "economic" (*camuka* or *poruḷātāra*, respectively), no one would actually use such a phrase in everyday speech. In addition, most people would be perplexed to hear it. Furthermore, in Indian English, "class" is just as likely to mean caste as socioeconomic class, as in the phrase "backward classes." (Note that *jāti*, the pan-Indian term usually glossed as caste, is itself ambiguous. Although jāti is generally taken to mean caste or sub-caste in everyday speech, its more precise meaning is genus or category, and jāti can be used to refer to a number of different classifications, such as people versus nonhuman animals, or women versus men.)

Takuti

To solve this problem in interviews and conversations in the early stages of this research—to the extent that I did solve it—I either had to clarify that I meant "social and economic class" when I was speaking in English, or use the Tamil term *takuti*. Takuti means level, standard, or social standing. Described more thoroughly, takuti is the amalgam of social and economic factors that combine to produce a person's standing and influence in a community. (It can also have the more restricted meaning of "qualifications" in the Indian English sense of the term, that is, educational degrees.) In Madurai it is cited as the most common basis for according people respect or deference. I often heard people say that "without takuti, no one gives you respect," and indeed people often spoke of takuti as something that, like mariyātai, is given or earned. My friend Usha, an upper-middle-class Brahman woman whose story appears in the following chapter, once pointed out that "the same person will have ten takutis," meaning that different observers will accord different takutis to the same person. It can be said that a person has a high, middle, or low takuti, but it can also be said that she has no takuti at all.

The factors used to determine someone else's takuti are said to vary in different places, especially from city to village, and according to the values of the person making the judgment (just as with mariyātai). People judge others' takutis based on a mélange of characteristics, including caste, political power, education, occupation, and wealth. In general, however, in the city, "money," the things it buys, and the tastes it expresses are overwhelmingly cited as the basis of a person's takuti. Yet takuti is not entirely congruent with the U.S. English term "class," since it draws on a potentially wider set of signifiers, and selectively so according to circumstances. Its multiple meanings appeared, for example, when I was told by a lower-middle-class Thevar man named Munusamy, "The people in the upper takuti, you can't tell their takuti" (*"mēl takutile iruk-kravaṅka vantu avaṅkaḷōṭa takuti ninekka muṭiyātu,"* which could be translated more thoroughly as, "The people in the upper level, you can't tell their class"). His point was that an observer cannot always tell the actual social and economic resources of someone who portrays himself as, and considers himself to be, a member of the elite, a point similar to the one about a "showcase exterior" that appears in chapter 4. The apparent paradox reveals the concept's nuances.

Nonetheless we can argue that takuti is the closest Tamil lexical equivalent to my understanding of class, for two main reasons. First, it draws on both economic and cultural forms of capital; in Weberian terms, it combines market situation and status distinctions. Second, when people talk about the different takutis in Madurai, they refer to categories that look very much like classes. Indeed, we might go so far as to say that takuti *is* what class is in Madurai—takuti is the form that class takes in this social formation, shaped as it is both by transnational capitalism and by local forms of hierarchy and power.

Yet by and large, when Madurai residents talk about class, they refer to specific class categories rather than to the abstract concept of class or takuti. In the United States, while many people deny that class is a major social division, virtually everyone can answer the question, "What class are you in?" at least with some hedging, even if they wish to disavow the topic's relevance. But to ask in Madurai, "What takuti (or pirivu) is your family in?"—even if takuti is modified by an adjective such as "economic" (e.g., *poruḷātāra takuti*)—can sometimes produce confusion and incomprehension, despite the fact that the term takuti is heard in everyday conversation about status. On the other hand, one can ask, "Are you poor, or middle-class, or wealthy?" and everyone can answer that question. If people are then asked to identify the larger concept to which those categories belong, they will most likely answer, "Money" (*paṇam*), rather than use another gloss for class. As I show throughout this book, however, there is much more to class than "money." While the concept of takuti captures well the multiple referents of class, nonetheless it is the concrete categories that people think with and respond to. These are relational categories that matter in everyday life and discourse. Over time, therefore, I gradually began to ask questions using these categories rather than invoking an overarching abstract concept. In doing so, I also came to appreciate the power of local terms to reveal meaningful indicators of and attitudes toward class (cf. Caplan 1987; Chambers 1992; Frøystad 2006; Parry 2014).

Current class categories in Tamil include *ēḷai makkaḷ* (poor people) or *illātavarkaḷ* (people who have nothing);[8] *naṭuttaramānavarkaḷ* (people in the middle) or *naṭuttara kuṭumpam* (middle family); and *paṇakkārarkaḷ* (monied people), *vacatiyānavarkaḷ* (people with resources or luxuries), or *periyavarkaḷ* (big people).[9] The class categories used by English speakers are typically "lower class," "middle class," and "upper class." When greater specificity is required, gradations such as "upper middle class" or *koncam naṭuttaramānavarkaḷ* ("a little bit middle class," i.e., the lower middle class) are also utilized. Terms like illātavarkaḷ and periyavarkaḷ suggest the condensation of economic and symbolic features in local understandings in the same way that everyday invocations of takuti do: illātavarkaḷ simultaneously evokes lack of money, possessions, and influence, while periyavarkaḷ alludes at once to wealth, command over resources, social power and importance, and cultural and political sophistication.

To summarize my argument so far, class can be seen as a "native" or emic concept in Madurai in three ways. First, the term itself is used in Indian English phrases of long standing when referring to lower, middle, and upper classes. Although the Indian English term "class" has a wider set of referents than do, for example, either popular or academic usages of "class" in British and U.S. English, this ambiguity cannot be used as evidence against the conceptual salience of class unless we wish to argue the same for "jāti" as caste. Second, as C. J. Fuller (1973, 6) and André Béteille (1974, 33, 49, 126ff.) have observed, the experiential relevance of class, even without a precise lexical equivalent, is reflected in indigenous socioeconomic classifications that are clearly class-based, such as the Tamil categories noted above. Finally, although takuti is not identical to class, and although its roots in prestige and influence mean that its determinants must vary historically and across social contexts, its meaning in contemporary urban Tamil Nadu is very close to class, both experientially and conceptually. The fact that the abstract term is used less in speech than are specific class categories may have posed challenges for the anthropologist, but it does not negate the presence and salience of class as a local frame for identifying and comprehending social relations, identities, and inequalities.

These, then, are both the abstract concepts and the locally recognized categories of class in Madurai. They inform the interactions I describe in this book; and, along with concerns for mariyātai and the desire for dignity, they can motivate those interactions as well. Identifying indigenous forms of class in this way is critical not only to understanding the local impact of class, but also to apprehending the reproduction of class as a system in this area.

The Locus of Class

In India, the family is the primary source of an individual's class. (By "family" here I refer, with declining relevance, to a person's co-resident kin [whether affines or agnates], to other members who live apart but make regular financial contributions to the household, to the family of origin if they are not co-resident, and to extended kin who are in at least somewhat regular contact.) This is so in two ways. First, other people judge an individual's class standing by looking at the individual's family, using signs such as family members' occupations, education, housing, consumer goods, and social networks. Second, it is primarily the family that provides and decides upon the resources and opportunities available to each individual (Béteille 1991). Family members share a pool of material resources, and the family head (usually, that is, the head of the co-resident family) makes decisions about how to divide those resources. Family members also play a large part in deciding how much education individual members receive, and which if any jobs or careers they should aim for, as we will see in the case of Anjali in the next chapter. Both immediate and extended family members choose a child's marriage partner, a choice that has a significant impact on the child's future class standing, and a choice that is shaped in large part by the family's current class standing (see chapter 7). Finally, each generation passes on cultural and social as well as economic capital—including knowledge, values, and social networks—to the next generation (Béteille 1991, 16–19; Peace 1984).

This argument counters certain other discussions of the locus of class in India, such as those made by Karin Kapadia (1995) and Selvy Thiruchendran (1997), both of whom argue that class is an individual phenomenon and must be defined for each person separately from the family. Kapadia, for example, argues that family members in the same household can be of vastly different classes, since in her assessment class derives from an individual's occupation and education (Kapadia 1995, 251–252). Others have made the related argument that class varies within households since gender relations determine "access to productive resources, and thus to incomes and to ownership rights," and therefore genders must be seen as distinct classes (Mukund 1999b, 1355; for somewhat related views, see Agarwal 1994, 14–15; Ram 1992, 47–48). These provocative arguments help to highlight the often widening gap in the opportunities available to women and to men, but for my purposes they do not isolate the locus of class effectively. Since individuals' class is interpreted by other people in conjunction with the class performances of those to whom these individuals are closely related, I regard family members as mutually shaping one another's class resources.

Class and Caste

Class is not, of course, the only form of inequality in India, as is already evident in this text. People confront and use inequalities built around gender, skin color, religious identity, and caste—among others—every day. Of these, the one most central to my analysis is caste, or jāti, which—like class—operates simultaneously as a form of identity and a system of hierarchy and inequality. Jātis are hereditary and endogamous. (Classes are neither hereditary nor endogamous, strictly speaking, although—as in much of the world—they in fact tend to be both.) Their ranking today is conceptually tied in large measure to local concepts of purity and pollution. The more inherently pure (or less inherently polluted) the caste, the higher the caste's rank, though economic power, particularly tied to landholding and business ownership, has also played a significant role in establishing rankings over time. Neither a person's caste, nor that caste's relative ranking, can be changed within a person's lifetime except in rare cases. (Class, on the other hand, is always *potentially* mutable, both upward and downward.) Although caste and class are somewhat overlapping hierarchies, they are viewed locally as distinct systems of ranking. Within small-scale communities such as neighborhoods and schools, most people know each other's jāti, but the markers of caste are less visible than those of class, and class is often more relevant in everyday urban interactions.[10]

Nonetheless, caste relates to class in multiple and diverse ways. Recent studies document the enduring, albeit imperfect, correlation between a family's caste and class rankings (e.g., Desai 2007; Deshpande 2003). Caste is relevant to my discussion of class in this book for several reasons. These include its impact on members' attitudes toward consumption and education, the historical privileges of and discrimination against particular castes that continue to affect access to education and occupations, and the ability (or inability) of caste identity to compensate for downward fluctuations in class standing. Finally, there is the ideological component that appears repeatedly in this book: the absorption of caste prejudices and identities into those of class.

Caste groups vary in their attitudes toward consumption—such as which kinds of consumer goods and practices are most valuable and prestigious, and particularly the extent to which those goods and practices should be displayed and enacted in public and at home. Such distinctions are commonly remarked upon, appearing in stereotypes that are expressed both by members of the castes themselves and by outsiders. Brahmans, for example, who rank at the top of the ritual caste hierarchy—but on the whole are somewhat below the top of the Madurai class structure—are said to avoid public display of their wealth and to have muted tastes in personal and domestic fashions. Some subcastes of the Chettiars, a high-ranked caste and one of the two wealthiest communities in Madurai, are stated to display their jewelry and expensive fashions in abundance at weddings, but often to skimp on luxuries in their homes and in daily life. Thevars put much of their wealth into their daughters' dowries, especially in gold, and some people said that Thevars' public dress and grooming may make them appear to be lower in class than they actually are (see also Fuller and Narasimhan 2014, 16–17).

Caste also affects the value that families place on education, and the historical privileges of and discrimination against particular castes continue to affect access to education (and thus to occupations) (Béteille 1991; Da Costa 2008; Desai and Dubey 2011; Desai and Kulkarni 2008). Nadars, for example, who rank low in the caste system, have used education since the nineteenth century to improve their economic circumstances and their overall social standing (originally by establishing their own schools, since they were not allowed to study with higher castes; see Hardgrave 1969); likewise Brahmans have a long history of extensive Western-style education, having been incorporated early on into British colonial administration. There is also continuing evidence that caste shapes effective access to education. Dalit children—members of castes that were formerly considered by some to be so polluted as to be "untouchable," and who are sometimes referred to as scheduled castes because of the lists, or schedules, that British colonial governments made of castes to be provided with protective benefits—continue to be discriminated against markedly by teachers in some schools (Desai and Kulkarni 2008); and schools established by specific castes typically (though not always) give preferential admission or scholarships to students of that caste.

Caste also appears to affect access to occupations that differ on the prestige scale. While most people in Tamil Nadu do not today carry out their caste's "traditional" occupation (if they ever did), occupations can be associated with castes in statistically significant ways (Desai and Dubey 2011). C. J. Fuller and Haripriya Narasimhan (2007, 2008b) have argued that Brahman men's and women's representation in software and other high-status institutional technology positions is highly disproportionate to their numbers in the state's population. In Madurai, some Chettiar sub-castes tend to specialize in business (as do many Nadars) more than other castes, and Dalits are said to hold almost all of the municipal sanitation jobs (which come with the benefits of government positions but also with the stigma of polluting and dirty work). These tendencies are important, in part because they suggest that entry into or exclusion from some occupations is affected by caste, even when education is controlled for (because certain castes are read as inherently more suited for the work, because they have or lack appropriate cultural and social capital, because they are predisposed to push their children toward certain occupations, or because of recruitment networks or caste-based occupational or business associations) (see, e.g., Basile and Harriss-White 2003; Carswell and De Neve 2014; De Neve 2005; Harriss 2006, 248–249; Harriss-White 2003, ch. 7; Mosse 2010, 1163). It is also important to note, however, that people of all castes work in a wide array of occupations, just as each caste contains members who range from the impoverished to the wealthy.

Not surprisingly, caste standing also affects the extent to which people emphasize their caste or their class identity in making prestige claims in a given social situation. The "stability" of caste means that upper-caste, middle-class people can anchor some of their prestige claims in jāti, using caste to compensate if they experience downward class mobility. (This may account, for example, for the relative lack of class anxiety found by Fuller and Narasimhan [2007, 2008b] among middle-class Brahmans in Chennai.) People whose caste is low but who belong to the middle or upper class can foreground symbolic markers of their class rather than caste identity, both in new social situations (where caste may not be known) and in longer-term social settings where caste is known or assumed (see also Osella and Osella 1999; Säävälä 2001). Sekaran, a middle-class Pallar man who is a linguistics professor, first told me in 1999 that he often uses his class and education as "a shield" to prevent people from asking him his caste. A decade later in 2009, he described his family's recent move from a small rented home to a large, luxurious house they had built in a new neighborhood. He commented that although all their new neighbors would certainly have used social networks to ascertain his family's jāti ahead of time, they nonetheless appeared to "have a good opinion of us . . . everybody smiles and says 'good morning'"—but this is because, Sekaran said, his home is the largest in the neighborhood. He described with some satisfaction how he hosted neighborhood association meetings in his living room and served the primarily Thevar and Pillai members water and coffee (though he has never offered them a meal), forcing them to be served by someone they might consider "untouchable." He concluded, "When you belong to a higher class, with a good education, a good appearance, owning a house and a car, dressing neatly, having an English education, that builds up your image. That very active overt [caste] discrimination cannot be enacted in that instance."

Finally, caste also affects class through its influence on the symbolic attributes used to perform and critique class identities. The ideals of the middle class that I discuss in chapter 6—including moderation, reasoned deliberation, and decency—are historically associated with the upper castes. Today these are held as ideals by lower-caste members of the middle class as well. Similarly, upper-caste stereotypes of the lower castes as dirty, uncontrolled, and irrational are now applied by middle- and upper-class people of all castes to the poor (see Dickey 2000b for examples), as we will see repeatedly in this book. Thus hegemonic high-caste ideals continue to inflect class attitudes, values, and practices. Caste prejudices, stereotypes, and attitudes have become widely euphemized (or rationalized) and adopted as class ones. As Fuller has argued, "class distinctions are constructed in cultural terms in all modern capitalist societies, and in India the language and practice of caste provide the most potent and pervasive terms" (1996, 16–17).

When Madurai residents discuss categories of "class" or "takuti" in the terms described above, they can easily distinguish them from caste/jāti. They speak, for example, about poor Brahmans and wealthy Thevars or Paraiyars. They also see caste and class as forms of ranking that, in a sense, compete with each other, or that can replace one another in certain social situations (as in Sekaran's narrative above). Bakkiyam, a poor Paraiyar woman who works as a servant, demonstrated this when she told me, "If there is money, caste will be far away, it will run away, it will go away, it will get lost." Her observation was echoed by Usha, who—shortly after moving from a government flat into a luxuriously constructed new home—remarked ironically that "when high class comes, caste tends to move off. A rich man's joke is always funny." And strikingly, of the fifty or so Madurai residents I asked between 1999 and 2001 (when I began this research project) whether class or caste had a greater impact on their lives, all but one said that it was class. Whether class has the larger influence on life chances is, I think, questionable, but the perception that it does is an indication of its salience in the urban imagination.

Despite these clear conceptual and experiential differences between caste and class, there are a number of ways in which many Madurai residents, like other people in Tamil Nadu, sometimes have difficulty distinguishing between caste and class, or feel no need to do so (cf. Ray and Qayum 2009). Often, for instance, when middle- or upper-class speakers continue to talk about class long enough, they may elide certain differences between class and caste. People often assign a particular character to members of different classes, as did Usha's husband Raman, a cardiologist, who explained to me that he and a butcher could not do each other's work because people of their classes have different natures. Upper-class people, he said, are "soft," tolerant, intelligent, reasoning, and forgiving, while members of lower classes fight, beat people, and otherwise act impulsively rather than reasoning things out. He described them as using their bodies rather than their minds. Of course, these are also substantive, embodied qualities associated with high-caste Brahmans on the one hand and low-caste butchers on the other (which was the point behind the criticism Lakshmi received for being possessed by the goddess). But Raman spoke explicitly of class when he explained these differences, pointing out that such lower-class behavior is learned, passed on from parents to children, "because of poor education, because of poor [upbringing]." Yet he also spoke of such qualities being inherited, saying, "They will inherit only those qualities or tendencies from their parents." It is difficult to distinguish where class ends and caste begins in accounts like this one.[11] Although some people (including Raman's wife Usha) do see behavior, character, and values as mutable because they are influenced more by upbringing, income, and education than by immutable sources, in common usage class-specific attributes are more often spoken of as being essential and possessing inherent sources such as "genes" or "blood," much as does caste (or race as it is commonly perceived in the United States, for that matter).

As Raman's characterizations illustrate, it can be difficult, for South Indians in their everyday lives and for analysts alike, to distinguish between the effects and articulation of caste on the one hand and of class on the other. Thus Mary Hancock asks, for example, whether urban Brahmans are perceived as educated and well-off because they are Brahmans or because most of them are middle class. As she points out, since class is "a cultural as well as an economic formation that encompasses competing meaning systems, modes of self-attribution, discourses of distinction (such as taste), and forms of consumption," and "insofar as [caste] derives from and is reproduced through these cultural practices," caste and class have to be seen "in dynamic interaction" with each other (1999, 46; see also Fuller and Narasimhan 2014, 17, 27 and Upadhya 2011, 184–185).

The overlay of caste attributes onto class differences is one striking example of the culturally specific nature of class categories and interactions in Madurai. So too are the particular class categories in currency today, which reflect recent economic change as well as longstanding local concepts and indicators of class differences. To understand how these emic understandings are used in practice, we will also benefit from applying the more abstract analytical concepts that I introduced in chapter 1. Equipped with an understanding of these conceptual tools and discursive categories, we now return to the concrete details of everyday lives.

3   *Four Residents, as I Know Them*

In this chapter I draw narrative portraits of four Madurai residents. They are the stories of Kannan, an autorickshaw driver; Anjali, a graphics designer from a poor family; Usha, who once helped her husband run his medical practice and now teaches English to aspiring IT students; and Jeyamani, a domestic worker. The focus is largely on the years in which our daily lives overlapped. My own class in India—which is not simply what my "class" is at home in the United States, but also includes my American nationality and light skin color, and presumptions about my modernity—figures heavily in our relationships and sometimes brings out aspects of these four people's class identities. The ways I came to know them, and the relationships we have developed, are detailed within each narrative. Each of these four people has been a crucial resource in my learning, enculturation, and ensconcement in Madurai, and I in turn have been a resource for them. Kannan and Anjali have become kin, Usha a close friend, and Jeyamani a fierce and caring interlocutor. While Americans in general are uncomfortable with the affective-economic mix, having close relationships with people in Madurai long ago taught me that the dominant American opposition between economic and affective relationships mystifies the actual material strategies that are part of most emotional relationships (cf. Constable 2003).

These narratives are not life histories. Rather, they are accounts of life experiences as they have been told to me and as I have shared in them. These narratives illustrate the compelling power and presence of class over spans of time. They reveal pointed differences in individuals' and families' challenges and opportunities, most of which are directly tied to class difference. They demonstrate the highly contingent nature of movement up and down in the class hierarchy, the stark impacts of inequalities and privileges, the intersections of capital, and the individual drive for dignity. Keep these themes in mind as you read; I return briefly to them at the end of this chapter, and thereafter I return to examples from these narratives throughout the book.

Kannan

I met Kannan on a day in 1999 when I flagged down his autorickshaw. I was taking Daniel, my infant son, to visit an old friend; and an autorickshaw ("auto" for short) was the fastest, most comfortable way to get there. Autos are three-wheeled vehicles with a motorcycle engine, a rigid shell with a windshield but no doors, and two seats—one in front for the driver, and a bench in the back for passengers (plus a meter, rarely used). These vehicles seat two or three customers comfortably, but autos can just as often be stuffed with eight schoolchildren. They are used primarily by people who can afford to avoid the crowded city buses, but who lack immediate access to a motorbike or car—or who don't want to park a car in a city center whose roads were not built with vehicle storage in mind.

That day, Kannan drove carefully and cautiously. I began taking his auto frequently, and eventually, Kannan came to know most of the people who appear in this book. Like most Tamilians, Kannan loves children, and as he took it upon himself to entertain my son, who adored the breezy bouncing auto rides, we began to talk about our families. Over the next several months, I came to know him fairly well.

Kannan, who was born around 1960, grew up in a family that was economically and socially better-off than his is now. He is typical of many people who find themselves struggling to hold on to what they and their parents have achieved. Wanting to improve their children's lives, but holding virtually no economic capital or savings, they know their lives can become more difficult at any time. Kannan's parents owned a small pappadam factory, where lentil-flour wafers were rolled paper-thin by hand, dried in the sun, then stacked and packed to sell.

Kannan and his wife Vellaiamma grew up on the same street. Kannan went to school through the sixth standard, Vellaiamma only through the second. They saw each other on the road occasionally as they went to do errands for their families, buying sweetened milky coffee to carry home in a stainless steel jug, or carrying water from a nearby well in a plastic pot. When they fell in love when he was fourteen and she was thirteen, they had a "love marriage" that shamed and angered their relatives.

Erotic love is unlike the love that builds up between two people as they come to know each other over time. It is thought to be dangerously uncontrolled; it prevents people from thinking rationally about such life-determining choices as marriage. For two children to make their own marriage is to reject the authority and wisdom of their parents, to deprive their families of creating a respectable alliance with another family, and to risk building the rest of their lives on an extremely shaky foundation. As usual in such situations, Kannan's and his new wife's families refused to give the young couple any further economic or emotional support. Their families were all the more angered because Kannan and Vellaiamma are of different castes; he is Maravar and she is Agamudayar. Though these two middle-ranked castes are very close in the local hierarchy, they are, crucially, not the same. The couple had to make their own precarious way without the help of parents and other relatives. Within two years, they had their first child, a son, then another son and then two daughters. Everything Kannan has—his job, his home, his health and his family members' health—is exceedingly fragile. I have seen all of them come and go over the years I have known him.

Shunned by his parents, Kannan began earning an income by driving a bicycle rickshaw, a physically demanding, even punishing, occupation. Later, he trained to drive an autorickshaw and earned his driver's license. He began driving by renting an auto at a daily rate. Kannan now rents by the month, but he has never (yet) owned his vehicle. Auto driving is higher status work than bicycle rickshaw driving: auto driving is not considered manual labor, it requires greater training and financial investment, and it brings in a higher income. Unlike some other lower-income men, Kannan brings almost all his money home, and lets his wife divide it up for family needs. Still, in the early years, on the many days that Kannan did not make enough money to cover his auto rent and gasoline, there was not enough food to feed the family. Kannan and his wife have never regained the social and financial well-being of the families they grew up in.

Soon after Daniel and I met Kannan, we were invited to his home for lunch. I—knowing the more complex obligations this could lead to, in a culture where economic and emotional ties almost automatically merge—accepted. The occasion was Kannan's younger daughter Prema's sixteenth birthday. The family lived in a small one-room home in the Singanalur neighborhood, a mostly working- and lower-middle-class neighborhood with small textile factories and shops mixed among the residential buildings. We approached their home down a narrow side street that was just wide enough to park the auto. The road was lined with adjoining single-room homes, all built of brick and concrete and covered with painted plaster. At Kannan's house, Prema was peeking outside, her high spirits spilling over as she laughed and hopped in the doorway. I stepped over the threshold, and Kannan's wife Vellaiamma placed a dot of red kumkum powder on my forehead. Prema and her older sister Bhumati found glass bangles to match my blue sari and eased them onto my wrists. Both girls and the younger of their two brothers, who was also at home, worked in a nearby towel-weaving factory.

Photo 2. Kannan with his rented autorickshaw on Prema's sixteenth birthday, 2000. Photo credit: Sara Dickey.

As most of us sat down on a reed floor mat—Vellaiamma preparing the food in the corner and Prema still dancing about—I looked around the room. Three shelves held small images and lithographs of deities, plastic flowers, and a box of matches. In a corner stood plastic water pots and a kerosene stove. Next to them a small metal bureau held all the family clothing. Soon Kannan was sprinkling water onto a banana leaf in front of me, and after I cleaned the leaf by drawing the water off with the side of my hand, he began to serve me. The meal was a feast—rice, lentil sambar, kesari pudding, green beans, pumpkin, cabbage, spinach, peppery rasam water, and sweet noodle payasam in a cup. I knew, of course, that this was not an everyday meal. Kannan poured the sambar on the rice and placed the kesari at the top of the leaf, and then Vellaiamma took over. When Kannan's older son came in later on, Kannan introduced the young man—who had also started work as an auto driver—as "the one I told you about, who is irresponsible, who doesn't give us any money."

Months later, Kannan told me that both his sons had studied until fourth standard, then dropped out of school. The younger boy was chronically ill, and the older was uninterested in studying. Prema and Bhumati stayed in school until the seventh and eighth standards, but that year they failed their year-end exams so Kannan sent them to work in the towel factory "as punishment." I asked Kannan why his daughters had failed their exams. He said regretfully, "They didn't have three meals a day. We couldn't afford mutton and chicken for them to eat, and so they couldn't concentrate." (A decade later, I recalled this conversation when a highly educated Brahman woman reprimanded Kannan, "Why did you end your daughters' education so early? Daughters are just as important as sons! You have to let girls get ahead too!" Kannan, who had just driven the two of us back from a visit with a wealthy business owner, looked rueful. But he only shook his head, and said that he and Vellaiamma could not afford to send their daughters to school any longer.)

By 2008, almost nine years after that birthday lunch, the two sons had moved out, one of them choosing a love marriage and the other separated from his wife and sometimes sleeping at his parents' home. By then Kannan had dismissed them as noncontributors to the family, even the younger son for whom he had a soft spot. He let them stay with him, and he fed them when they needed it, but he was disaffected by their irresponsibility. For his daughters, though, he kept a huge heart. Like most people of his generation and class, Kannan felt his primary duty was to arrange his children's marriages, and he both worried about and looked forward to these events.

Bhumati had married a man who worked as a mason's assistant in 2004. When I visited in 2008, she was about to have her third child. She and her parents lived in adjoining roof-top flats in the same neighborhood as before, and she had continued to work at the towel factory with her sister, leaving for work each morning after an early breakfast. Kannan would also leave early to wait for fares, and Bhumati's husband would head either to a job site or to a tea stall to hang around with friends. Vellaiamma, a loving grandmother, took care of Bhumati's children during the day. It wasn't easy for her to prepare the family meals, wash seven people's laundry by hand, and do all the other housework with two toddlers moving about. Some women I knew tied their small children to chairs to keep them safe, but Vellaiamma couldn't bear to do that. The younger boy had several times fallen down the three-flight staircase that began just outside their doorway and twisted unevenly down the dark middle of the building. All it took was one unbalanced step to tumble over the threshold. At age two the boy was tiny, and unable to talk.

My mother had joined me in Madurai for a short stay by the time Bhumati's third baby was born that year. We visited the baby and her mother in the private clinic Vellaiamma had chosen. We were ushered into a ward with twenty metal cots. Vellaiamma was seated on one, with her new granddaughter on her lap; only one other bed was occupied.

Two nurses carried Bhumati in and gently laid her down on a cot. We learned that Bhumati had hemorrhaged after having a tubal ligation, and was barely conscious. The baby was a healthy weight, but we were worried that Bhumati would not survive. Over the next two days, she continued to lose blood. The third day, as I was leaving Madurai, I called Kannan at home to ask how Bhumati was. Kannan was gone but Prema answered. She spoke faster than I'd ever heard a person speak, manic in her worry, and told me that Bhumati had been taken by ambulance to the Government Hospital for blood transfusions. Prema was about to leave for the hospital; their mother and Bhumati's parents-in-law were already there. Kannan would join them later. Government Hospital offers free quality care to all patients, but families have to bring food and buy medicine. For the rest of the next week, until we left India, we called Kannan every day. Bhumati was still in the hospital, alive but very weak. I kept calling once we returned to the U.S., and two weeks later, we learned with great relief that she had come home.

That year, Prema remained unmarried. This weight hung over Kannan. Prema was only a year younger than Bhumati, but the family had not yet been able to arrange her marriage because they had no means to pay her dowry and buy the requisite gifts for the groom's family. Between Kannan's and Prema's earnings, they had managed to put aside enough money to buy three small bits of gold for Prema's wedding. Kannan told me often that arranging Prema's marriage was his last major responsibility in life. "After that, I can die peacefully," he said. "I won't worry any more about leaving this life without finishing my final duty."

When I returned to do fieldwork the following year, I visited Kannan's family right away and found that the household was tense. Prema was not speaking to her father. Kannan had used her gold as collateral to borrow money from a finance company so that he could buy blood for Bhumati, who had continued to need numerous transfusions after she came home from the hospital. The finance company assessed monthly interest, and would hold the jewels for only one year, at which time Kannan either had to pay all the accrued interest plus the principal, or lose the gold. Kannan had made a heart-rending choice, weighing one child's survival against another's future, not knowing what impact his choice would have on either.

Bhumati by then was healthier, and delighted to be living in a new set of apartments. Her baby was a year old, almost as big as the now three-year-old son, who was himself laughing and skipping and starting to say a few words. The extended family had moved twice within the year to find a safer place for their toddlers. At first they had had to separate into two homes in different neighborhoods, but this meant that Bhumati had to give up her work at the factory (since her children were too far away to be cared for by her mother). Several months later, as Bhumati's husband finished work building two small apartments on top of a one-story house, the resident landlord gave him and his in-laws the first chance to rent the new homes. The rent would be a bit of a stretch, but it meant that Bhumati could earn money at the towel factory again, while her mother cared for the three children. They all moved into the entire upper story of the building, with its adjoining two-room apartments opening onto a shared front courtyard. The stairs climbed straight up the side of the building, ending in a wide landing. Once again, Kannan, Vellaiamma, and Prema lived in one apartment, and Bhumati, her husband, and their three children in the other. The front room of each home measured ten by twelve feet and was used for eating, sleeping, and visiting. On Kannan's and Vellaiamma's side, it had sleeping mats rolled up against the green-washed wall, the same small metal wardrobe for storing clothes, and shelves called a "showcase," with new plastic flowers, a radio, a photo of Kannan holding my son, and a knock-off light-skinned Barbie doll. Off of this room, behind a low half-wall, was a small kitchen with a metal drum of hand-pumped drinking water, pots stacked on floor-to-ceiling shelves, a counter holding a two-burner kerosene stove, and a concrete sink. Out in the tiled courtyard were red and blue plastic buckets for washing clothes, a line for drying, and—the real luxury—a walled bathroom for each apartment.

But while Bhumati was in better health and the family in a more comfortable setting, lighthearted Prema had become deeply unhappy. Every time I saw her, she sat glowering in the front room. While her sister had been rescued, Prema saw disaster in her own future. At twenty-six she was far older than most new brides of her Maravar caste. Without her gold, she could not be married. She knew it was unlikely that the jewels would ever be repurchased; for a family with barely enough income to cover food and rent, the combined cost of the loan value and the steadily mounting interest was nearly unthinkable. Prema's jewels had been the only real capital they had. Moreover, any potential groom whose family could give Prema some comfort and security would require more dowry than those jewels represented. Kannan certainly knew this as well. He was deeply relieved that his older daughter was alive, but crushed at being unable to create a new family for his younger daughter. And he was stung by Prema's anger. Every month, with the interest accruing steeply, Prema a month older, and no suitable matches in sight, his family's final security seemed to slip further away.

In past years I had watched the family survive Kannan's job loss, children's illnesses and accidents, troubled marriages, and a huge debt, and I found I could not bear to see this disaster overtake and overwhelm them. Two months later, I went with Kannan to the private finance company from which he had acquired the loan for Bhumati's transfusions. I paid the cost of the principal and interest. The plasticine bag held three tiny gold pieces—two stamped earrings and a pendant—which seemed a meager tie to security.

Over the next two years, back in the United States, I kept waiting for one of the 2:00 A.M. calls Kannan would occasionally make to us, expecting to hear news of Prema's marriage. By 2011, when there had been no word, I became worried there might be no wedding. Traveling through South India in January and February of that year, I tried to call Kannan on the old cell phone a regular customer had given him as a cast-off, but each time I heard only a recorded voice telling me the phone was turned off. That probably meant that the phone wasn't working, and that Kannan had no money to fix it.

The next day, as I continued making phone calls from Kerala, I reached my friend Anjali. "Guess what?" she said. "Kannan brought us a wedding invitation yesterday!" She told me the date so that I could arrange to be in Madurai for the wedding. And the next day, I learned that Kannan had indeed called my U.S. home at 2:30, 3:30, and 4:30 A.M. the night before, repeatedly awakening my partner and the three twelve-year-old boys spending the night for our son's birthday, none of whom spoke Tamil. But Kannan had called from a public call booth, and I still could not reach him on his cell phone.

Several days later, I passed through Madurai with a group of travelers. Kannan had learned from Anjali where I would be stopping for lunch, and he met me with a wedding invitation and a list of items he still needed to acquire. The list detailed everything that had to be presented to the groom's family by the wedding day. It had been drawn up by the groom's family, and agreed to by the bride's, during the negotiations that led to the marriage arrangement. There are technically two components to what is popularly referred to as "dowry" in India. The first includes gold jewelry, cooking vessels, and other gifts of household items bestowed upon a daughter. The second consists of cash, jewelry and other gold items, and large consumer goods given to the groom and/or his family. (Asking for the second type of dowry is illegal in India, but the practice is almost universal, as I discuss in chapter 7.) In practice, there is often little or no distinction between the two. The list in Kannan's hand, which the groom's mother had had written out and delivered, included both types of gifts. It read:

Things that need to be bought

1. 18 g of [additional] gold jewelry [then worth Rs. 27,000]
2. Bureau
3. Metal bed
4. Idli grinder [for idli and dosa batter]
5. Blender
6. T.V.
7. T.V. table
8. Table fan
9. Dowry—Rs. 20,000 remaining to give to groom's family

Looking at this list, I was overwhelmed. While I could afford to give one of the medium-priced consumer goods to the couple, most of these items were too expensive for their friends and relatives to purchase as a gift. Several of them would individually have surpassed what Kannan could save in a year. A huge amount remained for him somehow to come by in the final weeks. Kannan said that he knew he could get loans from certain acquaintances within three days after the wedding, enough to cover the remainder, but the groom's widowed mother had insisted that everything be presented on the day of the wedding itself. In any marriage, the bride's family bears the brunt of the wedding expenses. And because, in Indian hierarchies, the bride's family is ranked lower than the groom's, Kannan's family had to be very careful not to upset their new in-laws. They were worried that if the goods and cash were not acquired in time, Prema's new mother-in-law would shame Prema—not an easy beginning to a new marriage—or even call off the arrangement, which could end Prema's marriage prospects for good.

A week later, I was back in Madurai on my own. I went to see Kannan and Vellaiamma immediately, and they looked like they had not eaten or slept for a week. But the groom, they told me, was a good young man. His mother might be scheming, his younger sisters mean-spirited, but neighbors had insisted to them and their marriage broker that this boy was kind and hard-working. Although the two families lived in the same part of the city, they had not met previously, and Prema had seen the groom only once during the wedding arrangements. She was pleased that her marriage was almost a reality, and she was quieter than usual.

I ended up buying an idli grinder as a gift, along with some large stainless steel water pots. Kannan decided that I should bring the metal pots to their house the night before the wedding, since they were inscribed with my name and it would always be known that I had given them, but like other guests I should save my major gift for a formal presentation at the wedding itself. When I arrived at their house on the eve of the wedding, the family's greeting was warm, and Bhumati was especially welcoming as she took over for her exhausted mother. Bhumati tried to teach me what I should say during the wedding presentation. I was grateful for the instruction. It was a long recitation, delivered in formal Tamil quite different from the colloquial style of the language I was more used to speaking, so I asked her to write it down for me to memorize later. She tried to write the first word, then gave up. "I can't," she said, "I haven't studied." I was taken aback that Bhumati couldn't write easily after studying through the eighth standard, but I turned to Prema, who wrote out the speech without hesitation.

The next day, I went to the long-awaited wedding, along with Anjali. We were also joined by Anjali's friend Murugan, a professional videographer whom I had asked to make a wedding DVD for Kannan's family. There were about two hundred people in the wedding hall, an auditorium-like room with a low platform at the front. Most of the room was filled with chairs facing the platform, and along one side were two long rows of tables for the wedding feast, which went on throughout the event. While most of the lengthy series of wedding rituals took place in the hall, the central rituals, including tying the bride's *tāli*—a gold marriage pendant on a turmeric-colored cord—took place in a small Balamurugan temple down the street.

One of the other guests invited to the wedding was M. Chellasamy, a local industrial magnate, whom Kannan had met when I interviewed the industrialist in 2009. Two months before those interviews, Chellasamy had celebrated his own daughter's wedding with a public feast that Kannan and his family had attended, along with over a thousand other Madurai residents (as I describe in chapter 8). During my first interview with Chellasamy, I had mentioned that Kannan had spoken highly of the feast. At the end of our meeting, the industrialist made a point of coming out of his immense factory to meet Kannan. When I interviewed Chellasamy at home on another day, he sought out Kannan again and asked me to photograph them together in front of his grand staircase, which was modeled on the set for the 2005 Rajinikant film *Chandramukhi*. Now, two years later, Kannan and Vellaiamma had returned to Chellasamy's home to present an invitation to Prema's wedding. Kannan hoped Chellasamy would come.

Chellasamy did not. I had not expected that he would—but I was essentially wrong. After I left the wedding, one of Chellasamy's assistants arrived at the wedding hall. He explained that his boss was out of town, but had sent him to give Kannan Rs. 5001.[1] That night, I saw Kannan and Vellaiamma heading off wearily in Kannan's auto, on their way to buy a bureau, television, and bed. The industrialist's gift would go some way toward those dowry requirements. When I called Kannan late that night, he had just gotten home from delivering everything to his daughter's new mother-in-law, and he was eating for the first time that day. He had been able to acquire everything—some of it with additional loans that I did not ask the source of—except for the last 12 grams of gold. He was exhausted, but almost elated; by the end of that month, he said, after he had paid a deposit on an apartment for the new couple, he would be "free." He would still have debts to pay off to be sure, but he had done his life's duty. The last thing Kannan told me on the phone was that he cried when his daughter left with her husband that night. "After all," he said, "she has been with me her whole life."

But with his daughters married, Kannan could turn again to wishing for his own economic security. He still hoped to buy his own auto. Over the years, Vellaiamma had told me pointedly that I needed to buy him one, most recently quoting a cost of Rs.120,000 (which at that point was roughly $2,500). Owning an auto remained an impossible fantasy. When I first drafted this portrait a few years back, Kannan's story was one of a tenuous but constantly threatened hold on stability, more secure than he and Vellaiamma had been after their marriage, but still well below the class standing of their parents. Thereafter, however, Kannan had what may (or may not) have been a stroke of incredible fortune.

In early 2014, Kannan called and told me excitedly that he was about to get a bank loan for purchasing an auto. (The auto would cost Rs. 150,000, he said, and interest on the loan would amount to another Rs. 100,000.) I was stunned, because acquiring a bank loan normally requires economic, cultural, and social capital far beyond Kannan's reach (as I explain in chapter 5). When I visited Kannan again in 2015, he proudly showed me his bank loan book. The book was a graphic measure of his fluctuating income, documenting the principal and interest that he had paid in some months, but also the penalties and extra interest accruing in other months when circumstances prevented him from driving regularly.

I then learned the unusual circumstances that had enabled him to procure the loan. He told me that one of his regular passengers, the district head of a private bank, called a local bank branch, vouched for Kannan, and instructed the bank manager to give Kannan a loan. One day during my stay in 2015 I went to the bank with Kannan and Vellaiamma when they made their monthly loan payment. The current bank manager agreed to talk with me about loan rates and schemes, and while we were in the manager's office, Kannan casually named the district manager who had been his contact. The branch manager grew visibly upset and immediately interjected, saying that no, the bank officers *never* give loans based on people's recommendations, only based on the "viability and integrity" of the applicant. I was intrigued, and asked how the staff determined integrity. He shook his head angrily and said only, "Local integrity," refusing to elaborate. Nonetheless, Kannan, who lacked the steady income and substantial collateral that represent the minimal requirements for a loan, acquired one the only way someone like him possibly could have, through an unlikely access to powerful social connections.

Despite his (officially inadmissible) good luck, it is unclear to me how Kannan will maintain the monthly payments on his uncertain income. Gasoline price hikes, strikes, and political unrest often cut into his earnings, and he cannot drive when illness incapacitates him. If he defaults on the loan, he loses the tens of thousands of rupees he has repaid. He and Vellaiamma have suffered several medical setbacks in the past year, and by 2015 they had moved to a smaller home with fewer conveniences and sparser furnishings than at any time since I first met them; clearly they feel on a financial edge. If, however, Kannan can maintain payments steadily enough to save the loan, he and Vellaiamma will have gained an exceptional amount of financial security for those who count themselves among the illātavaṅka.

Anjali

Anjali was eight years old when I met her. After the day that I asked to take a photo of their compound's kōlam, Anjali and her younger brother Kumar were frequent visitors in my home. They would come down the street to my building in the afternoons, then settle into a broad window-sill in my apartment and read Tamil and Russian folklore books I had bought at the New Century Bookhouse, a USSR-funded venture. I keep a photo of them in my home office today. On the wall of their parents' home, where Kumar and his wife lived until the compound was razed two years ago, hung a photo of me that was taken around the same time. It is a paradigmatic "fieldwork" photo. Bent over a table, writing field-notes on a manual typewriter, I was wearing my usual sari, my long dark hair braided and garlanded with jasmine.

Anjali and Kumar had four brothers and a sister, all of them older. With their parents, the family had nine members, all living in a home that measured five by twelve feet. Their father made his living riding a bicycle rickshaw, and Anjali's mother worked as a housewife. The parents planned to educate all their children through high school (tenth standard) despite their meager household income. Their emphasis on education may have been partly due to their Pillai caste, a relatively high-ranking caste that stresses the value of education; but it also stemmed from their view, typical of the mid-1980s, that education was

Photo 3. Anjali and Kumar reading in my windowsill, dressed in their best clothes for the outing, 1986. Photo credit: Sara Dickey.

the single most important factor in improving their children's chances for the future.

Educating children is expensive, however. Private schools, especially English-medium, are popularly viewed as providing the best education and the strongest chances of succeeding on standardized examinations, and the fees for these schools can be extremely high. Even the Tamil-medium government schools that Anjali and her siblings attended, which do not charge high fees, require expenditures on uniforms, books, paper, pens, and other supplies. In addition, children who attend school cannot work for the small wages that in some families are crucial for meeting expenses.

When I first met Anjali and her family, Anjali was in the third grade and very interested in reading and in language. I remember sitting in her home in my early days of learning Tamil, when Anjali would teach me the contrasting literary and colloquial forms of the words she thought it was most important for me to know. (I had last studied Tamil as an undergraduate three years earlier, and I had much to re-learn when I came to Madurai.) Tamil is a highly "diglossic" language, which means that the written and spoken forms of the language vary not just in vocabulary, but also in pronunciation. They differ enough that people who do not read also often do not understand the literary language when it is spoken (as when someone reads a book aloud, or when politicians give speeches). So of an evening, while Anjali's mother and older sister cooked the family dinner over a small wood fire in the corner of the room, her father rested on the bench in the compound entryway, and her brothers went in and out on various errands, Anjali built on my interest in the rules of language.

Like most people without much money, Anjali's parents decided how long to keep their children in school by balancing each child's interest and success against the expenses of sending the child to school. Anjali wanted to study beyond the tenth standard, and her parents allowed her to finish the twelfth. This level was a prerequisite for college entrance, and Anjali passionately desired to go to college. Her parents were adamant that she take a job instead; the family needed her salary. But they compromised and agreed to let her take a typing course, and soon Anjali found a job as a typist. Her income and her unmarried brothers' wages allowed the family to put savings aside for emergencies and for crucial events like marriages, to pay off debts, and to buy a few conveniences like a metal cot and even a black-and-white TV. Anjali had grown up knowing that her family was responsible for supporting and helping her until she married, and that she was responsible for respecting and helping them as well. Family was central to her well-being and identity.

Anjali did not, therefore, defy her parents' decision. Instead, she enlisted her brothers' support. (By then, her sister had married and moved away.) She talked to her four older brothers about how much she wanted to go to college, and argued that she could support the family even more if she had a college education. Persuaded, her brothers helped convince their parents that Anjali could study for a correspondence degree while keeping her job. After protracted debate, her parents finally agreed. So Anjali worked at her typing job all day, and studied at home in the evenings while the rest of the family was socializing in the same room or talking right outside the house with passersby; then she would get up early in the morning to attend two hours of tutoring with dozens of other students in the nearby home of a university professor, before heading to her job again. The three years of studying for her B.Com. (a bachelor's degree in business) were tough. Anjali explained that it wasn't simply that she had no quiet place to read, but also, as she recalled in 1999, "There was no one at home who could teach me; they are all uneducated." No one could help her study, or empathize with the problems and pressures she faced in finishing a college degree.

But Anjali did finish, and went on to take a six-month computer certificate course. Her family was pleased when she found a job in a graphic design business only a block from their home. The proximity meant that, even as an unmarried young woman of a relatively high caste, she could walk to work unchaperoned. The business was small; the only other people working in it were the husband and wife who owned the company. They designed and printed calendars, wedding invitations, business cards, and school textbooks.

Anjali's position gave her family an additional Rs. 1,000 per month. It also placed her in a social environment that would have been inaccessible if she, like most other women of marriageable age, had stayed at home after finishing her education. The office on the floor above hers held a small videography business specializing in wedding and party videos, and down the corridor was a computer and Internet center. She made close friends with people her age working in these offices. Puri, who worked next door, taught her how to find affordable stylish clothing and to groom her hair in new ways. Both women became close friends with Murugan, one of the videographers. At that time, friendships with young men were rare for proper young women. Anjali's work gave her a new sophistication, which derived not just from her contact with computers, but also from her knowledge of fashion, casual friendships with men her age, a confident way of speaking, and an awareness of the world outside her family and neighbors. She was, in essence, experimenting with modernity, which in India is often an element of a higher-class image.

Anjali's arrival at this point had not simply been an individual accomplishment; it required the joint efforts and support of her family members. Her family was willing to support her because of her academic interest and success, but also because her education and computer-related career gave the family prestige and enhanced Anjali's prospects of making a "good" marriage. Through everyone's efforts, Anjali gained the education, work skills, sophistication, modern sensibility, and even social connections that could make her eligible to join a higher class.

In the meantime, with Anjali and her three brothers working, her family was becoming more comfortable financially. For a brief period, her mother—who managed the household finances—felt secure enough to stop worrying about how to make ends meet. She paid off debts, put money aside for her eldest son's wedding, and began to consider what kind of groom to find for Anjali.

By then Anjali was twenty-two, older than most unmarried women of her caste and class. Marriage is a crucial, life-changing event for almost everyone in Madurai. Not only is it the biggest responsibility that most parents bear for their children, it has long been at least as important as education in determining the stability and security of a person's life. And in most cases, it is not only the spouse who must be considered, but also the potential spouse's family. Marrying a person means marrying into that person's family too, especially for a woman; and marriages are alliances between families, not simply affairs between individuals.

It was time to find a marriage alliance for Anjali, a critical time for displaying family status to the social public. Most parents try to arrange a child's marriage with a family of similar economic means and educational background, believing that this will make it easier for the new couple and the two families to get along. In the case of a daughter, it also smooths her entry into the family she marries into. But, in a rare move, Anjali's parents were hoping that Anjali's education would make her a proper bride for a family of a civil servant or business owner, someone with much more financial stability than Anjali had grown up with. They faced a major hurdle in making such an alliance, however, because such grooms require a hefty amount of cash, gold, and household goods, equivalent to more than ten years' income for Anjali's father. (I describe their match-making strategies in more detail in chapter 7.) Anjali's parents had planned to use the dowry they had recently received from their second son's wedding to supplement their savings for Anjali.

Suddenly, though, her father was injured on the job. One day about six months after Anjali began working, he picked up a heavy parcel from an office for a delivery and was carrying it down several flights of stairs when he slipped and the box struck him on his upper spine. The family first rushed him to the Government Hospital, but because medical workers there were on strike, they had to take him to a private clinic, where they knew the costs of his care would far outstrip their available means. Because like most Indians Anjali's father had no health insurance or other "safety net," all the dowry they had received—plus some sizeable, very high-interest loans from informal moneylenders—went to cover the costs of his hospitalization and recovery. For three years, one person's wages—a third of the household income—went to paying off the interest and principal on the loans each month. Their father recovered somewhat, but he was never able to return to paid work. Anjali's parents were now faced with finding her a husband at a time when they had not only lost the father's income, but also incurred significant debt.

Soon thereafter, Anjali's employers decided to move their business to another office a few miles away, and Anjali was unable to continue working for them. As her parents pointed out, it was inappropriate for an unmarried young woman to travel unaccompanied through the city—at least if she hoped to marry into an honorable family. So Anjali proposed that she open her own design business in the old office, using a bank loan to start up the business. Given her experience and skills, and the added advantage of retaining much of the business's old customer base, Anjali was confident she could run the business on her own. Her parents agreed to let her take the risk. Anjali successfully completed the arduous process of acquiring a bank loan for computer equipment, aided significantly by her acquaintance with an old college classmate whose father happened to be the manager of the bank. She also obtained a new computer from the same classmate, who sold computer hardware and, aware that his father had already promised to provide the loan, trusted that the purchase price would be forthcoming. Anjali's education was already paying dividends in her class standing: it first enabled her to get a professional job, and then provided social contacts that gave her access to resources like loans (as well as customers).

In the meantime, Anjali's mother had stopped talking about finding a groom. When in 1999 I asked why, she said they were waiting to get the new business well established because they hoped its income would substitute for a portion of the dowry.

Unbeknownst to her parents, however, Anjali had fallen in love with a friend of her older brother. Her beau, Sundaram, worked in a shop across the street from her own office. He was from just the kind of family that Anjali's parents had been looking for—his father was a civil servant who owned a large home—but Sundaram belonged to the lower-ranked Thevar caste, so Anjali's brother could not suggest him as a potential groom. As Anjali's parents began proposing potential matches again, and Sundaram's parents simultaneously began the same process— proffering each candidate's photo, family information, and horoscope— Anjali and Sundaram rejected each suggestion as they kept in touch via cell phone. They rarely risked meeting, even though they worked just yards from each other. This went on for two years, as their parents became increasingly impatient with Anjali's and Sundaram's refusals to consider a match.

Finally, in 2001, as things at home became increasingly tense, Anjali and Sundaram told their parents they wished to marry each other. Both sets of parents were distraught. After a long struggle, with Anjali's brother and her friend Murugan acting as go-betweens, they finally convinced their parents to let them have an "arranged love marriage." This saved some face, since it could be said that the two families agreed to the marriage. It also prevented Anjali and Sundaram from eloping, which would have further shamed their families. Finally, although this was not an arrangement of their making, Anjali landed in the kind of life her parents wanted for her. After the wedding, Anjali moved into her husband's parents' home.

Anjali had sent me a wedding announcement in the United States, so I knew she had married. By the time I returned to Madurai in 2004, Anjali and Sundaram already had a son, who usually came to the office with them so that they could care for him while they worked. Sundaram, who has an M.A. and had established a moderately successful jute bag-making concern, closed his own company and joined Anjali's business shortly after their marriage, adding his computer and management skills to hers. The couple renamed the enterprise after their two fathers. I finally met Sundaram for the first time in their office, where I was also treated to a viewing of their wedding albums. The albums—produced by Murugan—included all the typical photos of a demure bride and somber groom, priests enacting marriage rituals, and relatives and friends presenting gifts. Anjali and Sundaram pointed out their many relatives in the photographs.

The next day, a Sunday, I had lunch with Sundaram's family in their spacious two-story home on the southwestern outskirts of the city, where Anjali and Sundaram lived. As Sundaram's father and I sat on cane chairs and conversed, I discreetly watched Anjali standing against the wall on the far side of the large room, the new daughter-in-law in vigilant attendance. The rest of the joint family—Anjali's mother-in-law; her two unmarried brothers-in-law; and two sisters-in-law, one unmarried and one widowed with a son—relaxed as they sat comfortably on the floor. Later, when we ate a meal of mutton curry, tomato rice, and many vegetables, Anjali was the one to run to the kitchen for whatever was needed. Both the photo albums and Anjali's deferential behavior signaled a standard arranged marriage to me, and it never occurred to me to wonder whether it had been otherwise. It wasn't until 2009, when I interviewed Anjali to update an essay I had written about her, that she and Sundaram told me they had been in love for years before marrying, and that Sundaram's caste was different from Anjali's.

By now Anjali had borne a second child, a daughter. Their business was doing well, and she and Sundaram were trying to expand it. In 2009 they bought an offset printer, a huge machine that fills half their office. I saw Anjali and Sundaram at the beginning of my four-month stay that year, stopping at their office as I always do when I am in downtown Madurai. Murugan was there, playing with their two-year-old daughter; her older brother was at school. When Murugan took the little girl out for the daily "round" on his motorbike, Anjali mentioned to me that she was having trouble getting enough loans to cover the high cost of the printer. I described bank loan programs I had heard about for women in business, but Anjali doubted whether she could get one since she no longer knew anyone who worked in a bank. Her classmate's father had moved on to a bank in another city, and personal connections are often key for getting loan approval even for people who possess the necessary collateral. Eventually Anjali and Sundaram managed to get private financing to cover the cost of their printer. Since few people are yet trained to run these printers in Madurai, however, it took them almost two years to find a reliable operator and see a steady income boost. They are now heavily in debt.

Anjali is much better off than her parents were. She has learned middle-class ways, and has integrated herself into her husband's family. First she was a daughter-in-law on tenterhooks, the only daughter-in-law in a large household, and moreover living with in-laws who hadn't chosen her. As her children were born and her business prospered, she slowly came to be seen as an asset to the family. In 2008, the last time I saw Anjali in her in-laws' home, she and her widowed sister-in-law and mother-in-law all gathered together in a side bedroom, sitting with me on the bed to show me wedding albums. Anjali's isolation and deference were by then much less marked.

Another major change occurred in 2010. Anjali and Sundaram moved out of his parents' house and into a small rented home near their children's school and their office. Their son had been attending one of Madurai's most prestigious English-medium grammar schools. After protracted uncertainty about whether they could afford the fees, they had enrolled their daughter in the same school as her brother, and Anjali and Sundaram cited their need to reduce travel costs as the reason for separating from the joint family.

Their new neighborhood is decidedly middle class. The rented house is part of a six-house compound, but it is physically very different from the compound Anjali grew up in. Like other buildings in the neighborhood, it sits on its own lot. It is entered through a gate, behind which bicycles are stacked on the left, and behind those is a staircase that leads to the roof; on the right is a shared hand pump for purified city water. An open hallway runs straight ahead through the building, with three homes opening off each side. The flat brick roof is used by everyone for drying chili peppers and laundry. Anjali and Sundaram's rented home has three small rooms—a "hall" or front room, kitchen, and bedroom, plus a private bathroom off of the bedroom—but they are nicely constructed with granite tile floors. While it is much less spacious than Sundaram's parents' home, it is comfortable and respectable. The bedroom has one metal double bed frame and two metal bureaus. One plastic-caned chair sits in the hall, and the puja shelves hold numerous lithographs, though not as many as lined the wall of Anjali's childhood home. The kitchen, stacked with pans, water pots, and lunch boxes, includes a tile sink with a faucet that brings well water directly into the house—a luxury unavailable to everyone on the street Anjali grew up on, and still well out of reach for Kannan's family.

On my last day in Madurai in 2011, after I had visited Anjali and Sundaram at their office a final time, Anjali made sure to walk out with me. She told me how worried she was about the debt they had incurred. They took out two loans amounting to over Rs. 200,000 to pay for the printer and its associated costs, one from a bank and one from a private firm using jewelry as assurance. They have been able to pay the monthly Rs. 10,000 interest payments, but nothing against the principal. She said that her children's school fees are also tremendously high, but then she asked rhetorically, "What can I do? I don't want my children to have a life like mine. If we educate them well, then they can get good jobs, not just some job in a printing office." Stunned, and troubled, I said, "But *this* is a good job, Anjali," thinking of the socioeconomic distance she has traveled herself. Anjali simply gave a half-smile.

Jeyamani

Jeyamani has worked in domestic service since her childhood. After her father died in 1965 when she was seven years old, her family lost their home and moved onto the street, begging for food and money. In an evocative phrase, Jeyamani once told me, "We even drank our *kanci* by begging." Kanci, a rice gruel, is a food associated with the poor.

Jeyamani recalled that as their days on the street wore on, she started to understand the world and their future in it. She thought often about "how we were when my father was alive, and how we were without him now." At the age of seven, she decided to support her mother and sisters by finding a job as a servant. Her first employers were a foreign family who worked for the Fenner mill in Madurai. Young children were often employed as servants then (and still are to some extent, even though a compulsory Education Act was recently passed). They are thought to be docile and malleable, and they require a far lower salary than adults. Eventually, Jeyamani said, her employers were persuaded that they were paying her too much (foreigners typically pay above the local wage scale); they cut her pay, and once again she had to worry about how to support her mother and siblings. She was then offered a job with a foreign family in the southern city of Tuticorin—probably on the recommendation of her first employers—and she went to live with them full-time. Her Rs. 20 monthly salary was several times higher than her previous salary, and most of her earnings were sent to her mother.

Jeyamani lived with this family for eight years, visiting her own family only once a year when her employers came back to Madurai to visit relatives. Jeyamani remembers these employers with great affection. "They beat me," she said, but "as much as they hit me, they also cared about me. If they gave me a beating, they would cuddle with me just like they did with their daughter." When Jeyamani reached puberty, her employers made her return to Madurai. She says they insisted she go home because "Tuticorin is a bad place"—they believed that the more conservative city of Madurai would be better for a girl who would soon be ready for marriage. Jeyamani said, "I did not want to come back to this place. They raised me as their daughter." Still, she returned to her natal family in Madurai, continuing to work as a servant, then marrying at age fifteen. Her young husband sometimes had work whitewashing houses, sometimes driving a bicycle rickshaw. The work was erratic, and Jeyamani kept her own jobs. In 1992 she told me, "Right from childhood I have been working in houses. I was toiling from my childhood. And I am still toiling."

By the time I met her that year, Jeyamani was twenty-seven. She had borne four children, one of whom died at the age of three. Her living children included two sons aged nine and seven, and a daughter who was three years old. Jeyamani and her husband previously had not been able to afford the school uniforms, notebooks, and pens required for the government school, so their older son had just started studying in the first standard. This made him three or four years older than most of his classmates. Jeyamani, though, was a fierce believer in education. She told me, "If my mother and father had given me an education, now I would be doing a teacher's job or a nurse's job."

I met Jeyamani while I was conducting interviews in S.S. Colony, a neighborhood in southwestern Madurai, just behind the housing colony where Usha was then living. Many of the neighborhood women were domestic workers. I was sitting with several of them in the bare and now crowded one-room home of an elderly woman named Agnes. Private conversations are not the norm in neighborhoods where many of the houses have no solid door, and where adjoining homes that share a thatched roof are often separated by only a partial woven-reed wall. So I was not surprised at having a group as audience or as part of the conversation. These working women were all at home because this was their mid-day break between morning and evening jobs. The employer's pots and pans were scrubbed, floors swept and swabbed, and any cooking tasks were completed; in the evening, these tasks would be repeated.

Agnes turned out to be quite taciturn. She either refused to answer most of my questions or deliberately misinterpreted them. For example, when I asked whether there was an organization for servants, she said, "An organization for white people?! Why would there be such a thing??" The Tamil words for servants (*vēlaikkāraṅka*) and white people (*veḷḷaikkāraṅka*) are similar, but easily distinguishable, and everyone else had understood. Agnes had turned the power dynamic in her favor, with a skillful subtlety that I appreciated. At that moment, Agnes's next-door neighbor came home from her morning job and walked in to see what was happening. She immediately picked up the conversation, and spoke for half an hour about her mixed experiences with local domestic workers' organizations. Then she invited us into her adjoining home, and we all moved as a group there; Agnes sat for a while on the threshold until she returned to her own home where, nonetheless, she could continue listening through the wall.

This new speaker was Jeyamani. Her home was as small and bare as Agnes's. She had a small hearth for a wood fire in the far corner, several cooking pots, three plates and two cups, two plastic water pots, a yellow rope strung across the top of the room with a few clothes draped over it, and a shelf that held a tiny mirror, a tiny container for kumkum powder, and a small lithograph of the Virgin Mary. Through a hook in a bamboo beam an old sari was looped to make a soft cradle for Jeyamani's youngest child.

Jeyamani was a powerful speaker. She was bold and outspoken, unafraid to criticize employers or social service workers or Americans, but she often infused an edge of warmth into her tone. All of us were compelled by the depth and articulateness of her views on the social world. As she began to answer my question about organizations (*caṅkams*, commonly spelled *sangams*) for domestic workers, she became very critical. She talked about the hard work she had put in for the sangam, attending meetings in Madurai, speaking at meetings in other cities, and fasting along with others to try to get land deeds for domestic workers. In the end, though, she felt betrayed by the sangam. Her hard work had gotten her nothing, no land rights or loans, because the sangam leaders said that Jeyamani was not poor enough. But Jeyamani charged that the land the sangam gained, the homes they built, and the money they made available for loans were only given to "those who have"—people who already have the resources that she lacks.

Jeyamani was employed in one home, working mornings 9:00–12:00 and evenings from 4:00 until about 7:00. She washed dishes, cleaned the five-member family's laundry by hand, swept, scrubbed the floors, and dusted. Her employers in Tuticorin had taught her to cook, and I asked Jeyamani whether she also cooked for her current employers. She laughed.

> They are Brahmans. Would they allow us to cook?! People like you would feel easy about having me cook. In my family we eat meat and fish, but they don't eat that food. A few Brahman households might go as far as telling a servant, "Boil the milk." That Brahman claims that he doesn't eat meat or any other nonvegetarian food. But he goes to a Muslim's marriage and sits and eats there in the feast. He eats it [mutton] and asks us to smell his hand when he comes home, to show us what he has done. In his lunchbox, he takes rice and meat. So he *does* eat everything. But if we go into the kitchen, he'll say that "they" won't like us to be in there.

"They" would be other members of the male employer's family, who follow orthodox Brahman rules about maintaining purity in the kitchen. Since Jeyamani is a Paraiyar, a caste considered by many people to be one of the most polluted, it is not unusual that a Brahman family would feel uncomfortable with her entering the kitchen or cooking their food. Similarly, most Brahmans consider meat too polluting to consume. Jeyamani, however, deftly revealed the hypocrisy of this Brahman man's practices.

Over the years I have observed Jeyamani's exceptional articulateness about the exigencies of hierarchy and inequality, and particularly about the burdens of poverty and the class system as a whole. In our first interviews, she made frequent contrasts between her economic and social situations and her employers'. In that initial interview, she told me, "You are those who have. You could eat whatever you want. You could cook anything you wanted to eat. Nothing bad will happen if you fall ill." On the other hand—as her own life had already shown, and would continue to illustrate in the years to come—for the poor, illness means crippling expenditures for medicine and treatment (or no treatment at all), lost wages, and death. And the poor must earn every day in order to be able to cook and eat even a meager meal.

In such situations, people who are poor must often borrow money to take care of unexpected expenses, or to buy food at the end of the month when the previous month's salary has run out. Jeyamani criticizes wealthy employers for being unwilling to raise her salary by even a small amount, or to give a minor loan. In poor families, women are more likely to earn a steady income than are their husbands. Lower-class men's work is often sporadic or seasonal; and men, who are expected to use much of their available cash on socializing with other men, generally put less of their wage toward family needs than do women (cf. Kapadia 1995, 42). A domestic worker like Jeyamani earns a monthly salary, most of which goes immediately to pay rent and to repay the previous month's loans—loans that typically accrue at least 10 percent interest per month. Men's wages are higher than women's, and more likely to be paid daily. Thus, even though a wife's income usually provides the majority of the house-hold's cash, a man's (or son's or daughter's) wage is crucial for daily expenses.

In the first interviews, Jeyamani repeatedly contrasted the circum-stances of the poor and the wealthy. In another example, she described the kinds of grooms that each can hope for when they arrange their daughters' marriages:

> *They* look for "officers" [civil servants]. But we look for house servants, rickshaw drivers, construction workers, etc. . . . In the future, the lives of our children will be just like ours. . . . How can we progress with this money? If we don't go to work for a day, we have to borrow money. But what do they do? Because they get a salary on the first, they stock up on rice, lentils, etc. Those provisions might cost 1,500 rupees, and they will have 1,500 rupees on hand. And having those 1,500 rupees [i.e., a large salary], they apply for loans, and they build big concrete houses.

Jeyamani also emphasized the mutual dependence that binds employers and domestic workers. If I had been asked at that time to describe this dependence, I would have said that workers depend on employers for wages, along with some material goods and perhaps the infrequent use of employers' social connections; employers depend on servants to main-tain the type of home necessary to keep up a middle- or upper-class standing, and also to serve as symbols of the household's standing. Jeya-mani, with a clear understanding of this relationship, went further, not-ing repeatedly that the relationship is hardly static: the rich "advance" and "progress"—using their money and capital—while for the poor, "the lives of our children will be just like ours." Despite their interdepen-dence, she was saying, the poor stand in place while the wealthy leap forward.

When I returned to Madurai seven years later, I went to look for Jeyamani. Kannan helped me find her house, twisting through brush and over rocky paths from one set of huts to another. But Jeyamani was no longer living there. She had moved twice since I had last seen her in 1992. People at her old place sent us to the next area she had lived in, and people there sent us to her current home. We found Jeyamani outside her new home pumping water. I could see that her circumstances had improved. She invited us in, but we stayed only briefly because the house was soon crowded with relatives who had come to attend a funeral ritual for Jeyamani's sister-in-law (her husband's sister). I gave Jeyamani some small gifts I had brought from the United States—scented soaps, maple candy, and hair clips—and we left.

A week or so later, Jeyamani stopped by my office to invite me to visit her sister-in-law's family. I came back to her neighborhood on the morning we had agreed upon. That day would turn out to involve a rather puzzling set of interactions. Later I would understand how typical they are of families where members are divided by class differences, however small.

Up until then, I had met only one member of Jeyamani's family other than her children and husband. This was Jeyamani's older sister—actually a cousin, in standard American kin terms, but they referred to each other as sisters. Her name was Mary. When I arrived at Jeyamani's home that day, Mary was there, and she told me that Jeyamani was still at work. Mary took me off to their brother's wife's house, a couple of blocks away. (Whether the brother was Jeyamani's or Mary's, or a cousin to them both, I never learned; it wasn't a relevant distinction.) This house was a great deal different from Jeyamani's small house of cobbled-together materials. Their brother's family lived in a solid masonry house surrounded by small plantings and shaded by a tall tree. Inside, there were several rooms, including a front hall with an upholstered couch and chairs, a television, and a cassette player.

I never saw much of the house, though. While Mary went inside to make tea for us, Kannan and I were greeted by the brother's wife, a teacher wearing a starched sari and carefully groomed hair. She and Mary directed us to sit in the entryway—on the tile step that separated the inside of the house from the outside. The social rules of house entry in Madurai are that higher-status visitors are allowed further inside than are lower-status ones, and if you are an invited guest, you normally enter at least some part of the house. The higher the guests' caste and class, the more likely they are to be allowed into the house proper, and Kannan and I had no reason to be kept out on either count (since, while for some people my castelessness makes me below-caste, this had never been the case with people of scheduled castes, like Jeyamani's family). Kannan and I sat on the threshold.

While we waited, the brother's wife brought us photo albums of family life-cycle rituals—a wedding, a puberty ceremony—a typical social activity for visitors. When the tea came, we remained sitting in the doorway, talking with Mary and her brother's wife, and looking through the photo albums. Our hostess pointed out various relatives who were carefully posed, such as her husband's father's brother's son who was an office clerk, and her own sister who was a housewife. I noticed Mary in one of the photos, but Mary's brother's wife pointedly neglected to identify the woman standing next to Mary. Like Mary, this woman wore little jewelry, and a simpler sari than most of the other women in the album. When I asked who she was, our hostess stayed tight-lipped, forcing Mary to answer that the woman was her own older sister.

Eventually Jeyamani arrived, and without so much as greeting her sister-in-law, she collected the rest of us and herded us all back to her house. It wasn't until we reached Jeyamani's place that I realized I had just visited the very sister-in-law I'd been summoned to see. The reason for that day's visit was indeed to meet Jeyamani's sister-in-law's family, but since Jeyamani had extended the invitation using the English term "sister-in-law"—which covers a much broader range of meanings than the nearest Tamil terms, which differentiate brothers' wives from husbands' sisters—I had thought she meant the family of the sister-in-law who had just died. This had been a command performance. We had apparently been called to enhance the status of Jeyamani's brother's family, or at least of his wife; or the sister-in-law might simply have been forcing Jeyamani to share the symbolic and potentially economic resource she had in this white foreign woman.

The moment we were back in her home, Jeyamani began complaining that she never visits her better-off family members because they look down their noses at her and don't even want to claim Jeyamani as family. Jeyamani and Mary said that their brother's wife disrespects them (*matikkamāṭṭāṅka*) because they are poor, and she refuses to visit Jeyamani's house. Although they are relatives, she sees Jeyamani as *maṭṭam* (disgusting) because Jeyamani does servant work. That explained why Jeyamani refused to speak to her sister-in-law. It also explained why we were not invited in; if we had been, Mary might also have had to be treated as a guest, or at least a semi-guest, whereas she is regularly called to work there when the sister-in-law needs extra domestic help. Jeyamani said that their sister-in-law should have claimed Mary's sister as a relative when she showed me the photos, but "she won't because she looks down on her for not having money."

While Jeyamani is less well off than some of her relatives, her circumstances were nonetheless more comfortable in 1999 than in 1992. She and her family now lived on free government land, in a home they built themselves. The house was made of corrugated steel, boards, plywood, and bricks. Jeyamani said they had bought the materials, but in some places the construction looked like such a haphazard combination that I guessed that certain pieces had been incorporated as they were scavenged from landfills and roadsides. Inside, the house had a partial dividing wall separating the main room from a good-sized kitchen. The main room served as a sitting area with a large work table along the outside wall. On the partition wall itself were shelves holding an old color television and two dented cassette players. Next to the shelves was a metal bureau. The television was bought second-hand, and its sound was poor. The two tape players were being repaired by her sons, Jeyamani said. Jeyamani's house had noticeably more *vacati* ("resources" or, here, "conveniences") than the home I first met her in. Their new home was on Housing Board land. In India, state and local governments regularly allow poor people to build houses on unclaimed land (purampōkku) owned by the government. Families who built homes, often called "squatters" (and their homes "encroachments") by wealthier people, were allowed to live there without paying rent, but Jeyamani said that a factory was due to be built there soon, and they had been given two eviction notices. (When the government builds on purampōkku land, residents usually shift to another vacant area, which they learn about either through information provided by the government body or through their social connections.) She had learned about this plot through other domestic workers she had met in the workers' sangam.

Jeyamani is Catholic, but she told me that on the official certificate that all children must acquire to enter school, her children are listed as Hindu Paraiyar. This allows them access to the "reservations," or affirmative-action type benefits, that are available to Hindu scheduled castes but not to Christians of the same castes. I remembered the first day I met Jeyamani and her neighbors, all but one of whom were Catholic, and they pointed out a Mariamman goddess shrine where they worshipped daily, as we walked along the path between their houses. This "mixing" of religions is not unusual for Christians in Madurai, especially those who are poor. Jeyamani distrusted the church administration and its hierarchies. In 2000, she and Mary both told me that they never attended the nearby church, just worshipped at a local temple.

A year later, when I returned to Madurai in 2001, Jeyamani was working for two elderly Anglo-Indians in the mornings for Rs. 500 per month. She had also just opened a small food stand along the road that entered the colony, selling idli (steamed fermented rice-flour cakes) and mutton curry. Her husband had been ill with a fever that might have been typhoid, which had left his joints too sore for him to work. Her sons had dropped out of school the year before, after finishing the ninth and tenth standards, but were unemployed. Her eleven-year-old daughter was in the sixth standard. Jeyamani was aggravated about her children's studies; she said she tried to make them study, but they wouldn't.

Mary soon joined us. After she commented on how thin I had supposedly become—a standard greeting that expresses caring and concern—I looked more closely at her and realized that she in fact *had* become much thinner. She told me that she had lost one of her two jobs, and could not find another to replace it.

I visited Jeyamani until 2005. When I went to see her in 2009, the land she had lived on had been cleared of its cobbled-together homes, and no one could tell us where she had gone. I have never learned how far her daughter studied in school, who or how her children married, or what work they did.

Usha

Usha, like Jeyamani, is a pointed observer of Madurai life. Her upbringing in cosmopolitan Bombay (now Mumbai), along with her innate interest in social processes, has made her a keen commentator on Madurai since she arrived in the city thirty-five years ago, even as she has molded herself to familial and social expectations in her new city. She describes herself as primarily focused on her family, but she spent most of her married life managing her husband's medical practice, and she now teaches English in a private language training center. Usha wears little jewelry, but she is always elegantly attired. Usha's family is Brahman, her parents from Tamil Nadu. Her father worked as a civil servant, moving his family to several Indian cities. They eventually settled in Bombay when Usha, the youngest of four children, was six years old.

By age twenty, Usha finished a B.Sc. in mathematics and statistics and was studying for her master's degree in statistics. Her studies were soon cut short by marriage. Her husband-to-be, Raman, was a distant relative, and had originally been engaged to Usha's sister, but he ended that first engagement in order to finish his M.D. before marriage. Usha herself intended to finish her graduate degree before marrying, but one day Raman's sister was visiting Usha's mother in Bombay, and took Usha's photo home to Madurai to show to her brother. The families checked the horoscopes and agreed that this would be a good match. Years later, Usha laughed when she told me that her first reaction on hearing the news was to tell her mother, "What did you give her that photo for? I'm not ready to marry any Raman-Aman from Madurai!" She was adamant that she would complete her M.Sc. before she married. But Usha's father was ill and bedridden, and her mother begged, "Get married now, while I am still healthy." Under pressure, Usha agreed, hoping that her in-laws would allow her to return to Bombay to finish the final exams for her degree. Her father-in-law, however, insisted, "Once you are married, your place is near your husband." When Usha recounted this over thirty years later, she laughingly added, "So he [Raman] is allowed to continue studying for his M.D., but I have to come and stay with him—and then help him in his thesis work!"

Usha married Raman in 1980 and came to live with his extended family in an old building in downtown Madurai. The joint household included Raman's orthodox parents, his two brothers, and his older brother's wife and two children. The ground floor of their property housed Raman's and his brother's medical offices. Their living quarters were upstairs. I spent a fair amount of time on the ground floor in 1985–1987, my first years in India, after Dr. Raman became my doctor. Entering the building, I would pass through the waiting room for Dr. Raman's older brother's practice, continue into the narrow hall that served as Dr. Raman's waiting room, and sit in one of the chairs arranged along the wall to face the receptionist's desk. Behind the desk was a narrow open stairway running up the wall. At some point I learned that these stairs led to Dr. Raman's family's home.

It would be over five years, however, before I met Usha. By then, she and Raman had moved to a different home. Raman had expanded his practice to open a downtown "nursing home" (a small inpatient facility). He also operated a medical store across from his office and continued his office practice as well. During that time, Raman's younger brother married and moved into the family home with his wife. As the downtown quarters became too cramped for the full joint family, Usha and Raman and their two young children shifted to a flat in an upper-income government housing colony. Shortly thereafter, in 1992, I interviewed Usha for my project on domestic worker–employer relations. We sat in their comfortably furnished front room. The caned couch and chairs were arrayed with colorful pillows. The kitchen was fitted with a two-ring gas stovetop and a refrigerator, and behind the kitchen the two small bedrooms were filled by beds, bureaus, and children's toys. Each building in the housing colony was made up of six such units. Although the residents were defined by the government as "upper-income," these flats were the epitome of what colony residents considered a middle-class home.

While living in the housing colony, Usha and Raman decided to close the nursing home and build a mid-sized hospital on the outskirts of the city. They procured a loan from a private lending corporation, which charged higher interest than banks but had a less stringent repayment schedule. They built the hospital in stages, first completing one floor, then being reimbursed by the loan company, and then following with another floor until the four-story building was complete. Usha helped oversee the building process, and then managed affairs at the hospital.

When I next saw Usha and Raman in 2001, after a gap of nine years, much had changed in their lives. Raman had suffered a heart attack at age forty-five in 1998, but he had recovered, and his work was flourishing. He and Usha had built a large new house near the hospital. This time they were able to get government loans from the State Bank of India, given their now solid credit history and the economic capital that the hospital provided. In fact, Usha said, loan officials had begun approaching *them* to offer loans. The house construction lasted over two years. When it came to their home, they decided not to compromise on materials, and used good marble and teak. Usha wanted to employ an architect to plan the house, an uncommon practice in Madurai, but Raman insisted on using less expensive contractors instead. Usha was pleased that they had nonetheless managed to create "a feeling of space" inside with the large windows and vaulted ceiling in the gracious front hall. When I first visited Usha in this house, I thought it looked like a palace. It was walled off with two grated gates opening onto a circular drive. There were small flower gardens front and back. Inside the light-filled house were many rooms, including a front room, dining room, spacious kitchen, and three bedrooms, one of which was on the balconied second floor.

That year I asked Usha where she would place herself class-wise. Usha replied that she and Raman had over the years moved from the middle class to the upper class. Raman's medical practice became highly successful with the launch of the new hospital. He had many influential contacts in the city and district governments, as well as in the press, which made for a number of well-to-do patients. As a result, Raman's income had grown, and their loans had been paid off. Now they calculated they would have enough savings to survive at least six months if Raman had another heart attack. Usha felt less tense about money worries, they had begun to save money for the children's education, and Raman now "splurged" on saris and jewelry for her.

I asked whether people's attitudes toward them had changed as their circumstances improved. "Yes," she said, "as you progress and prosper, people do change their attitude. I can see a lot of difference. People who probably would not talk to you much [before], come out of their way to come and talk to you." Their social circle had watched Raman's professional rise closely, perhaps especially because Brahmans are less likely to be wealthy than are some other caste groups in Madurai. As a result, Usha felt that there was "a lot of jealousy" among both medical colleagues and fellow Brahman community members. When Raman was recuperating in the hospital after his heart attack, Usha said, the head of cardiology "came out and said, 'Raman, half the people who came to see you, wanted to see if you are alive or departed.' That's what his own words [were]. Because people wanted to see whether this man is going to be a competitor or is he going to fall out of the rat race." Raman's mother worried that his heart attack had been caused by *kaṇ tiruṣṭi*, the evil eye, which she believed resulted from envy.

Barring another health disaster, all their savings were now slotted for their son's medical education. Usha explained that, being Brahman, their son would qualify for a merit scholarship only if he had extremely high scores on the entrance exams. She expected he would need 195 to 198 out of 200 points in physics, chemistry, and biology to clear the merit bar. Usha said, "That's because of being a Brahman, that's the price we pay here." But Usha and Raman would still be able to afford the tuition and other regular payments if their son did not receive a scholarship. The challenge, however, would be the bulk payment of Rs. 2,000,000 or more that must be paid before entering a medical program, which they were working to have reduced. Usha explained, "You have to use the right person to get it reduced, which we are trying to do. Somebody known to them, somebody through that circle, some politician. Somebody interferes." Raman, she said, had originally hoped that their son would study computer engineering or another less expensive field that would provide a job within five years. "But once we knew he was very keen on medicine, and not interested in maths and not interested in computers, we said, 'It's our duty, we'll see what can be done.'"

For people of Usha's and Raman's class, ensuring their children's education may be seen as even more of a duty than arranging their children's marriages. As a result, this education is carefully managed. Their daughter Mala, then in the eighth standard, struggled somewhat with math so Usha hoped that they could move her to a pure science group in secondary school. Usha was also willing to let her daughter study a humanities field, as long as the girl eventually earned a master's degree so that she could teach, but Raman was determined that Mala too would enter some type of medical work. Both parents were concerned that she be able to find employment.

Then, the worst happened. Raman died after suffering a second heart attack in 2002. A mutual friend wrote to me with the news, and I couldn't reach Usha from the United States. I worried for her, knowing how she had built her life around Raman despite her desires to study and to give more time to her children. The news of Raman's death was a painful blow. Raman's generosity, teasing humor, and skilled doctoring had helped both my son and me through serious illnesses. His friendship had often buoyed me, and I felt his loss deeply. As I remembered him, I kept returning to thoughts about Usha's life, wondering what she would do with the house, with the hospital, with her children's education and her own.

Eventually, Usha sold the hospital in order to finance her children's education and to provide the family with a more moderate but still comfortable income. Her son entered medical school, and is now doing his specialized residency in a prestigious hospital in the area. Mala received a bachelor's degree in business, and is now an aspiring VJ (video jockey) artist. Usha is hesitant about this field, but she is allowing her daughter to take a position with All India Radio as a stepping stone. Usha herself has taught English to aspiring IT workers and others for the past several years, her fluency in English and her sophistication making her a valuable employee. She is also at last carrying out research for a Ph.D. in psychology.

When my mother and I visited in 2008, we sat with Usha and Mala in the vaulted front room of their home. We were there a few days after Raman's death anniversary, and his garlanded photo dominated the wall behind us. Mala entertained us by reading her list of thirteen criteria for a husband, which included someone who would bring her coffee in bed and who owned a nice car. Usha and Raman had strategized for their children's futures, as Jeyamani, Anjali, and Kannan have too, but with many more resources at their disposal. Mala especially has options unavailable to her less wealthy peers. In 2011, when I visited Usha in her teaching office, she observed, "A woman's life must be focused on her family first. But you never know what will come of a marriage. I want Mala to be self-sufficient so that she can take care of herself as well as her family."

Placed side by side, the stories of these people and our friendships reveal stark differences in all of our lives. They show disparities in material conditions such as housing, labor, and consumer goods. They illustrate divergent divisions of labor within families by gender, age, and generation. They demonstrate the sizeable impacts of differential access to loans. They reveal that access to people who have power in the city, to education, and to health care are also widely divergent by class, with striking effects on long-term opportunities.

There are some similarities in these lives as well. All of these people recognize the importance of education for their children's futures, though they have varying power over the quality of that education and the ability to support their children's educations. All are concerned with arranging proper and advantageous marriages for their children (though, to return to class differences for a moment, this is of less concern for Jeyamani, who has few resources to husband or accrue through marriage, and even somewhat for Usha, whose children's education may be an even larger responsibility for her than are their marriages). The tensions of class divisions within families are significant for all four people. Perhaps most powerfully, the stories of their lives show the fragility of health and economic security, and the unpredictable contingencies of well-being.

To return to the concepts introduced in chapter 1, the four portraits also reveal numerous examples of the interactions of different forms of capital. For Kannan, insufficient economic capital meant that his daughters could not stay in school, and it nearly prevented him from arranging one daughter's marriage. His social capital, on the other hand, led him through me to a contact with an industrialist who became an occasional patron, while another customer provided him access to a bank loan. Anjali's social network enabled her to acquire the cultural capital of tastes, habits, and skills associated with modernity, which have supported her in widening the client base for her business, and to acquire the initial bank loan for that company. The economic capital of her business also played some part in earning acceptance from her in-laws, allowing her to continue to build the financial base of her business while she lived with them. Her income goes largely toward her children's education in a prestigious school, which will provide a great deal of cultural capital for her son and daughter and, she hopes, future security for all of them. Jeyamani received some access to loans through her volunteer work with the domestic workers' sangam, and she learned about Housing Board land through her contacts within that organization. She may have parlayed her relationship with me into some kind of help from her brother and sister-in-law. Usha used her cultural capital—fluency in a high-status version of English, cosmopolitanism, and ease in many kinds of social interactions—to acquire a position in an English-language institute. Her social capital ultimately helped reduce the fees for her son's medical education, and her economic capital allowed her to spend a great deal of time with her children supporting their studies, while the knowledge she had accrued through her own education facilitated this as well. These are only a few of the conversions made—or at least attempted—in employing capital to maintain class standing and, when possible, to improve it.

And finally, there is the aim to achieve dignity, a goal in and of itself. For many, dignity is a daily struggle. For others, the fairly constant regard of others makes the maintenance of dignity easier. The regard that is a prerequisite to dignity is fuelled largely by achieving class-based indicators, including all the forms of capital discussed above, as well as by maintaining caste, gender, and sexual norms. Jeyamani struggles to be treated with dignity by both her employers and her better-off relatives, while Kannan aims to gain regard from his paying passengers as well as his neighbors. Anjali faces the same process with her middle-class clients and her former classmates. And even though Usha possesses significantly more resources of all types than do Jeyamani, Kannan, and Anjali, she felt under scrutiny by Raman's colleagues after his heart attack, and has had to negotiate careful relationships with her employers and colleagues since being widowed.

With these portraits as backdrop, I now turn to a series of topics that allow us to look closely at how class is shaped by both mundane and dramatic events and interactions.

Consumption and Apprehension

CLASS IN THE EVERYDAY

When scholars study the impacts of class, we frequently look at the "big" things: the dramatic, the monumental, the long-term. We examine life chances, life histories, and longitudinal data. The focus of our work might be class movements, famous strikes, changing consumption patterns, the role of debt in impoverishment, the impact of educational attainment on occupation, or (as in chapter 7 of this book) the role of marriage in reproducing class. Class is indeed played out, experienced, and negotiated in these ways. But class is also lived in and through highly mundane processes. Examining the everyday ways in which class identities and relations are negotiated and enacted allows us to scrutinize the symbolic meanings that underlie class systems. More significantly for my interests here, it helps us comprehend the meaning and experience of class in everyday lives.

In this chapter, I examine some of the most mundane and ubiquitous items of consumption—clothing and cell phones—to see how they are used to present oneself to others with the aim of being seen as part of a certain class, and of being accorded social worth. That drive for regard leads me then to discuss one of the less instrumental purposes of such everyday consumption: the quest for dignity, itself both quotidian and intangible and therefore rarely examined in class studies. I open with those everyday, often fleeting, interactions with known and unknown others that can be crucial to people's sense of well-being. I focus in particular on the drive to be *apprehended* that shapes those interactions. In Madurai, people remark frequently on how the display of consumer goods affects the treatment they receive by others, and how they work to present themselves in ways that gain approbation from a salient audience. This of course implies that they too are judging others to identify those whose opinion matters or is irrelevant (cf. Frøystad 2006). What most people desire is to be *recognized* as social beings by those others whom they have already assigned that status, and to gain the dignity that recognition bestows.

Thus this chapter deals directly with a topic central to the relational approach to class: categories, the criteria for belonging, and the behaviors that attend interpreting and communicating belonging or its lack. It also explores the affective experience of class relations in the aim to achieve dignity. We will see that while the drive to appear above a class threshold and the drive to gain dignity can be enacted through the same process, they can also simultaneously be separate goals.

Hugo Gorringe notes cogently that "some groups have the capacity to *identify* others" (2006, 238). This "power to know"—to assign others to categories—is also "the power to judge" (Green 2006, 1121). Such "identification by others," as Richard Jenkins argues, "has *consequences*. It is the capacity to generate those consequences and make them stick which matters" (2008, 42–43). In this intersubjective production of identities, people define not only what it takes to be a member of a specific local class category, but also what it means to be treated as fully human. Here I look at the critical importance of visibility, recognition, and dignity in daily life, through the lens of embodied consumption and self-presentation.

Showcasing Class Anxiety

Questions over whether one will be visible as a social person often create a degree of anxiety among Madurai residents. Indeed, Vijayendra Rao has argued that "a deep anxiety about what others will think of them" means that "Indians face powerful incentives to regularly demonstrate [social] status, because their behavior is under constant, intimate, and structured scrutiny" (2001b, 87–88). Such anxiety manifests among people of all classes, since virtually everyone possesses a set of peers and higher-ranked social members from whom cordiality matters. In addition, the processual nature of class means that one's standing is never set forever; it must continuously be reproduced. While this anxiety is greater for some than for others—it may be especially heightened among people in the middle class, or among those trying to enter the middle class, as I discuss in chapter 6—people of all classes are vulnerable to it, because social approbation is frequently tied to the proper use of consumer goods. Because consumer goods change quickly, and since users must not only acquire an item but "know how and when to use it, and in style" (Brosius 2010, 264; see also Gilbertson 2014a, 146), this is not as simple a prospect as it may sound.

In 1999, as I was beginning to investigate local concepts related to class in Madurai, I interviewed my long-time acquaintance Jayanthi about class terms and identities. Jayanthi is a retired domestic worker who is a monolingual Tamil speaker. We were discussing which Tamil words were closest to the American English concept of "socioeconomic class." Jayanthi eventually settled on takuti (see chapter 2), by which she meant the social level ascribed to a person by others. In Madurai, she and many other residents contended, takuti is determined primarily by money and the goods that it buys. Showing me how the term can be used, Jayanthi explained that people who meet her might ask, "What takuti are you in?" Surprised, I replied, "Don't they already know that by looking at you?" "When we are outside," she said, echoing the point made by Munusamy in chapter 2, "we put on a 'showcase' exterior. I can look fine, but really, I'm suffering, so people who meet me ask what takuti we are in."

A prototypical "showcase" is the glass-fronted display case in the front room of most middle-class homes (and in some others as well, though homes with fewer resources are likely to suffice with a set of open shelves). In it people show off goods, as Kannan's family does—plastic flowers, ceramic figurines, Barbie dolls, small electronics, school trophies, folk art—and with them they make a claim to economic, cultural, and often social capital. The showcase is an apt metaphor for the surface, material performance that is enacted outside the home for a takuti-ascribing public. As Kathinka Frøystad has argued for the North Indian city of Kanpur, urbanites who encounter one another in public are "heavily dependent on visual criteria both when making class judgments of others and when attempting to communicate their own status" (2006, 179). And as Melanie Dean observes in Madurai itself, "In Tamil public life, the accrual of *kauravam* or 'status' is a fundamentally visual process. To gain status, one must 'conspicuously consume' in the sense of making one's wealth visible to others" (2011, xi). In Madurai, the "public" can include anonymous people in the city, one's neighbors and acquaintances, and even extended family members—anyone who evaluates one's standing and communicates judgment by seeing or by refusing to see.

Madurai residents state, often in so many words, that social existence depends on critical consumption practices. That is, a person who fails to display key material goods not only is unrecognizable and invisible but, in crucial social ways, does not exist. To be visible, to be seen, to be known (all condensed in the Tamil verb *teri*) are to count as a social being, to be a person of substance—and not just to be accorded inclusion in a particular class but, in this rendition, to be recognized as human. Here, a social person is one who is deemed worthy of positive apprehension—of recognition—by a relevant evaluating public. Recognition is a transaction that constitutes social substantiveness.

Soon after my early conversation with Jayanthi, I began to explore the notion of a showcase exterior, asking people why it felt crucial to present themselves in particular ways to a public audience that they hope will "take seriously the impression that is fostered before them" (Goffman 1959, 17). This conscious self-presentation is one of the tropes used to talk about the everyday experience of class relations and the construction of a class identity. Another frequent mode of conversation, which serves sometimes as a critique of oneself and at other times as a critique of others, is commentary on the role of specific consumer goods in constructing a social self. Both of these topics are discussed in this chapter.

Consumption and Class Membership

Consumption is a crucial process in the constitution of individuals' and groups' identities. As Daniel Miller argues, our use of material culture helps us to understand ourselves in new ways, just as our use of those objects (and our incorporation, or "sublation," of them into our identities) changes our understanding of the objects themselves (Miller 1987, 2010). The deployment of material culture is also widely recognized to "construct social identities and communicate cultural differences between individuals and groups" (Myers 2001, 3). These processes will be clear in the accounts below.

I am less concerned, however, about the identity that material culture helps to produce, than about the deployment of objects in enjoining others to *confirm* that identity, a key part of the process of class relations anywhere. As the linguistics professor Sekaran told me when I asked him why many people felt it was important to avoid consuming the same goods as those consumed by people of a lower class, "They want to tell others that 'I am not you, I am different from you,' or maybe, 'I am not them, I am like you.'" To be successful, either claim must be ratified by others. Thus, while most studies of clothing as material culture (to take one example) focus on the assertion of identity, we must recognize the fundamentally intersubjective nature of identity projects, at least in the construction of class relations. As Sophie Woodward elegantly notes, "We need to examine how clothing as a medium that relates surface to depth is as much the fibres that conduct the judgements of others to the inside, as the intentions of the self to the outside" (2005, 37). Madurai residents often reminded me of the Tamil saying "*āḷ pāti, āṭai pāti*"—the person is half, the clothing is half—and pointed out that while a person's character is important, it is the clothing that others see—and judge—first.

A great deal of attention has been paid in the past two decades to consumption and its cultural meanings and symbolic values in South Asia. Not only consumer goods are examined, so too are other items of consumption—food, domestic space, rituals, and experiences. This work often emphasizes the performance of class, the role of consumption in the production of class identities, and the transformation of cultural capital to economic capital. In his work on an emergent urban middle class in Nepal, for example, Mark Liechty has argued that "because of their ability to both include and exclude class others, and to both display and conceal class privilege, commodities (and their attendant practices) are the primary currency of middle-class life" (2003, 31). Such goods are key to the production and reinforcement of other class identities as well.

The use of consumption to create distinction has a centuries-long history in South Asia, playing a "core role . . . in the history of South Asia long before the advent of contemporary 'consumerism'" (Haynes and McGowan 2010, 4; see also Banerjee and Miller 2003; Greenough 1995, 221; Liechty 2003, 99; McGowan 2009; Srinivasan 2003; Venkatachalapathy 2006). So too, historical accounts tell us, do the self-fashioning of identities and the anxieties surrounding proper consumption (Haynes and McGowan 2010, 10). Contemporary consumption does differ, however, in the breadth of consumer goods available, their accessibility to a wider range of consumers, and the more finely nuanced distinctions that they enable. Each of these qualities has escalated since the beginnings of India's economic liberalization in the mid-1980s, and this "predicament of globalization has only made more obvious what was true all along: that objects and goods serve as deceptively concrete boundary-markers in the ongoing and ubiquitous struggle to establish definitive worlds of reference, belonging, and power" (Mazzarella 2003, 26).

Many of the goods that communicate class standing in Madurai today operate at the most mundane levels. Vegetables, cooking fuel, beverages, and newspapers, for example, are all sorted into finely graded scales that provide partial signs of the class level of their consumers. In addition, more durable consumer goods also communicate aspects of the user's identity in ways that are germane to future social and economic interactions. These goods have an enormous range, and include items such as radios, televisions, metal bureaus, upholstered furniture, bicycles, motorbikes, cars, jewelry, luxury saris, telephones, computers, pets, houses, vacation homes, and swimming pools, as well as less materially "durable" goods such as trips abroad or professional services. (A young architect named Salim—one of the few architects in Madurai, since most people employ contractors or masons to design and build—explained to me in 2004 how architects shape their clients' images: "Architects design lifestyles, the inner self, behavior," he said, "not just buildings.") All of these goods are among those "potent class signifiers" (Tolen 2000, 80) referred to as vacati.[1]

It is not just that consumption practices differentiate people, but that people of different classes have different relationships with material culture (see Srivastava 2015, 260–262). For the poor, for example, a sense of (potential) loss may shape the affect and meaning attached to goods that cannot be replaced when they wear out, or that may have to be pawned or sold to finance larger needs. Mukulika Banerjee and Daniel Miller (2003, 54–55) describe the sadness that poor women feel when their one decent sari kept in a trunk for "going out" becomes too worn to be respectable. Andrew Skuse, who explores the "social life and death" of radios in Afghanistan, writes that "the meanings and memories invested by the poor in items of material culture can be perceived as highly fluid, their experience of consumption being as closely associated with feelings of loss and alienation as with the pantheon of meanings invested through acts of consumption." Such loss and divestment, he argues, can create a potential "realienation of things" (2005, 124). As we will see, this realization can echo through the ways poor people talk about the goods they would need in order to be treated with respect or to be granted dignity.

Since the research I draw from in this chapter has taken place over fifteen years of changing consumerism, there have predictably been shifts in the material goods utilized in these modes of self-presentation. More intriguingly, there have also been striking consistencies. Through these years, the discussions I focus on in the following sections—of self-presentation and of the role of consumer goods in creating a social self—were each dominated by a specific topic: in the first case, the importance of looking "decent" when going outside the home (a concern primarily of lower-middle-class and poor people, for whom appearing decent requires disproportionate effort and expense); and in the second, the signifying value of one fetishized good—cell phones—which provides a frequent item of conversation among people throughout the middle class. These foci illustrate two striking features of contemporary modernity in Madurai, both heightened since liberalization: a) control and discipline of the body, and b) the role of material goods in defining a person. Of all the forms of cultural capital that are used to claim and interpret class identities, these two appeared most frequently in the commentaries I heard from 1999 onward, while they had been absent from widely condoned practices previously. In both cases, it is not just the possession of the material goods that signifies, but also the knowledge of how to deploy them as markers of status.

Appearing Decent: Missing and Passing Class Thresholds

Much of the affective weight of the accounts in this chapter lies in their emphasis on the importance of being recognized by others. I focus a good deal on the idea of recognition (and its conceptual twin, visibility) because the Madurai residents with whom I spoke frequently emphasized their strategies for gaining the recognition of others. They bore out Andrew Sayer's contention that "the everyday micro-politics of class are very much about recognition and misrecognition" (2007, 53). Madurai residents who act in order to gain recognition are striving to achieve what Sayer classifies as "conditional recognition" (2005a, 2007), and Tony Castleman calls "human recognition" or "positive recognition" (2011, 4, 5) (see also Honneth 1995; Taylor 1994). My usage overlaps closely with Castleman's definition of human recognition as "the acknowledgement provided to an individual by other individuals, groups, or organizations that he is of inherent value with intrinsic qualities in common with the recognizer, i.e. recognition as a fellow human being" (2011, 4). While the accounts below occasionally refer to a type of scrutiny and judgment that corresponds with Castleman's description of "negative recognition" (that is, "viewing an individual as lacking inherent value as a human being or not acknowledging this value" [2011, 5]), by far the more frequent contrast made in Madurai was simply between recognition and a lack of recognition. I thus retain the unmodified term "recognition" on its own.

The desire for recognition is felt across classes. The necessity of having both economic and cultural capital in order to present oneself in ways that merit approbation means that the likelihood of achieving recognition, however, varies by class. Thus while most poor people wish to appear respectable and be granted visibility, they face many difficulties in achieving this. Like others, they are sharply aware of the critical audience observing them, but less able to meet their observers' standards for counting. Anxiety over being accorded visibility is most heightened among those hoping to enter the middle class. I begin this discussion of visibility with excerpts from interviews with several people who feel they have no hope of achieving recognition, and then follow these with conversations with several others who continually feel on the verge of losing or gaining recognition.

The first of these interviews was held in 2004 with Indira, a construction worker (*cittāl*) in her fifties whom I had met as she walked to work down my street, and with her neighbors Rajkumar and Mallika. Rajkumar and Mallika are Thevars; I never knew Indira's caste. Rajkumar is a butcher, operating a stall in an outer-area market two days a week, and Mallika had done agricultural (*kūli*) labor before she and Rajkumar married. After marriage she had become a housewife; Mallika made it clear that this was her husband's and in-laws' choice rather than hers. Indira is married with one grown son, and Mallika and Rajkumar had two young sons whom they had not yet been able to send to school for financial reasons. After talking about the long stretches of difficulties in their lives, they turned to the treatment they receive from passersby, customers, neighbors, and family.

INDIRA: Here, it's all like, well-off people will only talk with us if we have vacati too. Even when they see us, they look at us like we are disgusting.

MALLIKA: They only give us respect if we have money.

RAJKUMAR: Nowadays, it's only money that's really important. Before, people put more importance on relationships and behavior, but now only money is important. Even the children we bear respect us, even the siblings we were born with will look at us and visit us, *only* if we have money.

INDIRA: Money is the most important thing in Madurai, even more than jāti.

RAJKUMAR: If a person is well off, people will look at him respectfully, no matter what his jāti is.[2]

This discussion highlights the operation of vision—of being looked at—in signifying respect. In addition, it centers on the fundamental importance of financial means—and the kinds of cultural capital (here, vacati) that economic resources generate, which then generate economic capital in turn—in determining social relations even with those to whom one is most closely tied, a point that recurs frequently in current discourse about social relations.

The importance of being seen and addressed was also highlighted by Vijayalakshmi, an impoverished thread factory worker belonging to the Acari caste. Vijayalakshmi, who in 2004 was thirty years old, is widowed and lives with her parents, two brothers, one sister, and the sister's husband and six-year-old daughter, all in a rented one-room home. The men are goldsmiths. Vijayalakshmi's niece is the first female member of the family to attend school. Vijayalakshmi complained that when she and her family members go out in messy or torn ("not-decent") clothing, rich people "won't speak with us. They glance right past us and scuttle off [*viruviruṉṉu pōyiṭuvāṅka*]. We have nothing, and they have a lot, right? So they hustle away." (To "go out" [*veḷiye pōka*], a common phrase, means going shopping, going somewhere public outside of the immediate neighborhood, or going to meet anyone other than one's closest neighbors, including the households of family members. It involves passing through and presenting oneself to the scrutiny of others.) Here, "rich people's" refusal to see is a refusal to ratify and to substantiate them as full social persons. Vijayalakshmi and her family members insist that "decentness" tells others nothing about one's character, only about what one can afford to wear, but they know that wealthier people regard them at best with the disrespect of indifference. Like Rajkumar, Mallika, and Indira, Vijayalakshmi emphasizes the near impossibility of getting wealthier people to mark her as worthy of respect through visual accord.

Their observations illustrate three key issues: 1) the importance of money/class as a source of respect, 2) the critical significance of being seen for marking a person's class standing, and 3) the range of others who act as a scrutinizing audience in these marking events.

They also bring up the importance of decency in the public eye. As Vijayalaksmi implied, one of the fundamental means of gaining the approving gaze is appearing "decent" to public onlookers. In urban Tamil Nadu, decency encompasses neatness, cleanliness, modesty, and suitability, qualities imbued with moral value.[3] In 2004 I was hearing a lot about "being decent," and I asked my friend Darshini, a Nadar woman in her forties who teaches high school and runs a small tutoring business, to explain what it meant. She replied, "Decent means being modest in speech, in activity, in the way [people] look and smile. A person shouldn't laugh loudly at other people's problems. They should be decently dressed, not exposing themselves. Not shouting to express themselves, especially girls. Those who don't want to be hygienic and healthy, they wear dirty clothes." Darshini then pointed out that dirtiness is often assumed by high-caste people to be inversely proportionate to caste rank (a point to which she served as a counterexample). I added that neatness and decentness are also associated with class. She agreed, and then confirmed my impression that today these values are more widely adopted (and adoptable) than in the past, especially when linked with consumption. "Nowadays all the poor," she reflected, "with maybe one or two exceptions, they dress up neatly. There are cheaper textiles available now. Construction workers used to have dry skin and hair, but now they have oiled hair and skin, pinned-up saris. When I was in college [twenty-five to thirty years previously], no one did. Today they wear neat blouses, not torn, not faded. Twenty years ago, they didn't mind wearing these. . . . And the poor and middle class people all have some minimal jewelry now—at least they wear gold-plated jewelry."

Darshini was noting not only the narrowing material gap in clothing and accessories between the lower and middle classes, but also the increasingly shared values associated with consumption, grooming, and hygiene. Thus even those in stereotypically lower-class jobs, such as construction workers, take care with their personal appearance—skin, hair, clothing, and accessories—in ways that surpass what even college students did twenty to thirty years ago. This was true of men as well as women; they had an equal concern with cleanliness and grooming, and more men in 2004 were beginning to "tuck in their shirts," Darshini said.

Being "neat" in this way is a part of being "decent." Both terms have moral connotations, since poverty itself is a moral issue (some Hindus, for example, assume it results from sins in past lives), and avoidance of public dishevelment is seen as a laudable character quality. But the moral issues involved go further than this; being "decent" also means dressing and behaving modestly ("not exposing," "not shouting"). "Decent" women must wear a gold chain (because to be without one is to proffer an inauspicious sight for others), but wearing an ostentatious amount of gold—ostentation being determined by what is appropriate for one's caste and class as well as by modern tastes—is indecent (see Dean 2011, 77). Neatness, hygiene, health, and suitability form a cluster of morally valued attributes all associated with control, order, and decency. Every one of these is a moral quality.

As I demonstrate in chapter 6, the contemporary middle class in Madurai has a heightened concern with control over bodies, desires, and consumption; but clearly decency is an ideal no longer monopolized by the middle class. This is evident, for example, in the manner in which most women manage their saris. The standard "neat" way of wearing a sari in most of southern India (as opposed to the more casual ways it is usually worn for domestic tasks or for extra-domestic manual labor) is to fold the final length of it into three or four lengthwise pleats as it crosses diagonally from the waist over the chest, and to stack the folds neatly onto the left shoulder to drape the end of the sari from there. Today, those folds are kept creased and ordered by pinning them all to the top of the left shoulder of the blouse. When I first lived in Madurai in 1985, no one in my neighborhood pinned her sari to the shoulder of her blouse. To do so was actually unnecessary to keep the sari in place, for the most part. Moreover, it would have been deemed artificial unless one was tying a sari for the first time, or perhaps if one was wearing a heavy Kanchivaram silk sari to a wedding, where both the hard-to-control weight of the fabric and the formality of the occasion might have made pinning acceptable. Some civil servants would also have pinned their saris to attain an air of ordered control (see Bannerjee and Miller 2003, 119–127). Today, however, almost any woman under a certain age who cares to appear decent when going outside the home will pin her carefully folded *pallu* to her blouse.[4]

"Decency" is clearly important to poorer people in Madurai, since being able to enact decency is a way of showing oneself to be part of the moral social order. It is key to gaining approbation in the public eye. And it is one of the primary attributes widely assumed to distinguish middle-class people from those below them, and thus to mark entry into the middle class (see also Frøystad 2006, 166). Decency is thus, not surprisingly, the quality that lower-middle-class people most often invoke when explaining how they try to present themselves to a watchful public.

Shortly after my conversation with Darshini, I interviewed Anjali, her husband Sundaram, and their videographer friend Murugan (who were all in their late twenties or early thirties at the time) about how the everyday world had changed since their childhoods. Anjali and Murugan are both economically better off than their parents were, and have achieved solid middle-class standing in their adulthood. Sundaram is somewhat less economically secure than his civil servant father was, but not drastically so. By the time they entered adulthood, the idea of "decency" had become a largely taken-for-granted notion—so much so that when I asked these young people what it means to be "decent," they found it hard to articulate an answer. Shifting tactics, I asked them to describe how someone who is *not* decent looks.

MURUGAN: It's someone whose clothing is dirty, unironed, torn, and unwashed, and whose hair is unoiled. They have no neatness [*nīṭṇas illāma iruppāṅka*].

SARA: What do you mean by neatness?

MURUGAN: Good clothes, new clothes.

SUNDARAM: If we wear old clothes, we feel really uncomfortable.

ANJALI: We feel like we need to wear new clothes. If we're going out, we'll wear the newest clothing we have.

SUNDARAM: If I went out to meet you, and didn't have a nice outfit on, I'd be embarrassed and feel like I should have worn nice clothing.

Trying to get at the behavioral consequences that regulate the necessity of decency, I asked them, "What would happen if you went out without looking decent?"

MURUGAN: If you're standing across the road from us, you'll think, "Poor things, they are suffering" [*pāvam, kaṣṭappaṭṭirukkāṅka*], and we mustn't have people think that way. They'll think, "Why did these people come out looking like this?"

SARA: How would you feel?

ALL THREE IN UNISON: Ashamed.

ANJALI: We don't want anyone to know we are suffering, so we go out looking neat.

SARA: If you are suffering, why shouldn't anyone know?

MURUGAN: They'll respect us less. If someone is suffering, no one respects them. They dismiss them, they think that person is beneath them [*ikalcci neneppāṅka, tālvu neneppāṅka*]. Their behavior won't be very nice.

SARA: How so?

ANJALI: They won't show much respect.

MURUGAN: Not from everyone, mostly just from some people—it's worst with relatives. Now, in our house, we have a girl who is ready to get married. [If we aren't decent] no one would ask for her to marry their sons. Lots of people are like that.

Here we see that, whereas certain kinds of consumption make a person "count" in society by making that person visible to a spectatorial public (see also Liechty 2003, 140–145; Srinivas 2002), the reverse situation—to lack and therefore be unable to deploy certain consumer goods in public—makes a person simultaneously pitiable and socially invisible. Just like the poorer residents I interviewed, Murugan, Anjali, and Sundaram emphasized the dismissal, lowness, and invisibility that improper or inadequate consumption results in, and both the immediate and long-term consequences of these. In Tamil, *pāvam* means both a pitiable person and the act of sinning, both of which are associated with poverty. (This association underlies Indira's earlier observation that any glance people give her is one of disgust.)

Both poor and lower-middle-class people talked about needing to keep at least one set of presentable clothing aside for shopping, visiting, or dealing with officials. Poor people especially struggled to achieve decency in public, and often spoke about their failure to do so. Nonetheless they emphasized the need to be decent when going out in order to avoid being treated with contempt (*alacciyam*) or disgust—though they rarely expected to be treated with regard (see also Banerjee and Miller 2003, 55). As Vijayalakshmi said, "If we wear a torn sari, the people who have [*irukkravaṅka*] will treat us with contempt. But if we go out in decent clothing, they still won't speak with us, they still won't respect us, because they know we are just thread factory workers. They'll think, 'They are just laborers' [*kūli vēle pākkravaṅka*]." Her observations underscore Arjun Appadurai's contention that "poverty is partly a matter of operating with extremely weak resources where the terms of recognition are concerned" (2004, 66). Though Vijayalakshmi and her female kin were perfect examples of the downward spread of "decency" that Darshini had observed, their poverty nonetheless remains marked on their bodies. Being registered enough to receive disgust or contempt signifies a kind of literal but stigmatized or negative visibility—that of the pitiable person (pāvam) or, as we will see, an insect. But it is not described by speakers in terms of visibility or recognition. In particular, it is not seen by recipients as a *knowing recognition*. Indeed, in the case of people like Vijayalakshmi, it may be described as an intentional practice of *non*recognition.[5] This is the systematic refusal to recognize a person as who she claims herself to be, or to accord a person the identity he claims for himself. Such denied existence is a class-based fear.

On the other hand, people who are middle class, or who desire to be, often emphasized their strategies for gaining a positive form of visibility in public. For them, the fear surrounding going out without looking decent is that they will not be "seen" by the people they pass through and approach. Chellamma, a Chakkiliyar woman in her twenties whose husband is a contractor, and whom I had known since her childhood, visited me often in 2004 and 2005 after her third child was born. She said that when she left her home to come visit me, and any other time she "went out," she would dress herself and her children in their best clothing, because otherwise "people won't see us" (*avaṅkaḷukku eṅkaḷai teriyātu*, which literally translates as "we will not be visible to them") and "they will not treat me with respect" (*mariyātai kuṭukkamāṭṭāṅka*). This is especially interesting in Chellamma's case, since proper consumption makes her "count" despite her Chakkiliyar caste (a scheduled, or Dalit, caste). Like the others, Chellamma aimed to be neat and clean and presentable, not to be fashionable. In these cases, fashion is far less critical than decency.

Fundamentally, then, a person has to be decent in order to be recognizable, to be worthy of respectful interaction—in sum, to count in the public eye. The structure of this encounter deserves some attention. Those who go out, wishing to be seen, are already "seeing" others as social beings. In the process of recognition, there is a reciprocal visual interaction, just as in *darshan* (*taricanam* in Tamil). "Taking darshan" is the practice of seeing and being seen by a deity in Hindu (and sometimes Christian) worship, an "exchange of vision" (Eck 1981, 6) and "visual intermingling" (Pinney 2002, 364). People can also take darshan of other humans, as they frequently do when viewing political and religious leaders or celebrities, and Madurai residents' descriptions of presenting themselves to be "seen" by empowered others resemble this practice closely. As with worshippers, people who are "going out" in Madurai represent themselves as the initiators of what they hope will result in a visual transaction. Vision accords recognition when it is an exchange; it need not be egalitarian, but it must be reciprocated.

Displaying Cell Phones: Substantiating Class Belonging

While being decent is often understood as the minimum standard for counting as a social being, by itself it is insufficient for ensuring a solid position in the middle or upper class. Other kinds of consumption, especially fashion-based consumption (and by this I mean simply keeping up with or ahead of trends, whether they be of clothing, technologies, or rituals), are necessary for being counted—or standing out—in smaller reference groups within the middle and upper classes. Interestingly, discourses around such practice often highlight the connection between consumption and *existence*.

Photo 4. Two of Kannan's grandchildren (Bhumati's daughter and second son), posing with their most "decent" clothing and a cell phone, 2013. Photo credit: Sara Dickey.

Of all the wide range of material goods that signify middle-class standing and its gradations—including clothing, televisions, refrigerators, motorbikes, gold, housing, etc.—the one that has caught the public imagination, and that for years has appeared most frequently in discussions of consumption and identity, is the cell phone. Cell phones are easily carried (thus of course "mobile") and displayed on one's person, and they signify taste and technological literacy, social networks, and relative wealth (and thus cultural, social, and economic capital).

India's telecommunications network, which is almost entirely wireless, is the second largest in the world (Department of Telecommunications 2015, 1). Today cell phones are widely owned across classes (see Jeffrey and Doron 2013). Both cell phones and calling options became relatively inexpensive in the mid-2000s. The resulting explosion of cell phone subscribers has meant a sharp rise in "teledensity"—the ratio of phone subscribers to population—in India over the past decade. Robin Jeffrey and Assa Doron have charted the growth of telephone ownership and access in India. In 1987, they note, India had three phones for every 1,000 people (including individual landlines and pay phones). By 1999, there were close to 23 phones per 1,000 people. By early 2010, the ratio had jumped to 510:1000—a ratio of more than one telephone for every two people—and, significantly, more than 90 percent of those phones were then cell phones (Jeffrey and Doron 2011, 399).[6] The most recent quarterly data as of this writing show that by March 2015, teledensity was 794:1000, 97 percent of it cellular (TRAI 2015, i). Notably, Tamil Nadu had the highest teledensity of any state at 1175:1000, and urban areas of Tamil Nadu averaged 1.4 phones per resident (TRAI 2015, 7).

Cell phones are not only widely owned, they are also finely graded in terms of quality and taste, making them useful for marking and imagining identities. This remains as true in Madurai today as it was when I began this research in 1999 (see also Dean 2011, 240). Such durability is rather remarkable, given the pace at which consumption signifiers change in contemporary India. The cell phone has both a "material presence" and a communicative function, along with other "inherent" uses such as information storage (Miller 2010, 111–113).[7] In other words, like other material forms of cultural capital, cell phones play both "instrumental and symbolic roles" in India (Donner et al. 2008, 333) as elsewhere.[8] Their material presence includes the location in which the cell phone is displayed on or near the body, the phone's appearance, its features, the data kept in it, and the sounds that nearby people hear when the phone "rings." In their talk about cell phones, Madurai residents tend to emphasize the phones' materiality, though the phones' function as a communication device does play a role in determining who should or should not be allowed to use a cell phone, as I discuss below. Like decent clothing and grooming practices, cell phones are incorporated into their users' selves, and they both shape and communicate an identity.

In 2004, Murugan had a cell phone. Anjali and Sundaram did not yet own one.[9] When I interviewed them all together that year, we talked about the increased availability of consumer goods since liberalization, which all of them viewed as a positive change. I asked them which goods it is most important to own. Murugan cited his cell phone and his motor-bike. Then, glancing at his friends, he quickly added that while he needs these for his business, "people who work in offices don't require cell phones." Despite this attempt at saving face, there was some embarrass-ment all around.

Later in the conversation, when I asked them what kinds of goods and resources (vacati) people typically acquire as they move from poverty to relative comfort, and in what order, they began with the basics of shelter and minimal household appliances such as a radio or television or blender. Then these three young adults—all familiar in some way with poverty—moved to the next levels of acquisition:

> MURUGAN: Before buying a house itself, the last important vacati would be a fridge.
>
> ANJALI: And after that, things for showing off [ātampara jāmān]. People won't use those things, they'll just buy them and keep them at home or carry them around. Like a cell phone—it's for showing off. [Laughs.]
>
> SARA: A cell phone is just a show, for some people?
>
> ANJALI: Yes, it's just a show. They won't *use* a telephone, they'll just keep one for others to see.

Sundaram then echoed Murugan's earlier statement by saying, "People who work in offices don't need them." Given the status enhancement that cell phones provide, I began to understand further why Sundaram and Anjali might be embarrassed not to own one.

The striking symbolic value of the mobile phone was evoked even more strongly by people who are positioned *higher* in the middle class. Renganathan, a Chettiar advertising company manager in his mid-fifties, talked in 2005 about why he needed a cell phone. Speaking in English, he said:

> Because I'm in marketing, I need a mobile phone. I may receive calls at any time. But frankly, owning a mobile has become a fashion, a status symbol. Like a car—if you are rich, you have a car. If you are middle class, you have a two-wheeler. And you also have a mobile phone,

whether you have any reason to get calls or not. You need a certain brand, a color monitor, all that. It means you are modern, and then people will respect you. Only if you have these things you are *recognized*. You *exist*, for them. Otherwise you are not recognized, you don't exist.

Renganathan's experience condenses Murugan's and Anjali's observations about cell phone functions into a unified critique. The phone's symbolic value, which communicates stature and identity, is more compelling to them than its inherent instrumental value of communicating verbal messages. It signifies the bearer's existence. Making an even more sardonic point, Sekaran said in 2009 that to lack up-to-date goods such as expensive cell phones means that "you don't get people's attention, you don't get their respect, and then you are just like a small insect crawling around." Note how this phrase evokes Vijayalakshmi's and Indira's descriptions of being seen as contemptible and disgusting. Sekaran's evocation goes further: humanity is removed. (Consider here Hugh Raffles's observation about museum-goers at an exhibit of/about insects: after their initial enthrallment, viewers were moved to "a deep, dead space without reciprocity, recognition, or redemption" [2010, 44].) Both Renganathan and Sekaran see themselves as upper middle class. For them, just as for those with fewer economic resources, to lack consumer goods is to be unrecognized and invisible—even less than human—while to display them is to make a claim to a social presence and to matter in the social body.

All of the accounts in these two sections produce a portrait of people self-consciously consuming in ways that they hope will generate recognition of them not simply as proper social beings, but more fundamentally, as beings who are fully human. If you do not consume in proper ways, you are not seen, perceived, or known (*avaṅkaḷukku eṅkaḷai teriyātu* glosses in English simultaneously as "they do not see us," "we are not visible to them/perceived by them," and "they do not know us"). People ignore you because you are beneath them (*tāḻvu*, a term that refers both to physical height and to social treatment), suggesting again that you are not within their field of vision. They dismiss you (*ikaḻcci kuṭuppāṅka*) because you do not count as worthy of recognition. You are less than human. If, however, your inadequate consumption abilities *are* noticed, you are seen as disgusting or pitiable (*pāvam*), a desperate, immoral, despicable condition. Recognizability requires both basic economic and cultural capital, in order to be decent and neat, while more finely graded forms of capital are required to substantiate oneself further. If you perform class properly, you will be recognized by a relevant audience, and you will be extended mariyātai, a term that means distinction and respect but also, just as significantly, denotes inclusion within a reference group (Mines 2005, 92). Being positively apprehended creates dignity, self-worth, and belonging.

Further Apprehensions

One of the anxieties that attends the drive for recognition is, of course, the scrutiny that provides the necessary field for visibility. Behaviors are watched closely, judged for signs of moderation or excess, and also for suitability. What is "suitable" for members of one class may be ridiculous for those in another class. But beyond this, consumption that is proper for one person of a certain class may be thought improper for another of the very same class. Age, gender, caste, and skin color commonly determine appropriate consumption. Lower-middle- and middle-class male college students in Madurai and Chennai, for example, demonstrate "style" with branded clothing that, in its mild transgressiveness, marks them as liminally located between children and adults and on the margin of "society" (Nakassis 2013). Darker skinned women, especially of lower castes, will be ridiculed should they carry umbrellas in the sun (a sign of high status, reserved for deities and light-skinned professionals who wish to preserve their fairness) (Dean 2013). Melanie Dean also writes about two Madurai neighbors, one a Dalit and one a Kallar, who were treated differently when they displayed their wealth by wearing gold jewelry or setting out ceremonial brass lamps. The Kallar woman was not criticized for showing her wealth, but the Dalit woman, who was both darker skinned and lower in caste, was—even though she was wealthier than her Kallar neighbor. As Dean notes, "not all displays of wealth are considered equal." Instead, "certain types of displays, adornments and comportments" are appropriate "only to certain types of bodies" (2011, 247).

In my own observations, cell phone use was governed particularly by gendered norms. Darshini pointed out in 2004 that she was criticized for carrying a cell phone. She said, "A man can have it, but a woman? She has to keep it inside her purse. One [autorickshaw] driver asked me, 'Why do you want to keep it in your hand? Why can't you keep it in your bag?' I said, 'Why *can't* I have it in my hand?' and finally he kept quiet. My sister's husband challenges me also. They think it is something like women's equality. They don't want women to speak anything in the public, other than with their relatives or their husband." In this socially conservative city, the same consumer good that produces status and belonging for men can lead to charges of immoral behavior for women. When I recounted this story to Anjali, she added that women are also criticized for using cell phones because unlike men, who "will attend to their calls and finish their business quickly and switch them off, ladies will keep talking for a long time, and disturb the people around them."

Unrestrained, unmonitored communication for women is at the least a social nuisance, and possibly a social danger. Studies in other Indian cities have noted similar patterns. Jonathan Donner and his coauthors observe that for some conservative Bangalore housewives, "modesty . . . meant not owning a mobile phone," and they argue that "rejection of mobile ownership reflects the traditional gender directive for modest women to stay close to the home" (Donner et al. 2008, 332, 333). Doron describes a similar understanding in Varanasi, where mobile phones symbolize social networks outside the control of patriarchal authority, and restricting women's access to mobile phones "reinforced social roles and gender ideology" within the marital household (Doron 2012, 422; for comparable findings in Tamil Nadu, see Jouhki 2013).[10] Here concerns for decency conflict with concerns to display fetishized consumer goods, as women's improper use of cell phones is character- ized as indecent.[11] Such examples indicate a gendered dimension to visibility, just as there are age, caste, and religious dimensions, among others.

In Madurai, then, while the proper use of consumer goods helps a person to become visible, material goods do not mean the same thing in everyone's hands; some people are more fully able to use these objects than others. The same markers that can give one the edge in performing to a group can attract attention or envy and draw kaṇ tiruṣṭi (the "evil eye") or verbal criticism, and the markers that are successful for one per- son may draw censure for another. It is a difficult balance. But what kind of balance? I would not argue that there is a single register or spectrum of visibility, in which an individual strives to be sufficiently but not exces- sively visible. Rather, people need to feel seen and recognized, to be accorded presence, in order to feel dignity and self-worth (see also Mines 2005; Sayer 2005a); yet simultaneously, many do not want to stand out dramatically—at least not to particular audiences, at particular times. Only certain people, in certain circumstances, wish to draw attention to themselves in this way (cf. Dean 2013; Nakassis 2013). To a great extent, the desire to be seen is the desire to be recognized by a larger public, both known and unknown. Here it is worth remembering the generalized references to "people" and "them" that Sekaran and Renganathan made when referring to observers evaluating their consumption practices, and the nonspecific "they," "you," and "we" invoked by Murugan and Anjali, all connoting a rather diffuse social body. On the other hand, the attempt to rise in status by *fashionably* standing out may be a bid directed to a specific and known group of peers.

Everyday Dignity

On the wall in her home in Hosur, Lakshmi has hung a page torn from her father Venkatraman's diary, written in Venkatraman's handwriting in about 2002:

> manitanukku mariyātai avaciyam
> malarukku maṇam avaciyam
> enku anpu irukkiratō
> anku āṇṭavan irukkirān

My translation:

> Respect is essential to humans [just as]
> Fragrance is essential to flowers
> Wherever love may be
> There God is

In this chapter, I have examined two of the most consistent themes in Madurai residents' discussions of class inclusion and exclusion: the critical importance of appearing decent in order to clear the lower threshold of the middle class, and the crucial significance of consumer fashions—particularly the cell phone—to signal belonging and exclusion for people of all classes. Such observations, concerns, and anxieties lie fully in the realm of the mundane. The hopes for recognition and the acts of judgment seem so small that they are easy to dismiss, yet they make up a good deal of the daily experience and impact of class for many people. Being accorded or refused recognition is closely tied to acquiring dignity.

As I have noted previously, sustained attention to intangibles such as dignity is rare in studies of class in India and elsewhere. Discussions of dignity do appear in other scholarly work, however, and in the literature on Tamil Nadu, they are found primarily in two areas: studies of the Self-Respect (Non-Brahman) Movement, and studies of scheduled castes. A brief review of these cases before I continue will clarify my usage of dignity and its significance in class relations.

The use of the concept in the Self-Respect Movement (founded by E. V. Ramasamy in 1925) was an egalitarian call for all people to recognize and act on their own dignity (*mānam*, "honor" and *cuya-mariyātai*, "self-respect")—akin to the category of essential human dignity discussed in chapter 1—and to reject a ranked sense of worth based on caste (see, e.g., Price 1996b; Ram 2009, 505–506). One of the movement's primary aims was to advance a group's sense of self-worth and social value (by according self-worth through markers other than those of an externally imposed hierarchical system) instead of a gambit to find a place *in* that hierarchical system.

Treatments of dignity closer to my own work are found in historical and ethnographic studies of rural scheduled castes' attempts to gain dignity by decreasing stigma and refusing degrading transactions. David Mosse (1994), for example, discusses a range of strategies that involve refusing or modifying exchanges, duties, demands, and transactions in a village in southern Tamil Nadu. Vijayendra Rao and Paromita Sanyal discuss scheduled and other low castes' use of *gram sabha* (village council) meetings to voice opposition to structural inequalities with the aim of acquiring "equal recognition as citizens" (2010, 159). (For other examples, see Gorringe 2010; Kapadia 1995; Mines 2005.) Because many of these efforts or the duties they contest have been tied to intermittent transactions, agricultural seasons, life-cycle events, and periodic civic and religious rituals, however, rather than to more continuous and mundane indignities, the deployment of strategies to circumvent them may be more intermittent than the everyday attempts to be recognized that I have discussed in this chapter. (In saying this I do not doubt that most lower-caste villagers face frequent and mundane indignities; my point is simply that the form of dignity captured in these analyses is somewhat different from the type I address.)

The form of dignity that I have found compelling in Madurai residents' discourse and behavior is instead both mundane and highly contingent on the regard of judgmental onlookers. One of the aims of my work is to demonstrate the importance of attending to intangibles such as dignity if we are to apprehend the quality of everyday life in a class society. Despite its absence from most studies of class, the desire for dignity frequently underlies Madurai residents' discussion of consumption in everyday life. Economist Avner Offer recognizes the fundamental nature of this desire when he writes that "interaction is driven by the grant and pursuit of *regard*" (2006, 77), citing a passage from Adam Smith's *The Theory of Moral Sentiments*: "What are the advantages which we propose to gain by that great purpose of human life which we call bettering our condition? To be observed, to be attended to, to be taken notice of with sympathy, complacency, and approbation, are all the advantages which we can propose to derive from it" (Smith 1976 [1759], 1, ch. ii.1, 50, as cited in Offer 2006, 77). "To be observed, to be attended to, to be taken notice of with sympathy" is precisely what Madurai residents try to attain from those around them. To be seen is to count, to have substance, visibility, and humanity; not to be seen is to be low, empty or void, invisible, and nonhuman.

While living in Madurai, I have frequently been drawn to what I observed as a drive to be treated with dignity. The question I asked of

Murugan, Anjali, and Sundaram—"Why shouldn't people know you are suffering?"—was intentionally naïve but sincerely curious. Independent of the experience of material comfort or deprivation, one of the most immediate daily concerns for many people is how they will be treated by the others they encounter. The desires revealed in the many answers to my often unspoken question demonstrate two parallel and often unrelated, even in some senses contradictory, aspects of living with class difference: the aim for (greater) equality for oneself and the aim for dignity and agency. These desires substantiate Michael Jackson's contention, raised in chapter 1, that people need to *feel* in control of their lives more than actually to *be* in control (Jackson 1998, 22). Jackson calls dignity a gloss for the "existential imperative" (1998, 206–207), the "truth . . . that people need to have some say in the world into which they are thrown, that they must in some measure choose their own lives and feel that they have a right to be here" (1998, 195). Anton Blok puts this in the negative: people, he writes, "require some measure of recognition and repute, lest they die a social death" (2001, 9). That social death is the invisibility that denies dignity.

Thus everyday well-being is intricately tied to the acquisition of dignity. My informants' comments in this chapter underscore the point that while material factors are important for physical and psychological well-being—at the level of, say, adequate housing and sufficient food—beyond that, subjective and immaterial factors play a major role. Thus they support Sayer's contention that "one of the most important features of class inequalities is that they present people with unequal bases for respect . . . [by virtue of] having unequal access to the practices and goods that allow them warranted respect or conditional recognition. Being able to participate in practices and such relationships and gain their internal goods if one so wishes is crucial for well-being" (2005a, 959). Affective well-being, and thus dignity (or regard, approbation, esteem, respect), should be important to analysts because regardless of the systems of inequality in which people are enmeshed, their sense of well-being is critical to their life experiences.

I have argued that this dignity is experienced as an end in itself, rather than "simply" as a tool for class advancement. It is also, however, linked to forms of capital, which in my analysis *are* instrumental. Dignity and capital are intertwined: not only may capital accumulation produce dignity, the accord of dignity may directly or indirectly result in the acquisition of capital. The compelling need to claim dignity and a place in the social body is one of the most conscious motivations for acquiring material goods and the knowledge of their proper use. The recognition bestowed by others also shapes life chances: "Human recognition transactions underlie and enable several other components that are central to poverty and development, such as empowerment [and] social exclusion" (Castleman 2011, 70). It shapes access to all forms of capital—symbolic, social, cultural, and economic—affecting a person's ability to become a member of a cooperative savings group, to be treated well at school, to be allowed into a bank, to attain any number of occupations, to find good marriage alliances. In other words, whether people are recognized as having what is needed to be respectable shapes not only their experience of everyday life but also their chances of gaining those goods that determine class standing.

My work demonstrates that indeed the desire for apprehension, recognition, and dignity is not limited to those people most disadvantaged by a system of inequality, but is also felt by those who have more privilege (as I discuss further in chapter 8). In my understanding, then, the drive for dignity in urban Tamil Nadu is not specific to a particular class. Rather, the struggle for dignity is related to class because it is about being recognized as a certain kind of person, which *accords* dignity, and in Madurai, the primary way of articulating this desire in everyday discourse has to do with class more than with any other form of identity.

Yet gaining a modicum of dignity also entangles people within the very hierarchical system whose effects they are trying to mitigate (cf. Appadurai 2004, 66). This is not simply because performing according to the rules of the game can reproduce the hegemony of class, but more precisely because it sets the performers up to be evaluated by—and to evaluate—others through the diffuse social gaze. In seeing and in presenting themselves in ways that invite being seen, these residents produce themselves as both subject and object in a field of power relations (Foucault 1978, 1980). The imprecise but all-encompassing sense of a disciplining audience is reflected in the nonspecific pronouns used when residents describe who observes and who is observed. Those quoted in this chapter, all of whom strive to be recognized regardless of how "high" they are in the class system, act as subjects when they themselves identify those by whom they want to be granted respect. They thereby continuously reposition themselves as objects of others' gaze and judgment. On the other hand, aware that they are offering themselves up to scrutiny, this behavior is also a means of "managing the gaze" (Staples 2003, 301). But there is a mutuality to this vision (in some ways akin to darshan): it is reciprocated. Such an exchange not only exercises power but also indicates belonging.

The self-conscious critique of the performance of class, in which participants are at once actor and audience, object and subject—a topic I address at length in chapter 6—suggests a level of awareness of the

engagement in a play of power. At the same time, the apparently contradictory drive for dignity, which is dependent on this very interaction
played out in this very way, remains key to the well-being of many
people.

This chapter has demonstrated the tactical usage of material goods in
achieving or maintaining class standing, and the use of those goods in
interpreting others' class. As always, it is not simply the possession of
boundary-defining goods that counts but the knowledge of how to use
them and the concern for "proper"—especially morally proper—
consumption. We have seen that gaining dignity is central to many
people's decisions about what and how to consume in a visible way. We
have also seen that many of the judgments Madurai residents make
about one another based on material consumption are about highly
moralized qualities—self-discipline, order, cleanliness, hygiene, suitability,
modesty, and regulation of sexual and material desire. All of these
features are related to control. So too are the even more heightened
moralizations made about the subject of the following chapter, debt.
Like consumption, debt is an issue that divides classes in practice,
discourse, and material impacts.

5 *Debt*

THE MATERIAL CONSEQUENCES
OF MORAL CONSTRUCTS

What happens when assumptions about entire categories of people are applied to their ability to borrow money, to invest it, and to repay? Debt is an exceptionally fruitful topic through which to examine class relations: not only is it by definition about relationships—since lending and borrowing create an ongoing relationship between two entities—it, more than any other topic in this book (with marriage being a close second), demonstrates the inextricably bound influences of symbolic, social, cultural, and economic capital. And it accomplishes these social functions in large part because of moral prejudices that are bound up not only with class categories but also with the idea of debt itself. In this chapter I focus on differences among types of loans, the varying costs and outcomes of debt, the gulf in the symbolic meanings and economic impacts of debt for people of different classes, and the effects these meanings and impacts have in perpetuating class difference.

We might think that debt is related to consumption in one obvious way: spending beyond one's means on consumer goods leads to indebtedness. This is accurate, so far as it goes. As Isabelle Guérin and her collaborators write, "consumerism creates norms which many households are willing to follow without having the financial means to do so" (Guérin, Roesch et al. 2011, 3). In addition, there are several other, perhaps less obvious, similarities between the ways that consumption and debt are implicated in class. First, each serves as both economic and cultural capital (whether positive or negative); thus debt and consumption constitute both indicators and sources of class. Second, both are everyday concerns for most households, and are practiced by people of all classes. Third, debt, like consumption, has material and immaterial meanings, costs, and benefits, including those that affect dignity. Finally, the practice and meaning of debt too are regulated by class, as well as by caste and gender.

Yet debt—unlike consumption—rarely makes a systematic appearance in qualitative studies of urban India. This is rather remarkable, because debt provides a fascinating lens on class for a variety of reasons.

For one, it turns out that a number of popular and scholarly assumptions about who holds what kinds of debt, why they take on debt, and what debt produces are incorrect. A common assumption in India and elsewhere, for example, is that only the poor are continuously indebted, whereas debt—including the chronic sort—is also assumed heavily by the middle and upper classes. Moreover, while debt is generally viewed as shameful, it nonetheless frequently produces both material and social gain, rather than loss and dishonor. (Indeed, debt is productive, just as credit is.) Guérin and her colleagues elaborate the complexities of this point succinctly: "Depending on how debt is experienced and perceived, and on the nature of the relationship between debtor and creditor, and the set of rights and obligations that link debtors and creditors, debt may be a mark of respect, a source of honour and distinction, or conversely a source of humiliation, shame and sometimes social exclusion" (Guérin, Roesch et al. 2011, 27). Patterns of debt, then, provide a stark representation of the discrepancies in the resources available to people of different classes, and of the divergent outcomes that result from identical activities—in some part because of class-based stereotypes about the people who take out loans. While debt is by definition quantifiable in terms of money, and thus objectively delineated (see Graeber 2011, 21), it nonetheless reveals how the tangible and intangible aspects of class coincide powerfully in the practices of and rhetoric around debt.

In addition, as these points already imply, examining the meanings of debt allows us to look closely at morality and class. Frequent, continuous, or "chronic" indebtedness is characterized as a social ill for at least one of two reasons: debt, it is said, destroys the chance to escape poverty, and debt reveals personal irresponsibility and short-sightedness. Thus, if only the poor were more disciplined and forward-thinking, they could avoid debt and "climb" out of poverty. As I will show in this chapter, debt is much more complex than such views allow. But debt *is* a highly moral issue, whether the invective's target is undisciplined, irrational debtors or scheming, greedy moneylenders. Looking at common assumptions, then, highlights the class moralizing at the heart of much everyday and political discourse around debt, and reveals themes that appear in the moral judgments threaded through class relations in general.

Debt, therefore, provides a powerful perspective from which to analyze class relations and identities. Examining debt practices and discourse provides tangible evidence of the long-term impacts of intangible aspects of class relations. And debt by definition, as I have noted, constitutes a relationship between people; the type of debt I write about requires that one must be in someone else's debt. It is the most obviously relational topic in this book. Finally, debt is arguably more highly moralized than consumption and even marriage practices, with significant consequences for individuals' dignity. It is "not only the economic effects of credit/debt that gives it its immensely powerful capacity to construct and destroy community borders or build social hierarchy. It is also the interminable debate about credit/debt itself . . . as people position themselves within the economic and moral spectrum of credit/debt relations" (Peebles 2010, 228).

My treatment of debt varies somewhat from my discussion of the subjects in other chapters for a key reason: it was not an intentional topic of my research. I did not think to ask about it in interviews, nor was it typically a polite subject to raise in casual conversation. Yet the subject of debt was raised spontaneously and fairly often, and it was while thinking over the trajectories of friends' and informants' lives, and reading through interviews and notes, that I began to recognize the role of debt in shaping class. Coming to the topic in this way had an impact on the types of debt I learned about—that is, specifically those categories that occurred to people as they recounted their livelihoods and survival strategies, spoke about recent events, or talked about class difference—but the frequency with which the topic appeared unelicited underscored for me what a powerful subject debt is.

To begin thinking about its social power, including the different value that debt carries for different kinds of people, consider the four individuals whose narrative portraits I drew in chapter 3. Kannan was able to acquire a loan from a private finance company to purchase blood transfusions for his older daughter because he had a modicum of property—his second daughter Prema's bits of gold—for collateral. He was unable to make the interest payments, however, and nearly lost their gold investment because of it. When Prema could finally be married, he borrowed money for the last of her dowry from acquaintances or local moneylenders. He never considered approaching a bank; banks were, as Stuart Rutherford has put it, "culturally too remote" (2009, 18). Three years later, however, something remarkable and highly contingent occurred: a regular customer of his, a district bank manager, provided a recommendation that enabled him to acquire a major loan from a branch bank. Yet the successful ending is still not guaranteed; Kannan struggles to make regular interest payments, and risks defaulting on the loan.

Anjali's natal family had taken loans from neighborhood moneylenders when her father was injured, and committed much of the family income to repaying them over three years at a high rate of interest. Later, Anjali herself was able to acquire her first business loan through a bank because her classmate's father was a bank officer. Her social capital in this realm was limited, however, and after the friend's father moved on, Anjali was unable to get another bank loan for several years. Although banks were offering loan schemes for women-operated businesses, she was unaware of these programs; when she learned about them, she was certain she would not be accepted into them. Eventually she and her husband were able to finance some of the cost of an offset printer with a bank loan on the basis of their income and business assets, but they also became heavily indebted to finance companies by using Anjali's jewelry as assurance to cover the remainder of the printer cost.

Jeyamani belonged to a domestic workers' sangam that availed itself of government loan programs for poor people, but the sangam (fairly or unfairly) did not deem her qualified to receive a loan. She complained that her employers too refused to give her loans. Instead, she borrowed both small and large amounts from local moneylenders, to buy food at the end of the month, to pay for her husband's medical expenses and her children's school uniforms, and to cover ritual obligations, all at the highest interest rates. Wealthier people like her employers, she charged, could get large loans at low rates to make major investments in property, such as a new home, carrying out the same practices as she—but with much more positive outcomes.

And this was precisely what Usha did. For decades, she and her husband had rotating car loans because Raman liked to replace his car every four years. Later they acquired their first building loans from a private finance company to build a hospital. Once they had successfully repaid the hospital loans, established a reliable credit history, and acquired extensive property to serve as collateral, they were able to obtain a loan from a government bank at a more favorable interest rate than the lending company had offered. The income from the hospital allowed them to pay off all their loans. After Raman died, the hospital served as security for his family; Usha was able to sell the business, keep their home, and continue to provide her children a stable economic and social life.

As these cases demonstrate, there are vast differences in types of loans, their costs, the uses to which they can be put, and their economic and symbolic outcomes. They vary according to the borrower's class, caste, and gender. In general—to focus on class for now—the higher a person's class:

> the greater the likelihood of that person obtaining a loan from a bank
>   or from another formal source with a relatively low interest rate,
> the higher the amount of the loan,
> the lower the nonmonetary costs of incurring debt,

the greater the likelihood that the loan will produce honor (symbolic
capital) and will be put toward an investment that directly produces
economic or cultural capital.

Thus poor people are generally restricted to loans that carry the highest
interest rates and the greatest dishonor, and they borrow smaller average
amounts. Furthermore, they typically acquire loans for daily living
expenses or for major ceremonies, rather than investing in income-
producing activities or prestige-producing commodities.

In the sections that follow, I delineate differences in loan sources and
their costs (monetary and nonmonetary), in the dishonor and honor
attached to borrowing, and in the uses and outcomes of loans. After a
rather extended iteration of such differences and their correlations with
class, caste, and gender, I turn to the public imagination of debt and its
moral panic.

Differences in Loan Sources and Costs

The major categories of loans available in Madurai include:[1]

Family members, friends, or acquaintances
Professional and nonprofessional ("local") moneylenders
Cooperative savings and loan groups, either entirely informal or con-
nected to banks
Pawnbrokers
Private finance companies
Public and private banks

In this chapter I focus on the four loan sources my informants discussed
most often: banks, finance companies, cooperative groups, and local
moneylenders. The following sections review the history of Indian banking, the forms of available credit, and their correlations with socioeconomic difference, all of which are key to grasping the pervasive impact
of debt inequalities and prejudices in Madurai.

Banks

In India, the most favorable interest rates and repayment terms come
from banks. (The one exception is loans from friends and family members, who sometimes charge no interest, though they may expect labor
on demand or a reciprocal loan in the future.) Bank credit practices have
changed a great deal over the course of independent India's history, and
this history has fundamentally shaped contemporary banking. The
government-controlled State Bank of India was created shortly after

Independence, but most banking services remained in the private sector for the nation's first two decades. These early banks catered to "industry . . . and trade and commerce" (Shah, Rao, and Shankar 2007, 1353), and less than 1 percent of villages had commercial bank services (Shah, Rao, and Shankar 2007, 1354).

In 1969, the country's fourteen largest commercial banks were nationalized. This process was politically expedient for then prime minister Indira Gandhi,[2] but also brought to fruition "a desire with a long history" among many Indian leaders (Austin 1999, 209). With the newly nationalized banks' deposits added to those of the State Bank of India and its associated institutions, public sector banks suddenly held 85 percent of bank deposits (Austin 1999, 215n. 18; Chakrabarti 2005, 3).[3] Having thus gained control over banking policy, the Indian government instituted a national turn to "social and development banking." These practices aimed to provide credit and other banking services to a much larger percentage of Indians, with a focus on rural populations. Banks were required by the Reserve Bank of India (RBI) to do three things: first, open numerous branches in "unbanked" and "under-banked" regions, primarily rural areas; second, extend credit to new "priority sectors," particularly agriculture; and third, adhere to RBI ceilings on loan interest rates (see Austin 1999, 209–200; Chavan 2007, 3219; Ramachandran and Swaminathan 2005b, xxii–xxiv).[4]

After the institution of economic liberalization in 1991, banking policy altered sharply once again. The market was opened to a number of private sector banks, foreign banks, and private finance companies. The government's official policy shifted away from "social and development banking" to the benign-sounding "financial inclusion." Despite the rhetorical similarity of these policies' names, however, the new regulations meant that, in a market-oriented economy, "banks have been asked to strive towards an equitable distribution of banking services, but without compromising on commercial considerations" (Chavan 2007, 3219). "Commercial considerations" meant following policies that were in banks' own financial interests. Interest rates became determined by the market rather than by limits intentionally favorable to the poor, and the location of bank branches shifted back to the "more profitable urban and metro areas" (Chakrabarti 2005, 3). It has been argued that the new policies represent "a clear and explicit reversal" of social and development banking (Ramachandran and Swaminathan 2005b, xxi).

Bank loans are thus once again aimed primarily at individuals with significant means. But even those individuals—people who have sufficient resources and meet all the formal requirements of lending rules— can find getting a bank loan very difficult.

There are several reasons for this. First, as Mary Shenk points out, professionals' "documented and stable incomes give them better access to banks and other credit-granting institutions than is likely to be the case among members of the working class, whose incomes may be unpredictable, off-the-record, or both" (2005, 93–94). These latter characteristics can be true of members of the middle class as well. So when Usha and Raman applied to a finance company for their first building loan for the hospital, they were able to provide the required three years of income tax reports and annual audits of their business and household finances. Murugan and his videography business partner, on the other hand, did not even consider applying for a bank loan when they invested in new equipment in 2007 because they had no documents to prove their income, such as income tax records (because "our business isn't big enough to pay income tax"). Instead, they took a Rs. 75,000 loan from a private finance company, and ultimately repaid Rs. 125,000 over two years.

Second, many formal loans (those from finance companies as well as banks) require collateral, such as land or jewelry. As the linguistics professor Sekaran told me shortly after he had received a bank housing loan of Rs. 800,000, "The *vacatiyānavaṅka* [people with resources] have the means to get loans. Getting a loan is not a small thing. You should have an adequate contact [at the bank], and then you should already have some kind of vacati, some money, some land or something which you can pledge as a surety. So you must already have accumulated some kind of a vacati or money in order to be able to apply for a loan."

Usha also pointed out that the amount of credit a person could qualify for depended not only on balance sheets but also on "the person's standing," meaning the applicant's reputation and social connections.

The third obstacle to acquiring a bank loan, then, is that the poor and lower-middle-class usually lack not only the requisite material capital but also the social, cultural, and symbolic capital required to obtain a bank loan. As Anjali too found, getting a loan may require knowing a bank employee. Or it may require a bribe, which requires not only cash but knowing how to give the bribe. Guérin and colleagues comment that "bribes and 'gifts' are the norm rather than the exception, and need to be given at the right moment to the right person. Familiarity with these informal rules speeds up procedures and prevents missteps. Knowing 'someone' within the branch or the bank network, or sometimes simply belonging to the right community, can help to avoid paying bribes" (Guérin, D'Espallier et al. 2011, 21).

Both Kannan and Anjali recognized that certain kinds of knowledge are necessary for a successful bank loan application. In 2005, Kannan told me about public sector bank schemes that were then available to enable auto drivers to buy an autorickshaw. When I asked him if he wanted a loan like this, he answered, "I want to get one, but first I need to go and find a politician and give him Rs. 5,000. I should also give something to the bank person. I don't have that kind of up-front money, so I'll wait for the grace of God and someday buy an auto from my income." Grace appeared almost a decade later in the form of his patron, the district head of a bank.

Anjali and her husband Sundaram viewed the process from a different perspective, that of people who *might* be able to negotiate their way through it. In 2004, when I asked them to talk generally about what uneducated people wouldn't know about how to use vacati—a classic cultural capital question—they immediately chose getting a bank loan as an example.

SUNDARAM: Educated people know the steps of how to get things done. If we need to meet a bank manager, we'll know whom to meet, how to meet him, the steps to go through to meet him, which of his juniors we need to meet. An uneducated person would be shy. They wouldn't know what to do when they get there, and they would hesitate to go.

ANJALI: They'll be afraid. If the manager yells at them, they'll be afraid. But educated people will speak back to the officials.

SUNDARAM: They [educated people] will say, "Why are you delaying my important work?"

ANJALI: They'll be bold, make an outcry (sound viṭṭu pēcalām)—"If you don't stop, I will file a [legal] case against you."

SUNDARAM: In the loan office they [the employees] will ask for lots of certificates, and even if we give them to them, they'll say to come back again. Uneducated people won't keep going back because they'll be afraid of being scolded, so they won't go back and get the loan. But educated people will keep going back and asking to get their loan papers.

I heard a confirming story in 2009 from Murugan and his business partner, who said that in addition to lacking the necessary documents, the reason they avoided getting bank loans (especially from government banks) was because the clerks "will speak in a way that just throws us out of the building."

Even Usha—who was exceptionally well educated, sophisticated, and socially connected—commented on the aggravations of dealing with bank officers. "The moment you go to apply for a bank loan," she reported, "they'll be very sweet to you. They say, 'Oh, no problem, sir. Tomorrow we will sanction a loan. Absolutely, no problem.' [But] the moment you go near them [with the application], they will want all the papers to be in order . . . they will ask you to [sign over] another building or a house as a collateral security. They may talk as if they would [help], but nothing comes easy." Only after repeated trips, each time being told to fix a new small problem in the paperwork, would the loan be sanctioned, Usha said. It is unclear to me whether these bank officers were hoping for a bribe or merely enjoying the pleasures of bureaucratic power. But taken together, these three descriptions of the actual or imagined loan process make it clear why getting a formal loan is an almost insurmountable challenge for people without the proper cultural and social capital. These loans require, in addition to substantial collateral and/or bribe money, some or all of the following: an understanding of the nuanced process of giving a bribe, the knowledge of how to speak to bank officers in a way that will elicit cordiality and approval, the confidence and know-how to respond successfully to bureaucratic roadblocks and power plays, and the social connections with people known to bank officers that make those officers more inclined to sanction a loan. Even if someone without the proper cultural or social capital is willing to enter a loan office (and witness both Kannan and Anjali, who at various points were unwilling even to consider applying for loan schemes formally targeted at people precisely like them), it is extremely difficult to emerge successfully with a loan.

Private Finance Companies

Private finance companies, which have expanded since liberalization, carry out many of the same lending activities as banks. For the most part, however, the companies are much smaller, less imposing, and less bureaucratic than banks, making them easier for a number of people to patronize. Many private finance companies also give out large loans, at higher interest rates than banks but often with longer or more flexible repayment terms. (In early 2009, housing loans, for example, were available from banks for 8–10 percent interest and from finance companies for 14 percent.) They also provide smaller loans against collateral. Such loans are provided for a certain percentage of the assessed value of the property (often 75 percent or 80 percent), interest is charged each month, and the full principal plus accrued interest must be paid back within a set time period (usually one to two years) or the property will be forfeited. Kannan's jewelry loan—the one against which he pledged his younger daughter's gold earrings and pendant—was taken at 18 percent annual interest in 2009.

Cooperative Savings and Loan Associations

Cooperative savings and loan groups, many of which are referred to as "self-help groups," have existed in India for centuries. Members must contribute their own capital in order to join. Although these groups were rarely mentioned when the subject of loans came up in interviews and conversations—an artifact of the way the subject of debt was raised—they are important and widely used vehicles for both saving and credit. In the Madurai area there are two main types, both requiring members to deposit fixed sums at regular intervals (usually weekly or monthly). In the first and less frequent type, rights to the funds are auctioned to members;[5] in the second, members take out loans at specified interest rates once enough funds have accumulated. (Some cooperative funds are for saving only, with no lending component. Jayanthi, the retired cook who talked about a "showcase exterior," had used such a "chit fund" in order to save enough cash to buy her first television.) Some funds are linked to banks, others are not. Fujita Koichi and Sato Keiko observed in Tamil Nadu villages that the middle classes are more likely to join this type of self-help group than are the wealthy or the poor (2011, 78), which accords with my own limited observations in Madurai. (For similar findings, see Abhijit Banerjee and Esther Duflo [2007, 157], who drew from quantitative surveys.) For the poor, up-front costs are often too high, and income flow is too irregular to adhere to the rigid schedule of installment deposits.

Local Moneylenders

Among the people I have known in Madurai, the most widely used source of credit is local (informal) moneylenders.[6] Both formal and informal moneylenders have, of course, practiced for centuries. The types, sizes, and terms of their loans vary a good deal, depending on the moneylender, the perceived trustworthiness of the borrower, and the urgency and purpose of the loan.

The group of creditors covered by the term "moneylender" is highly varied. To begin with, it includes both professional and nonprofessional moneylenders. In the Madurai region the primary professional moneylenders are the Nattukottai Chettiars, or Nagarattars, a mercantile-banking caste (see Rudner 1989; Schrader 1992). But in Madurai, moneylending is more commonly and popularly associated with a different caste group, the Thevar caste cluster, especially Kallars (see note 1 in chapter 8). Such "nonprofessional" or informal lenders turn their own savings to a profit by giving out loans.

Loans from moneylenders offer a number of advantages, and therefore they are used even by people who could acquire loans through banks or finance companies. Credit can be arranged much more quickly through a moneylender than through other sources, and lenders require no formal income documentation. Many moneylenders will make loans without collateral when they trust the borrower. Lakshmi had to take out a loan when her mother, who came to live in Hosur when she was widowed, became ill in 2007. "I had no money to pay for my mother's medical bills, but I need my mother. So I took a loan," she told me. Lakshmi has no gold jewelry, but she was still able to get a local moneylender to loan her the sum at 10 percent interest per month (if she had had jewels as collateral, she said, she could have gotten a loan at a rate of 4 percent per month). Finally, these loans are often the only credit available to the poor, to the lowest castes, and to women who have no husband or who are procuring a loan without their husband's knowledge.

Loans from informal lenders also, however, carry the highest costs. Interest rates can be 10 percent per month to 10 percent per day. Such rates reflect both the higher level of risk taken on by the lender and the "high costs of contract enforcement" (Banerjee and Duflo 2007, 155), as well as the monopoly held by local moneylenders over many borrowing populations. Interest may be taken off the top or charged on a daily or monthly basis, payable either at regular periods or when the term of the loan comes due. Such loans can come with other costs as well. When the moneylender is an influential resident of the area, debtors are often required to provide unpaid labor in the patron's home on an as-needed basis. Other types of local moneylenders verbally or physically harass debtors who are overdue, sometimes brutally and lethally; they may also confiscate property. Such harassment by creditors or their "recovery agents"—less formally referred to as "musclemen" or "goons"—can also occur with private finance companies and even banks.[7] Sekaran, talking about both private finance companies and local moneylenders, said, "You have to be careful of them. If you can't keep up with the interest payments, they will occupy your property, or take your daughter in exchange." He added, "The local guys [moneylenders] are the worst— the highest interest and the most brutal." These recovery risks—public confiscation of property, debasement of family members, and verbal harassment—point us to the subject of dishonor, the final difference in loans and their consequences.

Contrasts in Honor and Dishonor

In addition to these nonmonetary costs, which include responsibilities to the creditor and risks to one's self, family, or property, many loans also carry the potential for dishonor. The amount of dishonor can vary by type of loan or by lender. Some loans, however, can actually bring honor to the debtor. As with other costs and benefits of loans, the honor and dishonor of debt are distributed unequally among people of different classes, and affect a borrower's ability to be accorded dignity by others.

The dominant view of debt in India is that it is shameful. In a society that until recently has long viewed excessive consumption as immoral, value is still often placed on limiting spending to what is within one's available means (Radhakrishnan 2011a; van Wessel 2004). Debt, in contrast, suggests a lack of discipline or planning, dependence (and thus vulnerability), irresponsibility, unnecessary consumption, needs out of bounds with one's station, inability to care for one's family, and dissolution. (Here we again see an overlap in class and caste stereotypes. Guérin, Roesch et al. [2011, 15] note not only that debt "has pejorative moral connotations, implying surrender, dependence and even servility," but also that debt is stereotyped as a lower-*caste* "bad habit," along with alcohol, meat consumption, and uncontrolled female sexuality.) In general, then, debt is dishonorable and even stigmatizing.

Yet different kinds of debt carry different levels of dishonor, and today some kinds are in fact viewed as honorable. The amount of dishonor or honor attached to a loan from a moneylender depends largely on who the moneylender is—based, that is, on the lender's caste, reputation, and behavior (or the behavior of the lender's agents). Some non-Dalits refuse to borrow from Dalits, fearing especially the shame that would occur if the lender publicly harassed them for repayment. In Madurai, Chellamma's husband—a Thevar man named Palani, who was a contractor—frequently disparaged the behavior and habits of his moneylending lower-middle-class Chakkiliyar in-laws, and stated that he would never borrow money from such people. (On the other hand, I knew middle-caste women who borrowed from neighbors who were scheduled-caste women [see also Dean 2011], and did not appear to feel any discomfort.)

The potential for dishonor also depends on the identity of the borrower. As we have already seen, the poor are generally restricted to local moneylenders, whose loans frequently carry dishonor. Women who ask for informal loans on their own often fear disgrace. They have the fewest options for loan sources, and these sources carry the greatest potential for dishonor, partly because of the types of lenders and partly because of women's vulnerability. The high school teacher Darshini, who is divorced, modeled one way in which women become vulnerable when asking for informal loans. She told me that when she needed money for her daughter's wedding, she could not ask male friends for help, "because a single woman isn't trusted by men's wives. If she asks someone she knows for a loan, others assume she is sleeping with the man." The same judgment is made when women take loans from local moneylenders. In other words, some kinds of loans—just like some kinds of consumption—are not judged suitable for certain people. But even beyond such discrimination, the rules and prejudices that surround debt affect dignity because the lack of access to honorable debt prevents some people from being recognized as people worthy of regard, as I discuss below.

The situation with formal loans, and even with savings and loan cooperatives, is quite different. Both can provide honor to borrowers. Borrowing from a cooperative association brings regard because membership in the group not only implies mutual trustworthiness, it also carries the condition of saving money (again, a laudable act of self-discipline). But loans from banks and private finance companies appear to impart honor for quite different reasons. In 2004, Darshini commented incisively on this: "A person's status is now determined by loan eligibility. If you don't have it, it is a shame—it means you don't have proper employment. It used to be that taking out a loan was very shameful. Banks used to be for savings. Now they are for loans. Debt used to be a stigma, and now it is prestige." This change in the value of debt—for middle- and upper-class consumers—was deeply ironic to Darshini. She added that simply *saying* that you have a formal loan shows that you are part of the modern consumer economy and that you have the resources necessary to get a loan, and that both of these qualities bring "prestige." Similarly Parvathi, an M.D. who practices at Government Hospital, told me in 2000 that anyone who gets a bank loan can automatically be regarded as middle class. When debt is called "credit," then, it becomes a positive thing—an engine of the economy, a sign of personal worth.[8]

In sum, the loans to which the poor have access not only carry the highest interest rates and the highest nonmonetary costs, they also bear the greatest dishonor. It is not simply that poor people are criticized for taking on any debt whatsoever, but that the kinds of debt they must take on have the most negative social value, even among their peers. The same is true for women acquiring informal loans without a husband's participation. On the other hand, the kinds of loans that middle-class and upper-class people are qualified to take out often both attest to and provide positive cultural capital. This capital, as well as the visible consumption that loans often enable, helps create dignity and recognition. Thus the social meanings of loans—whether they serve as negative or positive cultural capital, and whether they produce dignity or indignity—vary a great deal according to the type of loan, the purposes to which it is put, and the class, caste, and gender of the person acquiring it. Moreover, as I will demonstrate below, the non-instrumental quest for dignity can affect the types of loans that people are willing to take on, and thus also shape the instrumental capital that they are able to acquire.

Differences in Loan Uses and Outcomes

Crucial differences exist in the uses to which different types of borrowers can put their loans. The economic and symbolic outcomes of debt vary directly by class as a result. Poor people take on debt for everyday living expenses and for major religious and life-cycle ceremonies.[9] (Life-cycle events include first birthday rituals, puberty ceremonies for girls, weddings, and funerals, among others.) Women who take out loans on their own are usually borrowing money for household survival. Many of the domestic workers I knew tried to get loans from employers at the end of their pay cycles to buy food for their families.

Everyday consumption and major ritual events rarely, however, generate immediate income. This point needs to be qualified somewhat for loans used for ritual responsibilities toward kin, which may still serve as long-term investments since such responsibilities should be reciprocated in the future; fulfilling one's ritual responsibilities also helps to ensure that family members will provide other kinds of support when necessary. The same could be said for loans taken out for school fees or school uniforms, since children's education is seen as an investment in one's own future. In addition, as I discuss in chapter 7, life-cycle ceremonies such as marriage (as well as religious rituals) can be used to increase prestige if they are sufficiently lavish, though lavishness is rarely possible for the poor; but in every case such ceremonies are critical, albeit intangible, indicators of class. Nonetheless, the vast majority of loans taken out by the poor produce no net economic gain.

In contrast, the wealthy and some members of the middle class are much more likely to take out large loans that enable investment in income-producing endeavors or in large durable goods, which serve to set them even further apart from the poor. Consumer goods also serve as cultural capital, as we saw in the previous chapter. Usha, Anjali, and Sekaran all provide examples, using their homes or businesses as collateral for future loans, income generation, and tax deductions. The same collateral, itself originally acquired through a loan, has also provided each with cultural and sometimes social capital. Usha and Raman made new social connections with powerful people after building the hospital, for example, and Anjali's graphic design business provided her with cultural capital. Sekaran was even able to use his newly built home, the nicest in his suburban area, to challenge the caste prejudices that surrounded him in his mostly middle-caste neighborhood, as I described in chapter 2.

Debt and the Public Imagination

Debt is a vivid part of the public imagination, and this imagination focuses obsessively on the shame of debt. Just as irresponsible borrowers are castigated, so too are lenders believed to loan money unscrupulously. As everywhere, "the ubiquitous moral debates surrounding credit and debt" are "coconstitutive of their material effects" (Peebles 2010, 225).

In this section I turn briefly to a discussion of moneylender stereotypes in order to consider further the shame associated with debt, and
then return to a discussion of the distance between debt in popular discourse and debt in actual practice.

Moneylenders have a particularly degraded image in the press and in
popular discourse.[10] They are depicted as abusive, usurious, greedy,
rapacious, and exploitative. David Rudner sums up one longstanding
stereotype of rural moneylenders as "coldly preying upon their cultiva-
tor clients, luring them further and further into debt, and finally suck-
ing them dry of surplus, savings, property, and liberty" (1989, 418–419).
Such views continue into the present, appearing in economic policy
discussions, laws, and political campaigns (for an example of the first,
see Jeromi 2007, 1). A centuries-long history of laws regulating moneylenders' practices, including interest rates and recovery methods, speaks
to the perception of moneylenders as a social menace. These laws
include the 1957 Tamil Nadu Moneylender Act and the 2003 Tamil Nadu
Prohibition of Charging Exorbitant Interest Act. One provision of the
latter bill was the "Abetment of suicide" clause whereby "if it is shown
that immediately prior to suicide, the debtor or any member of his
family was subjected to molestation by any person, the person who has
advanced loan shall, unless the contrary is proved, be deemed to have
abetted the commission of such suicide" (Tamil Nadu Government
2003, 172). The outcry against local moneylenders also provides a useful
political tool on occasion. In 2005, for example, part of Chief Minister
Jayalalitha's successful election platform was the strict regulation of
informal moneylenders, a position that was calculated to attract wide
popular support.

The avaricious moneylender is really, I argue, the complement to the
undisciplined poor borrower whose practice makes him vulnerable to
predation. The poor must be protected, but they must also be educated
(by NGOs), urged (by the government), or excoriated (by anyone who
has access to other forms of credit) to end their self-destructive borrowing habits. As I have noted above, moral discourse around debt also
impugns chronic debtors as irresponsible, unable to control their desires,
and (thus) morally dissolute. (Recall here that such criticisms are sometimes tied to caste and gender ideologies as well.)

My point is not that debt *does not* reproduce poverty; indeed, the
forms of debt available to the poor often contribute to entrenched poverty, at the same time as they help ensure survival (just as the forms of
credit available to the wealthy help to reproduce their wealth). The rhetorical and legal drama around indebtedness and informal lending, however, is meaningful in and of itself; it has both functional and symbolic

importance. For one thing, the common discourse about debt disguises very similar behaviors among the middle and upper classes, making it easier for people in those classes to marginalize the poor in private and public discourse. For another, the stereotypes it reproduces actively work to prevent the poor from gaining access to forms of debt with more favorable terms. This latter point is true at the federal level as well as the local. Stephen Young has argued that in the 1991 switch to "financial inclusion" banking policies, previous subsidies were "cut so that interest rates would be set according to the perceived hazards associated with particular borrowers. The failings of development banking were therefore implicitly attributed not to the absence of broader socio-economic reforms, in terms of land distribution or public insurance services, but to the moral irresponsibility of poor people who *chose* to default" (2010, 208–209; emphasis in original).

In the remainder of this section, I probe two related features of common wisdom that have appeared in this chapter, in light of the realities of everyday practice in Madurai. The first claim is that the poor are irresponsible, the second is that they (and only they) are burdened by chronic indebtedness.

I have discussed the near impossibility of saving money for people who lack a secure place to store savings or a regular enough income to contribute installment savings to self-help groups or other cooperative funds. But looked at in another way, a regular series of loans in fact functions as a process that Stuart Rutherford (2009, 20–24) calls "saving down." Borrowers receive a lump sum, repay it in installments, and then receive another lump sum when the first loan cycle has been completed; as Rutherford puts it, with both regular saving and regular borrowing "a pattern is created of swapping small pay-ins for occasional pay-outs" (2009, 24). This form of "saving" comes with a high rate of negative interest (from the perspective of savings), but moneylenders are generally the primary source of money available for the poor, who need funds both to cover the shortfall between meager income and modest consumption needs, and also (and here they are no different from most wealthier people) to cover large lump-sum costs for dramatic events such as weddings and funerals, or even for other smaller but still sporadic costs such as school fees. Very few of those people I knew who borrowed from local moneylenders complained about the loan rates, accepting these as part of the moneylenders' cost of giving loans without collateral (though they also were cynical about the wealth the lenders accrued), and they appreciated the flexibility that most moneylenders extended for repayment dates. The poor borrowers I knew tried to avoid the disgrace of borrowing from lenders known to be abusive, but otherwise their primary goal was to repay as regularly as possible in order to be able to take out additional loans in the future.

This leads directly to the issue of chronic indebtedness. First, most of my poor acquaintances accepted debt as an expensive fact of life. Few saw themselves struggling to get out of debt for any period of time; instead, they saw themselves living with cyclical debt while trying to maintain positive relationships with their creditors or potential creditors (see also Guérin, Roesch et al. 2011). When I asked the butcher Rajkumar what he did to buy food during the periods that his butcher stall made no profit, he said, "My life goes on only in loans [*kaṭanle tān pōkutu vāḻkai*]." His wife Mallika jumped in to say, "The people [i.e., lenders] will know that I am paying the money back correctly, so they'll give me loans." Rather than perceiving "chronic indebtedness" as the problem, for the poor themselves "it is instead the impossibility of taking on further debt that is considered a problem" (Guérin, D'Espallier et al. 2011, 13).

But intriguingly, the debt practices of the middle and upper classes are not entirely different. Almost everyone has to borrow money to pay the costs of major life-cycle events (see Shenk 2005), and many need to take out loans to cover major medical emergencies as well. And like the poor, wealthier people also borrow money to consume, though their consumption is beyond the level of household survival. Like Rajkumar and Mallika, these people too may see their lives progressing as a series of loans. Usha told me in 2001, after she and Raman had finished building their house, that in the days of the hospital and house construction, "My entire calendar was organized around which loan was paid on which day! Almost every day had a different loan written down." Because of their cars if nothing else, she said, "loans will always be there with us." In these important ways, the patterns of debt between the poor and rich are not terribly distinct. Though their loan sources, costs, uses, and outcomes differ significantly, both may be lifetime debtors. Socially, the differences lie in how visible their debt is in the public eye, how much social anxiety it creates, and most of all, *how their debt is judged*.

In sum, debt is tied to the reproduction of class in several ways. The poor pay more to borrow. Structural inequalities such as banks' loan policies (including qualifications based on income and the ability to verify it), and cultural inequalities such as dominant assumptions that the poor are feckless with their money, prevent the poor from paying less.[11] The middle and upper classes have access to lower borrowing costs, larger loans, and much larger gains in capital (both economic and cultural). Meanwhile, the poor receive less return from their loans; they generally *lose* cultural and symbolic capital by borrowing. In addition to the individual and family dishonor that borrowing from some moneylenders can engender, there is also the entrenchment of the stereotype that the poor borrow irresponsibly. This image of the poor feeds directly into their inability to borrow from formal sources—because they are "known" to be irresponsible, and therefore not only bad credit risks but also the types of people undeserving of access to banks.

The Class Relations of Debt

None of the patterns of the "social regulation" of debt (Guérin, D'Espallier et al. 2011, 6–7)—the systematic differences by class, caste, and gender in available sources and terms of credit—was lost on the illātavaṅka I knew. In concluding this chapter, I turn to something Jeyamani said when I met her in 1992. The conversation is ingrained in my memory: Jeyamani, back from cleaning her employer's house, was sitting on the dirt floor of her small thatched hut, occasionally rocking the hanging cloth cradle that held her three-year-old daughter. Tired but passionate, always a powerful orator, Jeyamani had spoken at length that afternoon about the inequities of the servant–employer relationship. Toward the end, she turned to the importance of loans.

> If [our husbands] don't drive a rickshaw one day, what can we do? We have to borrow ten rupees from someone. We would ask for ten rupees as a loan. They [the employers] would say, "Would you pay interest?" Okay, for the sake of the husband and children, we would take the money and boil the kanci. . . . We are asked, "Why do you pawn? Why do you borrow money?" Can I bring my children to your house if they are starving? You could offer food to only one of my children. Can you feed them all? No. Because you'd say, "With the cost of things today, how can I feed you?" I have to incur debt myself. How can I do otherwise?

Each of the lessons of this chapter—the patterned inequalities of borrowing, the moralizing about debt, the mutually determined relationships among classes, the intangible and tangible experiences of class, and the forceful impacts of the interwoven structural and symbolic elements of class—appears in this dense quote.

Jeyamani does not moralize about why people borrow. She recognizes its necessity for those who live under the constraints imposed by poverty—unsteady and low-paid employment, lack of health care, little access to good education—constraints she cannot alter. She also has a clear-eyed recognition of the financial and symbolic costs of loans; as a poor low-caste woman, she has only the worst loan terms. Her statement that "for the sake of the husband and children, we would take the money and boil the kanci" is especially poignant for two reasons. First is the reference to kanci (kanji, rice gruel), a food considered to be the last resort against starvation. Second is her insistence that she borrows money only for her family's sake, stressing that in order to provide, she must do something she does not want to do (because Jeyamani, like her wealthy critics, recognizes the financial costs of borrowing). Her employers' refusal to comprehend her need to borrow is also a refusal to see and to know Jeyamani, to recognize her as worthy of regard. Unseen, and known only as unworthy, she cannot gain dignity in this relationship. Her need to borrow money decisively shapes her subjective experience of class. Finally, she addresses the structural inequities of class that are exacerbated by current debt policies in India. Jeyamani emphasizes the stasis of her family's circumstances over generations, versus the mobility of "those who have." Her words not only construct a strong moral indictment of the failure of generosity; calling out the structural sources of class, they also make the claim that rich people's wealth is built directly on (and exacerbates) their servants' poverty. While Jeyamani does not see debt itself as immoral, she does see the hypocrisy of different approaches to debt—and their divergent outcomes—as immoral.

I argued at the beginning of this chapter that debt opens an especially revealing window onto the mutual relationships of economic, cultural, social, and symbolic capital. It also highlights the intersections of the tangible and the intangible, and the subjective and the objective. In this chapter I have engaged in distinct approaches to understanding class by analyzing structural, discursive, and phenomenological sources and impacts of debt. Unequal access to credit is a structural determinant of class. The moral discourse surrounding debt also produces patterned effects on access to resources and thus on the long-term chances of people of different classes. While debt is not a daily part of gaining regard to the extent that visible consumption is, it continually feeds into the taken-for-granted image of the illātavaṅka and affects how they are treated. In other words, the moralizing discourse of debt provides them less access to dignity. Simultaneously, the access to formal credit and the regard that this imbues shape the standing of the vacatiyāṉavaṅka and periyavaṅka. These processes, specific as their details are to Madurai and India, are nonetheless akin to such processes elsewhere, as Gustav Peebles describes: "By contributing to the construction of boundaries of exclusion, inclusion, and hierarchy, the moral tensions and asymmetries that reside within the indissoluble dyad of credit/debt are themselves elemental in helping to generate the specific material effects of credit/debt that unfold in any given ethnographic setting" (2010, 234). We cannot understand the impacts of debt on class—whether the material or the immaterial features of class—without taking these multiple approaches.

The construction of class difference that surrounds the discourse and practice of debt, and in particular the discourse of self-control, takes center stage in the following chapter on the construction of an emerging middle-class identity.

6   *Performing the Middle*

This chapter combines a continued focus on the moralized nature of self-control with a return to the display and interpretation of class, by turning directly to the self-conscious performance of class and the creation of class distinction. Concerns about scrutiny and subjective experience return as well. As we saw in chapter 4, Madurai residents of all classes can feel like they are anxious actors under the gaze of a critical audience. Members of the middle class describe themselves as being even more scrutinized than those above or below them, even as they lay claim to their position in the "moral middle" (cf. Gilbertson 2014b; Srivastava 2015), and the signs of their position include but are not limited to consumption practices. The middle class is a collection of people—like Kannan, Anjali, and Usha—who see their position as explicitly performative, and who belong to a class category that, in its current manifestation, is relatively recent in origin and figures as a critical player in the local and national imaginary of proper citizenship.

What does it mean to view oneself as a middle-class person in urban India? The "middle class" has been portrayed as a powerful social and political actor in India, particularly since the formal advent of economic liberalization in 1991, and "seems to have caught the public's imagination" (Desai 2007, 345). Yet we know little about how the middle classes see themselves and how they experience their lives as middle-class people. It may even be argued that we know little about who these middle-class people are, given the epistemological as well as ethnographic gaps in scholars' understandings of India's urban middle classes.

In this chapter, I explore both what it is like to be self-consciously middle class in Madurai today, and what this tells us about the perceived precariousness of class identity. It is both a pleasurable and an anxious position. Madurai residents view the middle class as a desirable place to be—but those who see themselves as middle-class also talk about their class position as a markedly uneasy and unstable place. Their accounts emphasize the *centrality* of the middle class, which is at once a position of social visibility and worth, a stage on which to be judged by critical spectators, and a site that simultaneously avoids, buffers, and is caught between behavioral extremes. This location contributes greatly to both the pleasures and the anxieties of being middle-class. Yet while middle-class people use the metaphor of place, as I have just done, there is little stasis in their descriptions of class experiences; rather, they emphasize the continuous need to perform behaviors that will support their claims to class standing. Class is not just a process; in cases like these it is a project, and often a fraught one. Thus, as the growth of India's middle class is lauded and its economic, political, and ideological power is trumpeted, the views held by the middle class in this city turn out to be less sanguine.

In this chapter I focus on the accounts of residents who *call themselves* middle class. As readers may already ascertain, this is a somewhat different set of people than those whom analysts include in this category, since many of those who claim middle-class identity in Madurai fall below the lower boundaries of standard objective definitions. Here again, my attention to subjective identities is not only a product of my research interests, but also a result of how I came to the topic. I was initially skeptical of the early fanfare over the growth of the Indian middle class. Despite the increased visibility of this class in India's national imaginary after the 1980s, as well as in media representations by other nations whose governments and manufacturers were eager for a liberalized Indian economy, reliable statistical documentation of middle-class growth took years to appear. Over time, however, I became persuaded of the significance of the middle class by a different kind of evidence: the increase in the number of Madurai residents who identified themselves as middle-class.

In 1985–1987, when I carried out research on class and film-watching in Madurai, I met almost no one who identified herself or himself as middle-class or who even recognized such a category. This was due in part to my social networks, which were concentrated in lower-class neighborhoods, but it also reflected the scant recognition then given to an intermediate class by the majority of the population. Several years later, while doing research on domestic service relationships in 1991–1992, I interviewed a number of people who recognized the middle class as part of Madurai's class structure. All of these individuals saw themselves as either middle- or upper-class, and they were overwhelmingly English speakers. On the other hand, those who described themselves as poor (almost all of whom spoke only Tamil) still recognized only two class categories in the city: the rich and the poor, or "those who have" (irukkravaṅka) and "those who do not" (illātavaṅka). By the time I returned in 1999, however, even poor people spoke of a class structure that comprised at least three parts, one of which was a middle class. Moreover, for the first time I heard many Tamil speakers refer to themselves as *naṭuttaramāṉavaṅka* (middle people) or as belonging to a *naṭuttara* kuṭumpam (middle family), terms that were not part of everyday speech even in 1992.

Such observations suggest that the middle is a much more widely recognized class category than it was in the early 1990s, and that more people identify with it than in the past. In short, "middle-classness" has become socially more significant, and culturally more elaborated, over the past two decades in Madurai. Few if any objective features of income, occupation, education, consumer goods, housing, or leisure practices, however, can be used to define this group. Indeed, because of my focus on self-ascribed identity, this "middle class" is even more heterogeneous than the Indian "middle class" that others have described as fragmented and divided (Deshpande 2003; Fernandes and Heller 2006). The only features that unite middle-class people in Madurai are their claim to the identity, the types of indicators they use to substantiate that identity, and the striking behavioral and attitudinal ramifications that attend it.[1]

Listening to middle-class people talk about their lives quickly creates an awareness of the extent to which these people see themselves as *performing* an identity. Here I employ the idea of performativity in a very particular sense, that of Erving Goffman's notion of the dramaturgical.[2] In Goffman's perspective, people, all with greater and lesser degrees of self-consciousness at different times, merge "selves" with the "masks" of social roles and see themselves as *acting* a part. The accounts of people in all class positions in Madurai reveal a direct attention to themselves as more or less secure or anxious actors, and attention to others as their evaluating audience. Middle-class people describe an even more heightened sense of being on a stage than people of other classes do. As in Goffman's discussions, there is a sense of both "cynical" and "sincere" performances, and especially a sense of the "fragility" of performance (see especially Goffman 1959, 19, 56, 252–253). This sense of being an actor—and of having an audience—is key to the precariousness expressed in subjective accounts of class.

As I have noted, the set of people who *call themselves* middle-class overlaps only partially with those people whom analysts have conventionally identified as middle class, typically based on income and assets, occupations, and/or consumption. In particular, even where analytical definitions are nuanced and precise, and differentiate carefully between, for example, the "new" or "new-rich" or "transnational" middle class and the "lower" or "local" portion of this class (e.g., Derné 2005; Deshpande 2003; Dwyer 2000; Fernandes 2006; Fernandes and Heller 2006; Fuller and Narasimhan 2007; Harriss 2006), the set of self-identified middle-class residents of Madurai includes many people who fall below the lower limits of these definitions of the middle class ("lower" in terms of occupational rank, income, material property, education, consumer goods, or dominantly valued cultural capital). (Those at the upper end of the middle class, however, correspond closely with the upper limits of analysts' categories.)[3] It will also become clear that those at the high and the low ends of the spectrum in Madurai do not agree that all the others belong. Despite this lack of correlation with analytical categories and the lack of local consensus on who properly belongs in the middle class, those people who identify themselves as such report a highly consistent set of criteria for middle-class membership, and of experiences resulting from their class identity.

There is a large literature debating the effects of liberalization in India, though little of it, until recently, has drawn upon ethnographic evidence. Thus while numerous studies assess the effects of liberalization on the middle class and other groups or categories of Indian society, only a relatively small portion have drawn extensively from the opinions of middle-class people themselves, or examined the nature of middle-class people's responses to economic liberalization (see Brosius 2010; De Neve 2006; Fernandes 2000b, 2006; Ganguly-Scrase and Scrase 2009; Jeffery, Jeffery, and Jeffrey 2011; Lukose 2009; Radhakrishnan 2011a; Säävälä 2010; Upadhya 2011; van Wessel 2004). Middle-class Madurai residents' reactions to the economic changes over this period are mixed. The predominant experiences they report are not the sort usually measured in studies of liberalization. Their accounts document shifting sets of economic possibilities in their lives. They also suggest how complicated the impacts of economic changes may be on a sense of well-being. Examining these accounts reveals ways in which everyday life experiences are shaped by socioeconomic structures and histories, as well as by emerging class identities. While numerous scholars agree that new middle-class formations are underway in India, this focus on local definitions of class identities suggests why we need to reimagine different ways of learning about class, comprehend which class contours are most relevant in specific communities, and grasp the consequences for everyday lives that are involved in the emergence of new class formations. Thus, this chapter serves as an invitation to consider what else we may learn by examining emic categories (internally contested though they may be) and local perceptions of class identities and differences.

In the following sections, I begin with very brief overviews of the impacts of economic liberalization on the middle class and of scholarly representations of the Indian middle classes. I then move to Madurai residents' own definitions of the middle class, the self-images they construct, and their accounts of the good and the bad of middle-class life. I conclude the chapter by considering the insights we gain into the construction of emergent class categories by focusing on self-ascribed identities and their performance.

Characterizing the Middle Class

India's middle classes are frequently portrayed as the primary beneficiaries of the 1991 liberalization policies, largely due to their growing purchasing power and the simultaneous increase in the quality and availability of the consumer goods for which they constitute the major market.[4] Yet despite the significant increases in measures of national wealth, including GDP and GNI per capita (World Bank 2008a, 2008b), the benefits of economic growth have been more narrowly distributed than is often assumed. Some members of the conventional middle class (including civil servants, professionals, and business owners), primarily its wealthiest segment, have benefited financially from liberalization policies. This group has been widely showcased as proof of India's successful modernization and globalization (see Fernandes 2000a, 2000b; Lakha 1999, 251). As several analysts have noted, however, the effects of liberalization have in fact been mixed for middle and lower classes alike (Desai 2007; Fernandes 2000b; Ganguly-Scrase and Scrase 2008; Ghosh 1994; Kothari 1995). For example, many public sector enterprises, such as life insurance and banking, have been privatized, making quintessentially secure middle-class jobs vulnerable to the uncertainties of private sector employment. And some data indicate that, while education levels are rising and the pay in some white-collar jobs is higher, the actual *number* of these jobs has not shown any significant growth, resulting in increased competition for more lucrative positions (Desai 2007). The ambiguous, and ambivalent, effects of liberalization policies are reflected in the everyday tensions reported by middle-class people in Madurai.

Estimates of the size of India's middle class (or middle classes) vary from 50 million to 350 million (roughly 5 percent to 35 percent of the population), though there is now a growing consensus that the higher figures are greatly exaggerated (e.g., Deshpande 2003, 134; Mazzarella 2003, 264–265; Meyer and Birdsall 2012; Shukla 2010; Vanaik 2002, 228). Size and composition depend on how the middle class is defined and which data are used to measure it.[5] The wide variety of characteristics used by analysts to identify an Indian middle class include income, durable property and assets, occupation, structural position (typically, relation to the means of production), consumption ability and/or expenditure, cultural and social capital, and attitudes.[6] Yet people such as Kannan, who see themselves as middle class, are not accounted for in such definitions.

Who, then, makes up the middle class in Madurai? Having come to this question by hearing people talk about themselves and others as middle class, my approach here is to gain a sense of what it means to see oneself as a middle-class person in a period of recent economic change. To begin to answer this question, I first review local terminologies for the middle class, examine the range of people who call themselves middle class, and then explore more closely how these people define the middle class and differentiate it from other classes.

In Tamil, as I discussed in chapter 2, current class categories include ēḷai makkaḷ (poor people) and illātavaṅka (people who have nothing); naṭuttaramānavaṅka (middle people) or naṭuttara kuṭumpam (middle family); and paṇakkāraṅka (monied people), vacatiyānavaṅka (people with resources or luxuries), and periyavaṅka (big people).[7] (Here I am using the colloquial forms of these terms rather than the literary ones; see note 8, chapter 2.) The class categories used today by English speakers are typically "lower class," "middle class," and "upper class." When greater specificity is required, gradations such as "upper middle class" are also utilized. Unless stated otherwise, I use "middle class" and "middle people" interchangeably in this chapter even though the two terms have slightly different lexical referents. That is, because terminology depends on the primary language of the speaker, and because people fluent in English tend to be higher class than people who are not, those who call themselves "middle class" will on average be invoking a slightly better-off group or category than will those who call themselves "naṭuttaramānavaṅka." The concepts are sufficiently close that, for my purposes here, they can be examined as near equivalents; both denote a class defined by contrast with an upper and a lower class, and most importantly, "middleness" is assigned the same behavioral and attitudinal features regardless of which term is used.

The Madurai residents I spoke with who identified themselves as middle class or middle people ranged from autorickshaw drivers, masons, and occasionally cooks; to small business owners and merchants, office clerks, and teachers; to bureaucrats, doctors, lawyers, and college or university faculty. These people represent a wide range of circumstances in terms of assets, security, and social respect. When they explained why they saw themselves as middle class, and how they differed from people of other classes, however, they not only used similar criteria to one another, they also focused on almost the same variables as analysts do— although they did not always agree with analysts (or with one another) on the values of those variables.

Differences of opinion about who belonged in the middle class most often centered on occupation, education, assets, and consumer goods. Recently, the ability to speak English has also become a critical marker for some. For example, a man named Paul, a principal of a small but prestigious school, quipped in 2005 that an autorickshaw driver could at best be a "middle-class wannabe." Paul, who with his wife owns a house, a domestic-model car, and a motorbike, and sent their children to an exclusive private school, added that owning goods such as "a television and a metal bureau" was insufficient to raise a person out of the lower class. Instead, in his view, such standing required substantial housing in the right kind of neighborhood and the right kind of English-medium education for one's children. Zakir, a successful businessman, had a different standard: "These days," he said (also in 2005), "really counting as the middle class means having a foreign-model car," since "lesser people" were by then buying domestic models. But some others who call themselves middle class (such as Kannan, Murugan, or the medical transcription students quoted later in this chapter) would have stated at that time that anyone who owns *any* kind of car can only be a member of the privileged upper class. Thus the category is a contested one; but not only is there agreement that occupations and consumption practices can place people outside of the middle class, the boundaries themselves (which vary predictably depending on the speaker's relative location within the middle class) are neither arbitrary nor highly elastic.

Instead, as the following accounts demonstrate, middle-class standing is defined by a family's economic and social security, its distance from wealth on the one hand and from mere survival or subsistence on the other ("wealth" and "subsistence" being, however, relative terms), the uses to which any discretionary income is put, and the ways in which individuals use the "goods" they acquire—in other words, how well they perform middle-class identity. Middle-class people stated that members of the upper class have substantial assets, including family wealth, capital, and other property, whereas middle-class people have a monthly income (or, in some cases, a reliable daily wage) and perhaps a small amount of property, and the poor at best have daily wages and sufficient earnings for a day's expenses.

These material differences were most notable, however, for the moral and behavioral characteristics that attended them. One of the first points to emerge below will be the moralizing themes that predominate when middle-class people talk about how all the classes *differ*: the ability of middle-class people to consume with moderation and deliberation, in contrast with the excessive acquisition, instantaneous gratification, and greed that characterize the rich, and the general inability to consume that typifies the poor.[8] (Note that this involves a more multi-sided set of moral distinctions than do discourses on debt.) In order to look more closely at how the middle class is defined, I turn to conversations with two women who identify themselves as middle class but who are at different ends of the spectrum.

Parvathi, the Government Hospital doctor, who is a member of the Pillai caste, distinguished the classes for me succinctly by explaining, "The higher class has money and wants to know what to do with it, the middle class has to search for money to get something, and the lower class cannot find the money even if it wants to get those things." Laughing at the sharpness of these distinctions, she expanded, "Here in the middle class, you have to *plan* everything, you wait for the money, and you say, 'Okay, I've got this amount, okay, I'll spend it this way.' But there [in the upper class], they don't have to plan everything. Whatever they want, they get it that instant. And here we're different from the lower class, because unlike them, we *can* get what we want."

Jayanthi, the retired cook who introduced me to the idea of a "show-case exterior," made more detailed distinctions. Jayanthi had moved across class lines in her life. At sixteen she married a homeopathic doctor and lived comfortably until he died six years later. She and her four small children then lived in severe poverty for many years until they all finally found steady employment. She described the classes to me this way:

> Well, rich people [paṇakkāraṅka], nowadays they go everywhere, they go out everywhere. Because they have resources [vacati], wealthy peo-ple will take a car, they'll take an autorickshaw. They have money. So that's how they'll travel. Middle people [naṭuttaramānavaṅka], they'll have to think first—"Can we go in a car? Do we have that much money? If we have that much money, perhaps we should buy something else. We could spend it on something we need at home." They'll think about that. Poor people [illātavaṅka] won't even be able to have the choice. Rich people don't have to deal with any of that. They have money com-ing in from everywhere, so they don't have to think about it. . . . Rich people won't bother themselves thinking about anything at all. They're pompous, Sara. Middle people don't have that attitude. They're more simple.

Parvathi and Jayanthi underline the middle class's ability to acquire necessary commodities through careful planning and deliberate spend-ing. They contrast this with the immediate gratification enjoyed by the rich, and with the inability of the poor to acquire desirable goods regard-less of their aspirations or strategic planning. Middle-class people are not wasteful or profligate; instead they deliberately sacrifice certain choices for others. On the other hand, there is no question that they *can* make those choices. Unlike the poor, they have literally (and morally) earned the ability to consume beyond mere subsistence.

As these points suggest—and as discussions of decency revealed in chapter 4—consumption choices and tastes signify not only the limits on resources, but also the values and attitudes of the people making those painstaking decisions. As Jayanthi said approvingly, middle-class people are more likely to make "simple" choices than to display the thoughtless excess of the wealthy. This idea was echoed by others I spoke with, who emphasized similarly the "plainness" and "ordinariness" of middle-class people. These characteristics form a cluster of related attributes that are used to depict and to judge the middle class. Simplicity and plainness are tied not only to a lack of pretension, arrogance, and excess, but also to "decency" and "neatness." In turn, all of these attributes mark a middle-class person as "ordinary" or "normal." In Tamil, the English terms have been adopted for almost all of these attributes, with the exception of the Tamil word *cātāraṇam*, which means common, normal, or ordinary (i.e., not inferior, superior, or otherwise extraordinary).[9] When I once asked Kannan his class (using the term takuti), he answered, "We are normal [*nārmalā irukkirōm*]. We eat three times in a day, but we don't eat or dress lavishly. We have no ostentation [*āṭamparam*]." Thus in their location between excessive wealth and utter lack of resources, these middle-class people represent themselves as ordinary people.[10]

While the concern about appearing decent in public was most marked in the lower middle class, women and men at all levels of the middle class talked about the importance of having their everyday clothing be presentable (clean and unwrinkled and fairly new, if not necessarily fashionable), neatly arranged, and modestly covering the body (see Dickey 2005; Gilbertson 2014a). Neatness and cleanliness are key middle-class values in other realms as well. For example, Renganathan, the Chettiar advertising company manager, explained that "the neatness of the home indicates whether a family is middle class and modern. That is the measure here. If a person is neat, then they are modern." Cleanliness and orderliness are standard, longstanding middle-class civic and domestic concerns, and are often cited by middle-class people in Madurai as distinguishing them from the urban poor (see also Hancock 1999; Harriss 2006, 458; Mazzarella 2005, 6–7; Nair 2005; Taguchi 2013; Venkatachalapathy 2006; Waldrop 2004, 97). All of these features of plainness, ordinariness, decency, and cleanliness—tied by nodes of order, self-presentation, and modernity, and directly linked to the definition of middle-classness as self-disciplined and moderate—are essential aspects of how middle-class people describe themselves as a whole, and how they aim to present themselves at home and in public to one another. These values and their enactment underlie both the pleasures and the anxieties of being in the contemporary middle class in Madurai, and are reflected in the accounts below.

The Good and the Bad of Being in the Middle

People who see themselves as middle-class report a consistent set of attitudes about what it is like to live in that class and to reproduce their class standing. The positive aspects of being middle class include having sufficient income flow and assets to live beyond a mere survival level and to partake actively in a consumer economy; to thereby be seen as "counting" in Madurai society; and to be in the culturally valorized position of moderate "middleness." The negative sides include the intense scrutiny of behavior by social onlookers; the need to perform a consumerist class identity with limited financial means; the excessive pressure to work and earn sufficiently to finance this consumption; the consequences of performing inadequately and the fear of downward mobility; and conversely, the fear of harm from envy and evil eye that results from upward mobility. For each positive aspect that emphasizes security and stability, there is a negative ramification or consequence that highlights the precariousness and potential instability of middle-class life.

It is hardly surprising that being middle class in a population whose majority is impoverished is experienced deeply—both corporeally and cognitively—as good. It means being able to take part in practices that require economic or cultural capital and enhance one's reputation in the local community, to participate in a consumer economy that is heralded in many public media, and to locate oneself in a position of moderate middleness that is socially and aesthetically desirable. To be middle class is to be *central* in numerous ways. While there are negative aspects to that centrality, its positive senses include being seen as an ideal normative citizen and viewing oneself as the norm, being central to public discourse and political policy (Deshpande 2003, 130; Fernandes 2000b), and avoiding behavioral extremes on either side of a moral middle.

Visibility, Regard, and Citizenship

The issues of visibility and social regard discussed in chapter 4 are also closely tied to the enactment of citizenship. To buy and display goods and to possess the knowledge to use them appropriately is to partake in consumption practices that both commercial media and government rhetoric represent not only as pleasurable but also as crucial signs of a desirable modernity. Purnima Mankekar notes that in India in the mid-1980s, "post-colonial modernity became increasingly articulated in terms of consumerism. In television's discourses, modernity was frequently equated with, and expressed through, consumerist aspirations and desires: consumerism itself became an index of modernity. The family, henceforth conceived as a unit of consumption, would acquire a modern lifestyle, and the nation, through the boost consumers would give to the economy, would also 'develop' and thus become modern" (1999, 48). As Arvind Rajagopal has observed, the pre-liberalization nationalist credo of "Be Indian Buy Indian" has since become "To Buy Is Indian" (2001, 73). Good citizenship thus requires the kind of consumption that will demonstrate to the world that India is a modern nation; conversely, "consumer citizens" gain the right to call on the state to protect their consumption (Lukose 2009). In Madurai, there is a more intimately observed reward for proper consumption: being recognized as a person with substance.

Furthermore, it must be stressed again that not only goods but also *practices* are key to consumption. One consumption arena frequently highlighted by middle-class residents is the performance of domestic rituals. As Minna Säävälä says of the middle class in Hyderabad, "religious observances are an important aspect of deriving distinction from monetary means" (2001, 303). In addition to marriages, family rituals such as first birthday rites and girls' puberty ceremonies enact middle-class standing by demonstrating the financial means necessary to carry out the ritual (including the costs of ritual supplies, religious specialists, and food and gifts for guests). They also display families' knowledge of current trends in ritual, entertainment, and food fashions, and of the technologies used to record events. Rituals may also be used to prove a family's community standing or influence by attracting high-status guests, including politicians, community leaders, and family members who are wealthier than the hosts. Like the possession and appropriate use of consumer goods, the staging of rituals can be used strategically in bids to be recognized by extended family, neighbors, or larger communities as belonging to a certain class. This is most dramatically true in marriage ceremonies, as we will see in the following chapter, but it is the case for smaller rituals as well.

The Rightness of the Middle

Finally, middle-class emphases on simplicity and ordinariness, controlled spending, and the lack of excess help explain another sense of "rightness" about being middle-class. The comments above reveal that "middleness" itself is valued for its *relativity*: it is neither high nor low; it is not extreme in any way.

Early in my research in 1999, as I began to hear more about the naṭuttaramānavaṅka, I asked Jayanthi to tell me what the word meant. She explained:

JAYANTHI: They are neither extremely rich nor extremely poor. They'll say they are in the middle. The middle doesn't fall on this side or on that side; it's right in the center. For example, when people come to

ask for my second daughter for a marriage, other people will tell
them that we neither have a lot nor are poor, we are in the middle.
So, it's a good word.

SARA: In what ways is it good?

JAYANTHI: It's a word without differences. People use it with affection.
Saying someone is in the middle doesn't sound the [pejorative] way
it does when you call someone high class or low class.

There is rightness and satisfaction at being in the center, at avoiding
extremes in both directions (see Liechty 2003; Säävälä 2010; van Wessel
2004).[11] This view is consonant with a dominant and historically high-caste
ideal that elevates gentleness, tolerance, reason, moderation, and control
of emotions and bodily desires over the gratification of physical needs,
expression of strong emotions, roughness and violence, impulsiveness,
and extremes of all kinds. The contrast that Raman, Usha's husband,
made between his own innate nature and that of a butcher is one
example of this (see chapter 2). In Hindu South India, moreover, these
oppositions are part of a broader set of themes in which coolness/
passivity and hotness/activity are linked to cosmological principles (the
passive male principle of *purusha* and the active female principle
of *prakriti*), gender (male and female), and associated foods, colors, and
states of health and illness (see, e.g., McGilvray 1998). All of these characteristics are used in explaining the moral superiority of the middle
class, and in expressing a sense of almost aesthetic pleasure at being in
the middle. It is interesting to note that, although the middle class is for
many people a new social identity, and certainly one that connotes
modernity, its protagonists have appropriated a much older social code to
express its moral superiority.

While middleness is a source of pride and pleasure, however, it was
just as often cited as a source of tension and difficulty for people in the
middle class. I often heard that middle-class standing comes with a higher
set of behavioral expectations than are placed on the lower class, but that
these expectations must be fulfilled without access to the financial and
social resources that the upper class commands. Such claims reflect the
tensions of middleness and the negative aspects of centrality—the sense
both of being caught in the middle and of being on stage, surrounded by
a highly judgmental social audience.

Scrutiny and Constraints

To understand this perception of being squeezed and scrutinized in the
middle, we must return to the topic of consumption. The significance of
consumption to middle-class identity, as well as the burden imposed by

the responsibility of proper citizenship, were reflected in the comments of Madurai residents. To explore the specific obligations of consumption for the middle class, I turn to a discussion with a group of young people who were at the heart of the economic changes creating a "globalized" service sector in India. In early 2000 they were training for employment in medical transcription, then a growing field in India. These young adults had enrolled in a certificate program in medical transcription at the Centre for Entrepreneurial Development (CED, then affiliated with Madurai Kamaraj University).

I first met these students at their CED course. The medical transcription instructor at the Centre had asked me to talk to her class of about twenty students, to help them become more familiar with an American English accent. After speaking to the class, I invited the students to visit me at home sometime and talk further. A couple of weeks later, six of them, four women and two men, came to my home and we spent several hours talking (though mostly in Tamil) about a variety of topics concerning India and the United States. These students were all in their twenties. They were from families that had been in the middle class for at least a generation, were unusually well educated, but were located near the center of the middle-class spectrum.[12] They all identified themselves as middle-class, and came to a consensus that being middle-class means having a monthly income, own-ing a small amount of property (such as a house), and having a two-wheeler (a scooter or a motorbike). When I asked whether one could be in the middle class and have a car, they said immediately, "No, that is upper class."

When I asked the CED students why they wanted to work in medical transcription, the two men answered, "To eat." After some delayed laughter, the students said that the degree would give them opportunities in a new field that has many openings, quick placement, and good pay. I then asked whether, given their educations, other good jobs might be available without this transcription course. They were vociferous in denying this, and their answers revealed much of their vision of the middle class's predicament.

They explained that in Madurai, the highest salary they could get from the types of jobs for which they already qualified, such as teaching or engi-neering, would be Rs. 1,500/month (at a time when the small apartments or houses they lived in could be rented for Rs. 1,000–1,500/month). Medical transcription, on the other hand, would pay Rs. 3,500 "plus perks," and more with experience. Here is how they described their situations:

PRIYA: We've studied so much, we ought to be able to get a good job.
KUMARASAMY: Nowadays everyone has studied—it's compulsory. But there aren't any jobs.

LALITHA: And even if you work, you don't earn anything. There's no income. The jobs are a lot of work, and the income is very low [*vēle nereya irukkum, income koreyā irukkum*].

RAJENDRAN: If we had a different job [other than medical transcription], we would work ten hours per day, and even then make only 1,500 rupees a month.

LALITHA: Even if you have a good education, if you have only one job, and there's only one person working, you really suffer. You have to have some kind of thing on the side.

RAJENDRAN: Nowadays in Madurai, if a person has only one job, he can't make it. You have to work two or three businesses on the side. Part-time jobs. Take my father, we have a stationery store, on the side he works as an agent for a real estate agency, and then we have started a meat shop. We have looked after three businesses.

SARA: What would happen, then, if you didn't work all those jobs?

RAJENDRAN: If you don't do all that work, and if you [still] want to be in the middle class, you don't eat. Really, you can't stay in that status. You'll have to change, you won't be able to buy things, you will feel very bad [*manacu kaṣṭamā irukkum*, your heart/mind will suffer]. "But look, they don't have money, the children are starving," that's what people will think. Right now, we're doing okay. We are ordinary [*nammatān ārṭinēri mātiri irukkōm*].

Thus despite their educations and their parents' assets, these young people felt that they could not maintain middle-class standing with only one job and only one family earner. In their minds, the jobs simply were not available, and they were turning to a new field in hopes of beating others to what they perceived as a wealth of positions.[13]

From the only half-joking comment about the necessity of this job for subsistence, to the description of how they will be pitied—and demoted—socially, the images these young people invoked portray the sense that they cannot "survive" in the middle class without an occupation like medical transcription (or, alternatively, without three traditional middle-class positions). When Rajendran says that "you don't eat" if you want to stay in the middle class without such employment, he suggests that it is at some level imaginable to give up food in order to keep a flat, a two-wheeler, good schools for one's children, fashionable clothing, and the right household appliances—that is, all the necessary signs of the middle class. This is a performance that is, in Rajendran's view, an empty front, like Jayanthi's showcase. When Rajendran and the others associate starvation with the lack of middle-class resources, they exaggerate, but they make a poignant point in doing so. They too suggest that if they cannot buy what they need to maintain their standing, they will be written off as if they are poor and pitiable. The consumption of commodities is deemed to be as crucial as the consumption of food. These students remind us again of the palpable fear that those who cannot acquire and maintain the *visible signs* that legitimate middle-class standing—education, occupation, and commodities—will become as socially invisible, insignificant, and despised as the poor.

Thus one of the difficulties often complained of is the seeming impossibility of making ends meet in a middle-class household even when its members have strong educational credentials and good jobs. The long hours of work required for this struggle are a hardship. Compounding this stress is the continuous public scrutiny of one's position. When people spoke of what it is like to be middle-class, they often focused on the acute pressures they felt from belonging to a distinctly recognized and closely scrutinized social group. While people in many different social groups and categories (castes, occupations, and religious organizations, for example, as well as classes) feel constrained to behave in particular ways because of the judgments of watchful communities, middle-class people identified these constraints more vociferously than anyone else I heard. Furthermore, such complaints were voiced by middle-class people from a broad range of castes and economic circumstances.

Munusamy, a Thevar man who works as a clerk in a university office, complained that upper-class and lower-class people have great leeway in their behavior: both can do whatever they want, and "no one says anything"—the former because they have power, and people let them do as they wish; and the latter because no one cares what they do.[14] The "middle people," however, must do everything just right. They cannot drink in public, they must wear clean clothing, and they must marry within their caste, because otherwise "everyone will talk about them." In his mind, and in the views of many others, middle-class people are held inordinately responsible for performing dominant social mores. While the poor are excused because they do not count, and the wealthy are excused because their money and power make them less susceptible and less accountable to social judgments, the middle class feel the pressure of having to do things right. These students' comments reflect the pressure to be proper citizens as well. While national media link this performance to the consumption of modernity, here we see that just as the middle class must be modern consumers—spending, as the local model goes, on modern goods but with moderation—so they must behave in accord with the dominant values of modernity (proper hygiene and clothing) and moderation (thus neither alcohol in public nor the disorderly behavior it leads to).

Srinivasan, Lakshmi's younger brother, had temporarily migrated to Sri Lanka in the 1990s to help his natal family gain a tentative foothold in the lower-middle class, working there as an accountant in a gold shop. By 2001 he had returned to Madurai to work as a factory clerk and had recently married into his comfortably middle-class in-laws' family. Contemplating the upcoming rituals that he needed to carry out for his young daughter (rituals that should have been paid for by his father, who could not afford to contribute), Srinivasan said, "When you are poor, you don't do these things, and when you are wealthy, you have the money to make it easy. But in the middle, there are all these expectations to show that you belong where you are, and it is very hard to be able to afford to do everything right."

The CED students had similar laments. Like Srinivasan's complaint, theirs emphasize the need to reproduce class through proper performance. Here is what they said, for example, about dowry:

> KUMARASAMY: If you're upper-class, giving a good dowry is no big deal, because you have lots of money. On the other hand, if you're lower-class, you don't face the problem because that group doesn't ask for a big dowry. But in the middle class, it's a big problem. Dowry demands are high—money, gold, scooters, refrigerators—and we don't have enough money to meet these demands without huge trouble. It's a big problem. We suffer a lot. But the wealthy people . . .
> JANAKI (cutting in): Whatever problems they have, they can solve them.
> LALITHA: While the lower class stays within its limits.

The middle class feels pressed to stretch beyond its limits to provide the dowry and gifts required for a respectable marriage, while imagining that the people above and below them have demands that fit comfortably within their resources.[15] While they in particular must reflect the morality of their society by enacting its behavioral codes, they feel they possess insufficient means to meet the exceptional responsibilities demanded of them.

The Fear of Losing Status

Another anxiety felt by the middle class is the fear of downward mobility. To some extent, this fear reflects the predictable economic shifts that have long been faced by most lower-middle-class (and poor) families throughout the domestic cycle, as well as unexpected accidents and illness. But even where households have enough assets to weather economic difficulties, the sense of precariousness is acute.

Although evidence suggests that most families now in the middle class have not experienced significant downward mobility in recent generations, there can be real economic consequences to households and/or individuals for failing to perform middle-class behaviors properly. As we will see in the next chapter, one of the landmark sites for confirming class standing is marriage arrangements, when families demonstrate publicly that they are willing to create alliances with one another. Middle-class people with unmarried children often spoke about the need to control household members' public behavior in order to create an image that would be salutary when marriages were arranged. These ideas underscore both the social value of decency and the concept of a watchful community. Two college faculty in their twenties, one a Brahman and one a Nadar, each with a lectureship in social work, gave me lengthy descriptions of the kinds of expectations their middle-class neighbors had about proper dress and comportment for women their age. When I asked these professional women why their neighbors' opinions were so important to them and their families, they said that these opinions would weigh heavily at the time of their upcoming marriage arrangements, when prospective spouses' families would ask acquaintances about their character. "Acceptance in the neighborhood will gain you acceptance in your future household," one of them explained. In another instance, two Chettiar women of the Nattukkottai sub-caste told me that, whenever possible, they avoid attending gatherings at a local Chettiar social "club" because they would be asked to donate money for the organization and its projects. It was not the cost of the donation per se that concerned them, but the fact that if they failed to give the right amount of money each time (it had to be a dauntingly large amount, but not so huge as to seem above their standing), people would speak badly of them, making it difficult to maintain the social image that they need in order find suitable marriage partners from the Nattukkottai community for their remaining children. It was better to avoid such situations entirely than to risk attracting public criticism.

Schools and colleges are another crucial arena for the generation of class futures. In addition to producing a great deal of cultural capital, they can also be significant sources of social capital. Classmates become the social networks that may secure a job, and teachers can provide assistance or pose obstacles in career searches. My research assistant Revathi, a young middle-class Brahman woman, described one instance in which her college classmates were affected by teachers' judgments. Girls who were on scholarships would try to prevent the teachers from knowing their financial situations, Revathi explained, saying, "At college they are daily nagging us for Rs. 50—for functions, lunches at competitions, farewell money, birthday parties for seniors. It's compulsory—you can't say you won't give. If a girl says, 'I can't donate, I come from a poor family,' the teachers will say, 'So why do you want to go to college, why don't you go get a job, or go get married?' The girls' friends will help them, and then the girls pay their friends back later when they can earn some money." In order to be treated as deserving an education and job recommendations, a girl must act as though she already has middle-class resources. Like Rajendran and Jayanthi, Revathi emphasizes the importance of presenting a surface that the actor "knows" is insubstantial artifice, yet is prerequisite to gaining the social and cultural capital necessary for earning the economic capital to help stabilize a middle-class role.

Economic, social, and cultural capital interact in numerous settings. Onlookers must be compellingly convinced and persuaded of one's class identification. This may especially be true in a newly emerging class for which the material and processual indicators are in great flux. The need to convince others of where one stands is especially acute among the different layers of the middle class, and perhaps most so among those whose families lack certain forms of social and cultural capital (such as conventional middle-class jobs for two or more generations, tertiary education, and/or high caste). Qualitative studies of the middle class in South Asian cities reveal that many members of the middle class report such anxiety, though some do not (such as the IT professionals studied by C. J. Fuller and Haripriya Narasimhan [2007], among whom unassailable educational credentials were more significant in determining status than was consumerism, and a large number of whom were Brahmans).[16] But for most people in the middle, the performance of class is, in Goffman's words, "a delicate, fragile thing that can be shattered by very minor mishaps" (1959, 56). Such points highlight how both dignity and class standing are affected by the judgments of a relevant community. In the accounts reproduced here, that community includes neighbors, kin, classmates, teachers, potential business partners, and civic organizations, among others.

The awareness of others' critical gaze is heightened by these actors' consciousness of their own roles as social spectators. Murugan and Rajendran evoke the pitying-and-critical audience most explicitly. In much middle-class discourse, the poor serve as a cipher of what the middle class, more or less insecure in the economic moorings and cultural production of their standing, fear they could become. While the poor have a negative presence because of their social invisibility, that is, their nonexistence, they simultaneously stand as a substantive reminder of what the middle class must work to avoid becoming.[17]

The Fear of Envy

Paradoxically, anxiety can also be created by upward mobility, and discussions of this anxiety also invoke the watchful attention paid to class.

Just as middle-class people perceived themselves to be under exceptional scrutiny for the behavior that helped them maintain middle-class standing, so they felt deeply and dangerously scrutinized when they prospered. When a person achieves something uncommon for her status, or something unusual among her peer group, she may fear the impact of others' envy. In South Asia, envy is known to harm a person who possesses a coveted good or quality, regardless of whether such harm is intentional. Focusing on, admiring, complimenting, or desiring something that is attractive or appealing can draw misfortune to the bearer or owner of the good or quality, or to the object itself; this casting of a harmful look is referred to in English as the "evil eye" and in Tamil as *kaṇṇūru* or kaṇ tiruṣṭi. It has been argued that envy is felt between status or structural equals, not between those who are hierarchically dissimilar (Dean 2013; Pocock 1992; Warrell 1990). David Pocock contends that the evil eye "is most to be feared when those who should be equal are not so in fact" (1992, 62). When a peer or near equal achieves something out of the ordinary, desire and its ramifications become a concern, and people who advance within their social reference group feel threatened by others' envy (see also Säävälä 2001, 313).

In Madurai, I heard worries about the evil eye from middle- and upper-class people who had experienced both small and large improvements in their material or social circumstances. Many middle-class people said that fear of the evil eye would be unlikely among the poor, who were deemed to have too few resources to be jealous of one another, though I am skeptical of this view. (The possession of "resources" and "advantages" is far more relative than the typical middle-class view admits. Indeed, recent research by Melanie Dean [2011] demonstrates the pervasive presence of evil eye concerns among poor residents of Madurai.) Nonetheless, the new opportunities for mobility provided by economic liberalization (such as loans, investments, and capital accumulation) that enable people to enter and rise through the middle class, and the media images and political rhetoric that promote the accumulation of goods now crucial to a proper middle-class life, may make this broad swathe of people especially subject to envy. Envy comes about when people do not play their proper roles in the hierarchy—in other words, when they get ahead of those whom they are supposed to be like—and peers are highly attentive to such deviations in the often close quarters in which urban people reside and work. Thus unusual achievements must be hidden from the eyes of neighbors, co-workers, and sometimes extended family members.

Both Anjali and Usha provide examples of the fears that can develop around upward mobility. When Anjali, then in her early twenties, applied for the loan to open her own computer graphics business, she and her family took care to keep the news from their neighbors, which was especially challenging in the crowded quarters of their residential compound. During a visit in 2001, they spoke to me in whispers whenever talking about the new business plans. Once Anjali attained the loan, however, all their neighbors came to know about her ambitious plans. Just days before the opening of her new business, she was knocked down in the street by a cyclist and broke her right wrist, making it impossible for her to use a computer keyboard. She told me that the accident must have been caused by the evil eye—since bicycles rarely knock people down, and when they do, such a fall never breaks a bone. She was certain that an envious neighbor had caused the harm, in this case maliciously.

More dispersed peer sets can be equally attentive, as Usha experienced when her husband had a heart attack in his forties, several years after they had built the new hospital and their large new house. Although Raman was not involved in politics, he had become well connected to many of the powerful politicians and bureaucrats in Madurai, who patronized him as one of the few cardiologists in the city. Raman's mother was concerned that her son's heart attack had been caused by others in their social set who were jealous of Raman's marked professional and economic success. Usha, dismissive of this idea, nevertheless did believe that their peers—other doctors and their families, and other successful professionals with whom they socialized—had watched Raman's rise closely to see whether he made any mistakes on his way.

Whether it was neighbors or a more dispersed social network doing the watching, in both cases, envy—and thus the danger of the evil eye—arose because Anjali and Raman began to stand out from their peers. Where they had previously been relatively equal to others in these communities, Anjali and Raman gained greater resources (education, a government loan, a new business and potential income in Anjali's case; greater income, success, political connections, and professional stature in Raman's case) than those who considered themselves their peers.

Thus, at least from one perspective, the anxious instability inherent in middle-classness derives from the two sides of a performative coin: failure to perform well enough means falling in class, but performing too well creates harmful enmity. The possibility of losing a foothold in the middle class constantly looms, and so do the hazards of upward mobility. Such feelings of insecurity cannot be measured by standard indicators of downward mobility; indeed many are at most tied only indirectly to the objective risk of falling in class. They result instead from the energy it takes to keep up, to prevent envy, and to negotiate the tiny daily judgments by others as well as the more massive ones. Underlying all the accounts in this chapter is the awareness that having a proper job and a sizeable income is not enough to maintain a middle-class position. Those who wish to stay in the middle must secure their class standing by convincing their audience that they deserve the role.

Performing, Naming, and Classifying

I have argued that a person's place within the class structure is flexible rather than static. In Madurai as elsewhere, class is a continuous process of remaking an identity and convincing others of its validity. If this sounds like a superficial or inconsequential aspect of a system that fundamentally shapes people's lives, the accounts provided here argue otherwise. Class location is unstable not simply because major financial losses or gains can precipitate a change in standing; rather, class positions must be accepted by others, and onlookers (both intimate and anonymous) must be persuaded of them on a continuing basis. Much of this reproduction requires the performance of proper class behaviors such as language, consumption, ritual practices, public comportment, and hygiene. Madurai residents "in the middle" emphasize their sense of being on a stage where their choices are scrutinized and judged every day. They echo Christiane Brosius's observation that many members of the middle class "depend on visibility, visuality and performativity, as well as on a culture of circulation and a competence (e.g., taste, 'being cultured') to manage and decode them" (2010, 24)—albeit often with uncertainty about the success of their performance. The ambiguity of middle-class boundaries, the newness of many of the class fragments, and the ongoing changes in signifiers of class underscore the fact that maintaining a class identity is a *process*, one that for many families and individuals requires significant work, effort, commitment, and sacrifice.

The accounts recorded in this focus on subjective identities also highlight the relational nature of class. It is produced in interaction; a successful class identity is both claimed and ascribed. Being in the middle class may feel especially precarious because of the emphasis on enacting a role that, even when highly "interiorized" (to borrow Ian Hacking's term [2004, 294]), must be seen as authentic by others. There is always some risk.[18] Assessments can pass fleetingly—as in the glance given by a seatmate on the bus—or they can rupture a moment or a life, as when a professor tells a student that her family is the wrong sort to attend college, when interviewees for a multinational IT position are turned away because of how their clothes are arranged and their English is accented, or when a bride's family declines to make an alliance with the kin to whom she has been promised since childhood because the intended groom did not pass his medical school exams.

All serve to alter or reinforce a person's worthiness, opportunity, and belonging within a class.

Roles, in Goffman's sense, shape who we are, and we become some of them. But to the extent that we recognize them as performances, we can easily be open to doubt about whether we are *really* what we portray ourselves to be. Without taking the performance metaphor too far, it seems reasonable to argue that such self-doubt may be especially prevalent when social life is seen as so explicitly performative as in Madurai. People in the middle do not spend every moment thinking of themselves as acting or as taking on a role that is artificial. And yet, as we have seen, they are highly aware of the critical audiences around them. They describe themselves responding to these audiences, anticipating them, and hiding negative evidence from them. In presenting themselves "neatly" and "decently," taking on multiple jobs or training for new ones in order to gain the means to acquire and display signifiers of middle-class standing, hiding signs of growing or waning resources, people who wish to be seen as middle class are trying to perform that class in a way that will be accepted by onlookers, and in so doing gain the rewards of relative dignity, social networks, and everyday security that are accorded people in different sections of the middle class.

This chapter demonstrates the recent spread and development of a class identity, and the attributes of value, security, danger, and precariousness that attend living with and reproducing that identity. The pleasures and the anxieties of being in the middle exist in tension alongside each other. While this could be said of any class in Madurai, "middleness" today is both structurally and culturally constructed to heighten the good and the bad of being in the center. The common features of local middle-classness highlight this tension. On one hand, the distance from and centrality between the poverty of mere survival and the excess of wealth imply material and moral comfort. To "count" as a person on the social stage, to reside in the moderate middle, and to claim regard as fundamentally decent and ordinary are all desirable. The pleasures of being in the middle are about social, economic, and cultural security. On the other hand, the negative aspects of the middle have to do with the insecurity of maintaining this position in the face of critical social judgments, unstable signs of membership, and inadequate financial means—the stressed resources of performance.

There is some disjunction between scholarly and native categories of the middle class. Including attention to local identities enhances an understanding of how changing economies and class processes shape everyday lives. Finally, we must consider the possibility that "naming has real effects on people, and changes in people have real effects on subsequent classifications" (Hacking 2004, 280). If, in performing middle-class identities, people who would be denied class membership by some city residents nonetheless demonstrate a sufficient command of key class values and styles to convince others, they may also succeed in expanding the categories of who is "ordinary" and who "counts," a possibility that animates the narrative of Murugan in chapter 9. As carefully defended as these concepts are in any highly hierarchical community, shifts in their content can reveal alterations in the processes by which classes are formed, challenged, and maintained.

As this chapter shows, the drawing and policing of class boundaries are highly moralizing endeavors. In the next chapter we turn to forms of display and performance that have especially high stakes, those surrounding marriages, which are decisive in determining individuals' and families' socioeconomic standing over the long term.

7 *Marriage*

DRAMA, DISPLAY, AND THE
REPRODUCTION OF CLASS

Marriage is one of the most singular events in Madurai residents' lives. Like debt, however, marriage is a subject of heightened public concern, since the high costs of weddings and of dowries are often decried for plunging families into debt. Marriage does have a dramatic impact on individuals' and families' class positions, in both the near and the long term, though in much more complex ways than public discourse suggests. While getting a child married can indeed be very costly, requiring the greatest expenditure of most families' domestic cycles, large weddings and dowries also create positive capital of all kinds for families; conversely, inadequate ceremonies and gifts produce negative capital. Marriage as a whole plays an even broader role in the production of class. It serves as a foundation of an individual's and family's class standing, and it continues to play that function throughout a person's life. In addition, because of the critical role that extended family plays in determining a person's class in India, one's siblings' and children's marriages may *also* affect one's own class. Marriage works through financial resources as well as the unquantifiable elements of display, regard, and social alliances to produce families' and individuals' class, with long-term and intergenerational impacts.

If we think about Kannan's daughter Prema's marriage, much of this is already familiar. Providing a dowry was a considerable challenge, and if Kannan and Vellaiamma had not been able to produce as much dowry as they did, Prema would almost certainly have married into a poorer family. The dowry itself made statements about both families' class, just as the wedding ceremony displayed their social and economic resources to relevant onlookers. In addition, the marriage alliance created social ties and provided resources for the new couple and their families.

In this chapter I will draw extensively from my experiences with three other families in order to demonstrate the several roles that marriage plays in the production of class. This chapter is the longest of the book in part because marriage is highly celebrated in Tamil society and it (unlike debt, for example) was raised frequently in interviews and everyday conversations. But in particular, because to my knowledge no one else has analyzed how these separate elements of marriage impact class in conjunction with one another, I support my arguments with lengthy narratives and interview excerpts.

My analysis addresses marriage in several of its aspects: 1) as a social institution, 2) as an alliance that creates long-term relationships, 3) as a ritual event, and 4) as a set of negotiated transactions. The everyday Tamil term for marriage—*kalyāṇam*—also conveys each of these meanings.[1] All four aspects of marriage display status claims and help to produce class standing, though each does so in different ways. In the first case, because families typically marry their children into other families of a similar class, marriage as an institution tends to reproduce class standing, though in rare circumstances it can also be used as a tool for significant class mobility. Second, the alliance of families in marriage creates enduring relationships that impinge on one another to influence outsiders' interpretations of the families' status. The alliance may also be used to create economic and social capital; thus the creation of those affinal relationships can be both a short- and a long-term investment. Third, as a ceremonial event, marriage displays and dramatizes claims to family standings more publicly than any other event. Finally, the transactions that precede and accompany the marriage (and often continue after it) display the families' wealth and tastes and also their standing.

Thus marriage tends to *reproduce* class intergenerationally. It *ratifies* a family's current class standing through a public alliance with a family of similar standing. It *displays* class publicly through the dowry and wedding ceremonies. And it provides *resources* for the continued development of class capital, through dowry and through the cultural and social capital of the allied families. Marriage is thereby one of the key mechanisms through which class is formed and re-formed. I will turn to each of these points in detail, following a discussion of marriage patterns and practices in South India.

From Kinship to Class: Changing Ideals in Marriage Arrangements

Heterosexual marriage is almost universal in India, and the great majority of marriages are arranged by parents and other close kin of the spouses, often with the input of the potential spouses themselves. (Patricia Uberoi [2006, 24] notes that "an estimated 90 per cent" of Indian marriages are arranged.)[2] Marriage is almost always seen in India as an alliance between families rather than simply a romantic partnering of individuals. In South India, a number of principles determine appropriate marital partners: among others, these include families' religion, caste, reputation,[3] kin relations and responsibilities, and social and economic resources; and individual partners' physical attractiveness, education, occupation, and (among most Hindus and some Christians) horoscope.[4] As Anthony Good and others point out, some of these principles are *prescription* while some are *preference* (Good 1981; also Fuller and Narasimhan 2008a; Kapadia 1995). For example, marrying inside one's religious and caste or sub-caste group is almost always required, while for some communities marriage with parallel kin is prohibited, and thus these rules are prescriptive where they occur; and marrying cross kin is often preferable, but rarely prescribed. Yet other rules can be either required, preferable, or entirely optional—for example, matching horoscopes closely is prescriptive in some Hindu and Christian families but only preferable or even irrelevant in others. Moreover, each family (and, when permitted a voice, each potential spouse) weighs the relative importance of all these criteria differently.

Anthropological and sociological studies provide evidence that class considerations have steadily replaced certain other preferential criteria for marriage alliances over the past century. Kinship obligations in particular have become less emphasized. In the past, siblings often promised their children in marriage when possible (that is, when the potential spouses were of similar enough ages, when their horoscopes matched sufficiently, etc.). Such potential partners had a *murai* relationship—a "right" to or a "claim" on one another. (Murai can be glossed as right, claim, order, kin, rule, law, custom, and tradition—all of which reveal something about the term's meaning in this context.) These preferred marital partners were often specific kin, and these kinship relations still remain relevant to varying degrees. The ideal partner among many Hindu and Christian castes is a cross-kin relative, usually (for a woman) a maternal uncle or his son, and (for a man) a sister's daughter or a paternal aunt's daughter.[5] Among Muslims, close-kin marriage is more likely to take place between parallel cousins.[6] (Cross kin are people related to one another through siblings of different genders. Thus a person's cross cousin could be a mother's brother's child or father's sister's child, but *not* a father's brother's child or a mother's sister's child. The latter are examples of parallel cousins—cousins related through siblings of the same gender.)[7]

An ideal differs from a statistical norm, however, and social rules never determine all behavior. In fact, empirical data suggest that marriages between closely related kin have almost always been in the minority in southern India. (Thomas Trautmann, reviewing twentieth-century studies of Dravidian marriage patterns and the incidence of cross-cousin and uncle–niece marriage, concluded that "the general run falls between, say, 10 to 30 percent" [1981, 219].)[8] Still, the ethos of murai relationships—the "preferential spouse" or "spouse by right"—carried significant moral weight in many communities until recently.

Over the past several decades, however, as economic considerations have begun to replace the kinship responsibilities that formed the ideal in choosing spouses, a relatively wealthy adult sibling is likely to refuse a murai obligation with a poorer sibling, especially among upwardly mobile families and communities (Clark-Decès 2014, 126; De Neve 2006, 38; Kapadia 1993, 38–43, 48; Kolenda 2003, 371; see also Good 1981, 126).[9] Instead, the better-off sibling will look for an alliance with a wealthier and more prestigious family. As Karin Kapadia noted over two decades ago, "kinship obligations and their moral order are being increasingly viewed as obsolete" (1993, 50).

Another significant shift in marriage arrangements lies in the gifts and payments given at marriage, and this shift is also closely tied to the increasing weight placed on class considerations in marriage arrangements. Both the amount of money and goods given by one family to the other, and the *direction* in which the gifts and payments travel, have changed in recent decades, as dowry has replaced bridewealth. As late as the mid-twentieth century, most South Indian families paid bridewealth (gifts/payments from the groom's family to the bride's family).[10] Dowry (which is given by the bride's family to the bride, the groom, and/or the groom's family) was previously associated largely with Brahmans. Now, almost all marriages involve not bridewealth but dowry. And the size of each of the dowry's components—including, as we saw with Kannan's daughter's wedding, a cash payment, gold jewelry, utilitarian household items, and consumer goods—has increased greatly. Dowry is often one of the primary factors that families consider when making a marriage alliance.

The increase in the size and importance of dowry, especially of those portions that are given to the groom's family rather than to the bride, has been linked to the decline in murai marriages (Caldwell, Reddy, and Caldwell 1983, 347–348; Heyer 2000, 18–19; Meinzen 1980, 1140–1141). When alliances were created between relatives, requests for cash and gifts to the groom's family were minimized (Clark-Decès 2014, 41–42; Iyer 2002, 105), and the need for conspicuous display was less significant (cf. Bloch, Rao, and Desai 2004). The shift from the kinship marriage ideal also places greater emphasis on a key aspect of contemporary marriage arrangements: parents' desire to settle children with a partner whose family is of a similar class.

With this historical background in mind, I turn in the following sections to an exploration of the importance of marriage arrangements and alliances, wedding ceremonies, and dowry transactions in displaying and producing class for married couples and their families.

Family Alliances and Class Reproduction

Many factors are taken into account when parents and other kin make marriage alliances.[11] In the great majority of cases, families aim to find their children a partner and in-laws who will support them well. Today, as companionate marriage becomes more of an ideal, the partners' congeniality is also of concern. The potential spouses often have a say in this decision as well (and sometimes a good deal of say, particularly in upper-middle- and upper-class families) (see Desai and Andrist 2010, 669; De Neve 2011, 93; Donner 2008, 71–72; Fuller and Narasimhan 2008a, 737; Gilbertson 2014b; also Wilson 2013, 44–45). Families also want to make a prestigious marriage. Each family, often including the children preparing to be married, takes these issues into account, along with dowry offers/requests and the prescriptions, proscriptions, and preferences mentioned above.

Marriage is an exchange—not just of children, but of resources in a strategic building of alliances. Families make decisions that they believe will be in their own best interests as well as their children's. Some families are better at bargaining than others. But, and this is a crucial point, all are trying to gain something. And here I need to note that this is just as true of the groom's side as of the bride's. Intriguingly, however, the literature on marriage and dowry in India focuses almost entirely on women's families' motivations and ignores what men's families are gaining from the marriages. This is likely due in part to the fact that marrying a son presents less of a "problem" for families than does marrying a daughter (since the son rarely must adjust to a new life in someone else's family; he has much more latitude in the age at which he can marry, so his parents face less pressure to get him married within a short time frame; any premarital sexual activity is less likely to make him unmarriageable; and the bride's family will bear the brunt of the marriage costs). And, in South India as in the north, the groom's family will be accorded the deference due to the higher ranked wife-taking affines.[12]

But in life if not in scholarly renderings, the parents of a son are equally concerned to make a good match and a good alliance—to find a spouse who will make positive contributions to their household and produce grandchildren, to make fruitful connections with a new family, and to find a family whose standing and whose daughter reflect well on them. The alliance reflects on both sides, and since most families have both sons and daughters, the son's wedding may influence the marriageability of any of his unmarried sisters. A social system in which marriage is endogamous and even ideally consanguineous, and in which caste hypergamy is not practiced, places a logical limit on the extent to which one side or the other can systematically "move up" in marriage. My discussion of marriage arrangements in the remainder of this chapter will illustrate how important it is for both brides' and grooms' families to gain a variety of "goods"—respectability, status, fertility, contributing household member, productive alliances, material items—and that many of these goods are common goals of both sides. This point is crucial for understanding how marriage reproduces class.

Searching for a Match for Miriam's Son

To illustrate the process of looking for a match, I begin with an extended excerpt from a two-hour conversation with my friend Miriam, who was trying to find a bride for her son Parthiban, her only child, who was twenty-eight years old in 2009. Miriam was widowed, and she and Parthiban lived in a small apartment in a middle-class building complex. Miriam, a Catholic Vanniyar, manages an upscale catering firm in Madurai and speaks pristine English, though we normally speak Tamil together. Parthiban had a master's degree, worked for an international hotel chain, and had traveled internationally for work. He was very light-skinned, tall, of average weight, good-humored, and well spoken. All of these qualities made him an attractive groom; in addition, he had no sisters whose marriages he would have to help finance. His position in the corporation, however, while very respectable and modern, did not come with a high salary, and he could not easily relocate to another city. For a variety of reasons, Miriam had not yet found a good match. She had added Parthiban's name to the registries of prospective brides and grooms in two Catholic dioceses, and she had placed an ad on a major matrimonial website. Although she had by then gone so far as meeting with two girls' families, neither had proved suitable, and she described why.

> MIRIAM: My son and I have only each other. So it has to be a family that will be supportive of him. The girl can work or not; that's her choice. I don't care, I just want a good family.
>
> We found a girl in Bangalore who has an M.Sc. in biochemistry and is working in [a multinational pharmaceutical firm]. We said we didn't need to meet her right away; my sister is in Bangalore and she can check out the family and meet the girl. The girl is a bit dark, a bit short. But the family is very good. So we were going to the first meeting, to talk about sovereigns and dowry. We went and met them [in Bangalore]. A good family. I said to the girl, "You need to talk and make sure you like the boy." First they have to like each other, then we could speak about the rest. Afterward, when we called them that evening, they didn't say anything about whether the boy and girl liked each other. Instead, the father immediately said, "We didn't know Parthiban was going to be working in Madurai." Parthiban said, "But that's in my

registry profile." The father sent a message the next morning saying, "We want to respect your son's feelings. We wish him all the best."

SARA: So they were saying, "We don't want this boy."

M: Yes. My sister had said that they were asking if Madurai was like a village! I told the father that they should have been looking for a groom in Bombay or Chennai or Bangalore. It has to be what the children desire in their own minds. Otherwise, there will be a life problem [*vālkai piraccinai*].

Then we went to look at a girl in Trichy. We had already asked my friend's brother to look into that family. He said they have their own house. We knew from her biodata that she had done the first year of an M.C.A [master's of computer applications]. Everything looked very positive. The photo looked nice too. We had talked on the phone with the girl's mother, but not directly with the girl. My brother's friend had talked with them, but he is aged and wouldn't ask the same questions as a woman. When I talked with the mother I said to just have the girl wear casual clothes, nothing fancy, wear the clothes she wears when she goes to college. But when we went to their house, she was wearing a ghagra-choli and skirt.[13] Full of beads and spangles, so shimmering and jiggling! [Laughs.] It was overwhelming to look at. And the beading on her dupatta was so heavy that it kept falling to the ground.

They had us sit in a veranda-type room, like a passageway, not in a drawing room as is normal. There was only a rexine sofa. Before we started talking, the girl came and sat down—they don't usually do that. And she sat really close. Not a respectful distance. [Laughs.] So then they took us inside, to the next room; it was like a dining room. There was only a dining table, and we sat around it like at a conference. [Laughs.] They served these huge plates of food—a massive plate of jalebis, another of mixture. We thought of this meeting as a small event [*cinna vicayam*], but they treated it as a big fancy thing [*periya vicayam*]. The TV was blaring. Normally you turn off the TV when people arrive, but they didn't turn it off. Then the mother, when we were all sitting together, kept asking me again and again, "Do you like her? Do you like her?" Everyone was still there when she did that. *Everything* was over the top.

Afterward, Miriam and Parthiban went to a restaurant to talk over what had happened.

MIRIAM: I was upset. Parthiban said that the photo is so different from how the girl looked. She is like a little girl. Even though we talked to her in English, she spoke in Tamil. I understand, I went to a Tamil medium school as a girl myself. She could have said, "I know only one or two words in English, I am sorry, I prefer to speak in Tamil." But she didn't say anything about that. If she acknowledged these things, we could mold her if we brought her home, but she didn't. It would be very difficult.

So we have seen two girls—one at each extreme.

Miriam's narrative reveals a variety of important things. Her very first point is that her son must marry into a family that supports him emotionally. Second is her evident concern that the children themselves be comfortable in the union that is arranged. Her primary goal is finding a "good family," based on character and reputation. She also mentions the girl's physical features and the family's dowry expectations. But the foremost theme of her discussion is finding a future daughter-in-law who "fits" with them in terms of sophistication, modernity, and class-based lifestyle. A girl who sees Madurai as a village and whose family wants her to continue in her high-paying job in Bangalore, rather than take a less prestigious and lower salaried job in Madurai, is not right for them. But neither is a girl whose family lacks sophistication, reveals poor taste in their domestic consumer goods, and misses the mark by overdoing everything. Miriam is willing to train and "mold" the girl so that the girl meets their standards, but she admits that this would be hard on both her and her daughter-in-law.

As Miriam's account demonstrates, the emphasis on class in marriage arrangements is not simply a feature of matching the social and economic attractiveness of a groom and his family to the wealth that a bride's family is willing and able to transfer. It also reflects an enduring belief that the child will be most comfortable if marrying into a family of a similar class (cf. Caplan 1984, 227), especially if that family happens not to be close kin, and reveals that both cultural and economic capital go into the considerations of class. A girl in particular will avoid on the one hand the privation resulting from marrying into a poorer family, and on the other the ridicule meted by wealthier in-laws for her failure to act and think in class-appropriate ways—which is also a potential danger for a boy who marries "up." In addition, both sets of parents want to be comfortable with, and assured of being treated well by, their new affinal relatives, and they want their future grandchildren to be raised in the "proper" way.

This point about class matching is important, given the tendency in the literature to emphasize status mobility strategies or "hypergamy" in match-making, a practice that I rarely found when paying close attention to marriage arrangements. Informants themselves confirmed that most families prefer to marry their children into households of a similar class. Valli Mahentiran, an educator who administers her Nattukkottai Chettiar family's philanthropic organization, talked with me about class mobility in the course of discussing philanthropy in Madurai. At the time, Valli was also beginning to plan her first son's wedding. In talking about the difficulties of upward mobility, she observed:

> Even in marriage, if you are born into a family of a certain class, your family will do all it can to make sure that you are married into a family of a similar class, or higher. Though if you marry into a more upper-class family than you are, their expectations may be [too] high for your child, which is a problem for all of you. But if it meant a family of a lower class, *no* marriage would probably be better. [Sara: Really? Than marrying into a lower class?] Yes. Because by doing that, that affects your birth family's class also. They thereafter lose a little of their status also, because they have given a daughter in marriage to a lesser class.

While, as Valli then noted, some people would insist that they were only concerned to marry their child into any family that is "good people, honest people," in practice (as she argued, and as I observed with friends like Miriam), the great majority of families are uncomfortable about the prospect of creating an alliance with a family of a different class—either lower or higher.

This isn't to say, however, that families don't *also* try to make the most prestigious match possible for themselves. But every family makes its own calculations, and no family will accept a match that scores too low in its own calculus of considerations. While each side is attempting to make a prestigious match, there is typically an upper limit on social climbing because both sides are equally interested and invested in the alliance. Where a bride's family's reputation, occupation, or education is more meager than desired, a large dowry or strong political ties may make up the difference. But ultimately there is some sort of equivalence, and the result is that young people rarely marry into families that are highly different from one another economically and socially.

Thus the most basic way in which marriage is tied to class in Madurai is that families normally prefer to arrange marriages for their children with families of roughly equal social and economic status. This practice acts to pass families' current class standing on to the next generation. (I say "current" because, as we will see in the history of Lakshmi's and her siblings' marriages below, the socioeconomic standing of the family at the time of the marriage arrangements plays more of a role than does its past class standing, if they differ.) Other authors have noted this matching strategy as well, in numerous settings and communities in

South India—among middle-class Christians and Vattima Brahmans in Chennai (Caplan 1984, 227; Fuller and Narasimhan 2008a, 745), the Maravars in rural southern Tamil Nadu (Good 1981, 118), elite families in coastal Andhra Pradesh (Upadhya 1990, 43–44), Lingayats in a northern Karnataka town (Bradford 1985, 289), and Muslims, Hindus, and Christians of all castes in southern Karnataka villages (Iyer 2002, 97–98), among others. Marriage thus plays a major role in the *reproduction* of class by allying families of roughly equal means and producing new families that, all other things being equal, are likely to be of similar standing. Examples of this process of class matching will appear in a discussion of Lakshmi's family's marriages in the second half of this chapter.

Much more rarely, however, marriage can produce class mobility (upward or downward) for a spouse who marries into a family of significantly different means. Although unusual, this is one logical outcome of attempting to make the most prestigious match possible, especially where a family judges the potential gains of upward mobility to outweigh the likely discomfort. Even then, each side *must* see the marriage as in its own interests. Anjali's family attempted to marry her into a family of much greater means, and their efforts are recounted in the final section of this chapter.

Weddings, Dowry, and Display

In addition to reproducing class by allying families of (usually) similar standing and combining their economic, cultural, and social resources, marriages are also used to *display* the two families' class in highly public ways. Marriage and dowry arguably form the most public dramatization of almost all families' class standing (Roulet 1996, 93; see also Heyer 1992, 429; Jeffery 2014; Nishimura 1994, 265). Considerable expenses are incurred for the wedding ceremonies, which fall far more heavily on the bride's family than on the groom's. Francis Bloch, Vijayendra Rao, and Sonalde Desai call marriages "a signal of status," a "symbolic display" (2004, 679). In Madurai, the lavishness of weddings reflects positively on both families, and the dowry is understood to communicate both the bride's and groom's families' standings to the community as a whole— the bride's because her family can afford such a dowry, and the groom's because their son and their family are attractive enough to warrant such a dowry.

Weddings and dowries can both be considered forms of conspicuous consumption. Indeed, Uberoi has called weddings "the most visible sites of conspicuous consumption" in South Asia (2008, 231). Thinking of them in this way allows us to see marriages as part of a continuum of visible consumption, from the highly quotidian forms discussed in chapter 4 to the singular and exceptionally dramatic form at this end of the spectrum. Not only are marriages obviously much rarer events than everyday consumption decisions, they are also by far the most costly expenditures in most people's lives. In my observations, the costs of daughters' weddings and dowries typically amount to at least five to ten years of a household's income for each daughter.[14] Indeed the costs are so dramatic, and the goods achieved so apparently "nonfunctional," that many analysts see them as an irrational form of spending that mires millions of people in poverty. While loans accumulated to enable the kinds of visible consumption discussed in chapters 4 and 5 are lamented as indebting households frivolously or at least unnecessarily, the indebtedness that almost always results from financing daughters' marriages is often lambasted with greater passion and vitriol. As I will demonstrate, however, weddings, dowries, and the alliances that they create are in fact critical for the "positive" production of class standing.

Wedding Ceremonies

Those few analysts who attempt to explain the socioeconomic utility of lavish wedding ceremonies explore the critical importance of "status" or "prestige" as both a social and an economic good. Thus, for example, Vijayendra Rao argues that "Indians are strongly driven by status and rank, and the status and rank are not simply a matter of individual or relative wealth but are derived from the size and influence of their familial and social networks and from the public demonstration of access to these networks" (2001b, 87; see also Caldwell, Reddy, and Caldwell 1983, 557; Heyer 1992, 430). These public demonstrations, he contends, occur most efficaciously in life-cycle and community rituals (see also Dean 2011; van Hollen 2003, 108–109).

The display of wealth, taste, and social connections at weddings has a number of effects, which appear to hold across classes and throughout most of India. "Publicly observable celebrations" like weddings, Rao argues, "have two functions: they provide a space for maintaining social reputations and webs of obligation, and they serve as arenas for status-enhancing competitions" (2001b, 85). Uberoi notes similarly that "historically, marriage has always been the occasion for making status claims in terms of the relative social status of the intermarrying families, the lavishness of the hospitality and entertainment offered, and the number and importance of the guests in attendance, as well as the value of the gifts given to the daughter and transferred through her marriage to her husband's family" (2006, 26–27). Roger Jeffery, Patricia Jeffery, and Craig Jeffrey observe that "weddings of daughters and sons alike offer opportunities for display, and successful marriage arrangements establish tangible evidence of a family's social equivalents" (2011, 156; see also Guérin et al. 2012, S128). Thus the "status-enhancing business of marriage" (Uberoi 2008, 244) plays anxiously to, and depends fundamentally upon, the scrutiny of audiences: those who have the power to grant or deny the recognition examined in chapter 4, and those whose critical gaze unnerves many middle-class people as we saw in chapter 6. In the rest of this section, I describe the ways in which wedding rituals play this role.

Wedding ceremonies are complex, sometimes multi-day affairs that are "read" by guests and passersby in a number of ways. The division of costs borne by brides' and grooms' sides varies a great deal, but the great majority of expenses are paid by the bride's family, typically including fine clothing for their own relatives and for their new affines, priests'/officiants' fees, ritual supplies, musicians, food and drinks for all guests, rental and decorations for the venue(s), and invitations for their guests. In any event, the wedding requires substantial expenditure, though far less than does the dowry. (Marriages may also initiate a series of expensive gift-giving at festivals and life-cycle events that continues for years, the costs again borne primarily by members of the bride's family [Dean 2011; Dumont 1983, 80ff; Heyer 1992, 426–427; Kodoth 2006, 3n6; van Hollen 2003, 102].)

Marriage rituals are usually held in a combination of spaces, including domestic and public or semi-public venues (the wedding hall and/or temple, mosque, or church). If a wedding hall has been rented, most or all of the public activity takes place there. As the long series of minor rituals takes place, all the guests—indeed everyone except that moment's central participants—will participate in a variety of social interactions and rituals of their own. They will typically spend a good deal of time sharing stories and gossip with other guests while watching the bride and her attendants duck in and out of the changing room and meantime viewing the gifts that have been given and displayed on the site. During some part of the ceremony they will also eat the wedding meal(s) and observe the ongoing "gastro-politics" of seating and serving, since "the lavishness and harmonious conduct of such feasts, and the maximization of the number of satisfied guests, are crucial determinants of the future status and reputation of the bride's family" (Appadurai 1981, 502). Much of the time at the wedding will be spent scrutinizing the other guests to see who has come, looking at the women's saris and judging their cost and fashionableness, admiring the decorations, giving *moy* (in Hindu weddings, a formal cash gift, given in an auspicious amount, which is written down in a register along with the giver's name, and often announced over a microphone), glancing over the register to see how much moy other guests have given, listening to the music of the wedding band, examining the quality of the photographer's or videographer's equipment, and posing for photographs with the wedding party. Before even arriving, the guests will have noticed how stylish the invitations were, and which individuals were listed as sponsors of the wedding. In sum, the activities that attend the wedding are a social performance, carefully watched and played.

All of these elements combine to produce an overall evaluation of the ceremony and of the family that has put it on. After Kannan's daughter's wedding, my friend Araci and I walked home. Araci, a domestic worker (and daughter of Jayanthi, the retired cook), commented that this had been a "poor household's wedding" (*ēlai vīṭṭu kalyāṇam*), the kind that "people who suffer like us" put on. It was the opposite of "grand," she said wistfully. "They put on a wedding without any pomp or grandeur (*taṭapuṭal illāma kalyāṇam*). This is the way it happened for Kannan's daughter." Araci observed that Prema's wedding jewelry was rented, her own jewelry was meager, and her family had given the groom only a gold ring and bracelet and no heavy chain for his neck. "The food was fine," she added, but only a few of the guests wore heavy silk saris and substantial jewelry, and "everyone else came simple, like us." Araci was not there when the industrialist Chellasamy's assistant arrived with the Rs. 5,001 gift, which would have impressed her and nudged up her assessment of Kannan's social connections. But it would not have made much difference in her overall judgment of what the wedding said about Kannan's family or his new in-laws.

Any discussion of wedding displays would be incomplete without one final element, the visual records of weddings: photo albums and video recordings, such as those that Anjali's friend Murugan produces, which long outlast the event itself. One of the standard practices when women visit friends they have not seen for some time is to look at the family's most recent engagement and wedding albums, and sometimes even to watch the wedding recording. These artifacts themselves are a marker of class, since they are fairly expensive. When I brought Kannan and Vellaiamma the recording of Prema's wedding that I had commissioned, they were thrilled to watch—and to own—the DVD. Neither they nor their older daughter Bhumati had had the opportunity to acquire a recording of their wedding, they pointed out, but now Prema did. Their pleasure was due not only to the anticipated enjoyment of continuing to watch the DVD in the future, but also to being able to display a prestigious marker of status. For others, the albums demonstrate additional forms of cultural, economic, and social capital. In 2009 when I visited Fatima, the gregarious daughter of a friend, she proudly presented the colorful albums of her recent wedding and pointed to the visiting

Photo 5. Wedding guests, shown in one of the photos I used to elicit conjectures on class and caste, 2000. Photo credit: Sara Dickey.

dignitaries, the well appointed hall with its plush seats and chandeliers, the lavish decorations, the gold that she and her groom wore, and the women's silk saris (with the latest designs) and the men's silk jibbahs.

Such photo albums had suggested to me a research strategy before I even started this project. When I first began to look systematically at the symbolic communication of class in Madurai in 1999–2000, I took photographs at four weddings and, with the wedding party members' permission, I later showed the photos to twenty interviewees of different castes and classes, none of whom knew anyone depicted there. In terms of grandness, the weddings ranged from the marriage of poor middle-caste villagers in the Meenakshi Temple to the lavishly decorated celebration of a lower-middle-caste couple's wedding in the city's most expensive wedding hall. Without providing any background information about any of the marriages, I asked each interviewee to view the photos and try to ascertain the caste and the class of the wedding party members. My aim was to get an initial sense of the visual cues that Madurai residents used when judging class and caste. It was not an ideal measuring tool, since the images were static and many everyday cues were therefore missing— speech, bodily comportment, and interactive style in particular. But no one thought it was a pointless or even artificial exercise, everyone entered into it enthusiastically, and each respondent believed that he or she knew the caste and class of each wedding party. Of the twenty people I asked, only two guessed a single wedding party's caste correctly; the other seventy-eight assessments of caste were incorrect, often wildly so. But *everyone* assessed each wedding group's class correctly—that is, in the same terms that the wedding party members used to identify themselves. This contrast between reading caste and class was remarkable in its own right. But its utility for this chapter's topic derives from the visual information that interviewees used to assess the class of the wedding party. This information included the wedding's venue, decorations, the bride's and groom's jewelry and attire, the wedding guests' jewelry and clothing (especially saris), the guests' grooming and their style of wearing their clothing, and the body types of the main participants (primarily height, weight, and skin color). In short, it was an abbreviated version of the qualities that Araci and others use when they view weddings (and wedding albums in the future), the qualities that proclaim a message to the public.

Dowry

Dowry is another crucial means for communicating and displaying family standing. "Dowry," in its colloquial Indian usage, generally refers to the total set of transactions (both goods and payments) made by the bride's family for the occasion of her marriage. Dowry, however, has multiple components (see, e.g., Beck 1972, 327; Caplan 1984, 217). These include 1) the household and personal goods given to the bride, often called the *stridhana*, *cītanam*, or *cīr* in scholarly and everyday speech,[15] and 2) the jewelry, consumer goods, and cash given to the groom and/or his family, often called groomprice by scholars, and *varataṭcinai* in Tamil (though varataṭcinai is also used colloquially to refer to the entirety of the dowry).[16]

In everyday discussions, displays, and interpretations of dowry, however, people in Madurai rarely distinguish between these components, and the lines between the two are frequently blurred (cf. Donner 2008, 76). For example, the bride's portion is often in fact controlled by her husband or in-laws (her jewelry might be given to her husband's sisters for their dowries, for instance), and key items such as gold are today seen as both cīr and groomprice. Therefore, when I discuss dowry in this book, unless otherwise specified I combine its two portions (see also Ram 1992; Waheed 2009).

Dowry is consciously used to display the class of the family who gives it and the family who receives it. (It is also important as a means to establish and cement the alliance between families [Roulet 1996, 92; Upadhya 1990, 45].) The amounts given as gold, household goods, and consumer goods are publicly known. Much of the dowry is on prominent display in the bride's family's home before the wedding and in the groom's family's home afterward, and sometimes key items will be on display at the marriage ceremonies as well. Thus there is a visual drama that wedding guests, neighbors, and often casual passersby can view. But there is also a great deal of open talk about the dowry. Brides' families acknowledge freely the size and components of the dowry—including the amount of gold jewelry, the household items, the cash, and other gifts. Talking about the dowry that has been requested or given is a standard way for brides' families to make prestige claims as well as to complain about the "demands" of the groom's side. Grooms' families are less likely to talk as openly about the dowry (especially about requests for cash), largely to avoid being seen as greedy, but they typically acknowledge the amount of gold involved. (As Kannan's future affines demonstrated with the list they presented, they may also be just as open about the demands as are the bride's family.) They are also eager, as Sekaran's wife Annam put it pointedly, "to show off big items at the wedding because this gives them *perumai*, prestige, and they can't be without that." Acquaintances of the spouses' families are often intimately familiar with the details of what was requested, what was given, and what perhaps remains to be fulfilled. (Although the Dowry Prohibition Act of 1961 made it illegal to request payments and gifts for the groom and his family, this has had little if any impact on either actual practice or its public acknowledgment in the South. It should be noted, however, that dowry is not a matter of such public discussion in some other parts of India.)

As Marguerite Roulet has argued for North India, dowry "is not merely an institution confined to the valorisation of marriage, but serves more importantly as a central institution to define social prestige and status and thus becomes an important dimension of people's representations of themselves and others" (1996, 91; see also Caldwell, Reddy, and Caldwell 1983, 357). Dowry, she argues, "stands as a uniform, public symbol that says something about the status and prestige of the bride and groom and their two natal households and families" (1996, 93). As dowry has become prevalent in different South Indian communities over time, a number of scholars have observed its capacity to display, make claims about, and help others interpret families' class standing (Caplan 1984, 225; Gough 1956, 834; Heyer 1992, 429; Nishimura 1998, 264; Srinivasan 2005, 602; Upadhya 1990, 45; also see Roulet 1996). Judith Heyer emphasizes the pressure that this places on brides' families, observing: "It is daughters' marriages, rather than other things, that have become the status symbols, the markers of reputation or prestige. Spending substantially on daughters' marriages and dowries, and/or marrying daughters into successful households, confirms or raises households' reputations. *Not* spending substantially on daughters' marriages significantly *lowers* households' reputations. Daughters' marriages make important statements one way or the other. Households with marriageable daughters cannot escape this" (1992, 429; emphasis in original).

It is important to reiterate that although the importance of the dowry to the groom's family's prestige is rarely mentioned in the literature, the groom's family's status is also signaled by the amount of dowry, since the dowry is essentially one measure of the groom's and his family's worth. Carol Upadhya, who along with Roulet (1996) is one of the few analysts to acknowledge the symbolic value of the dowry to the groom's family, makes the point succinctly: "The size of a dowry reveals much about the social and economic statuses of the two families as well as about the qualities of the groom. To say that a man 'got' a dowry of two lakhs is to say something about his social and economic worth" (1990, 45). (See also Heyer 2000, 21; Nishimura 1994, 260.)

The Shift to Dowry

Yet the practice of dowry was almost nonexistent in southern India a century ago. How, then, has it come to acquire this role? The striking shift from bridewealth to dowry represents a changing set of criteria for matching spouses—or changing ways in which old criteria are weighed—with a heightened emphasis on economic assets, education, and occupation. These changes underline its importance in helping us to understand the role of marriage in the production of class.

The reasons for the shift to dowry and for its persistent growth bear some consideration if we are to understand fully how dowry is related to the ratification and display of class. To my mind, no definitive explanations of the increased prevalence and size of dowry in South India have been provided, although many hypotheses have been offered (see Dickey n.d.b). An adequate explanation needs to take into account demographic and economic changes correlated with the rise of dowry, as well as the communicative function of dowry.

Three causes appear most likely to have shaped the transition from bridewealth to dowry in South India: emulation of elites' marriage practices, a scarcity of grooms relative to the brides eligible to marry them, and the rise of consumerism and the attendant need to make consumption conspicuous. None of these possible explanations is entirely supported by large-scale quantitative studies or by a breadth of ethnographic studies, but each does fit the available data and, in conjunction with one another, they can reasonably be argued to be causally related to the rise of dowry.[17] Because each of these three explanations tells us something about the increasing involvement of class in South Indian marriage arrangements, and the pressure that families feel to provide and request large dowries, I will review them very briefly.

In South India there is solid evidence that the practice of dowry began with elites—originating with Brahmans, possibly at the end of the nineteenth century (Srinivas 1962, 54)—and spread systematically downward through the caste structure (Caldwell, Reddy, and Caldwell 1983; Epstein 1973; Kapadia 1995; Srinivas 1984; see also Billig 1992; Ifeka 1989, 266; Nishimura 1998; Srinivasan 2005). Brahmans are the prototypical elite in most of Hindu and Christian South India, even where (as is often the case) they are not the wealthiest or most powerful caste. Kapadia explains that, in southern Tamil Nadu, "upwardly mobile groups hope to acquire the cultural capital that distinguishes the upper classes. And because upper-class behavior is perceived as being Brahminic in style, a 'Brahminization' of behavior tends to occur in these groups" (1995, 47; see also Basu 1999, 255). Thus one of the explanations for dowry is that it was taken on in emulation of elite practices in a time when socioeconomic characteristics have become increasingly important as determinants of social standing.

Others have pointed out that selective access among men to education and professional employment made some potential grooms more attractive than others. At about the same time that dowry began to be practiced by economically dominant castes, some men among these communities began to be formally educated. Because women in these groups were not yet provided with formal education, the most desirable grooms became "scarce" relative to the brides whose families were looking for alliances (Gaulin and Boster 1990, 997; Heyer 1992; Lakshmi 1989, 190; Rajaraman 1983, 275; Srinivas 1984, 21; Upadhya 1990); and "in a sellers' market, created by relative scarcity, there was no alternative but to offer a dowry with one's daughter" (Caldwell, Reddy, and Caldwell 1983, 347).

Finally, the increase in the incidence and size of dowry has been tied to changing practices of consumerism (though authors disagree on the advent of widespread consumerism, varying its timing from the colonial period to the latter twentieth century [see, e.g., Nishimura 1994; Srinivas 1984; Srinivasan 2005; see also Jeffery 2014]). Whatever the timing, it is feasible that the importance of visual display of consumer goods, both at life-cycle ceremonies and seasonal rituals as well as in the kinds of everyday presentations of self described in chapter 4, has gone hand in hand with the increase in sizeable consumer goods as a part of dowries.

Taken together, these three factors—elite emulation, scarcity of desirable grooms, and consumerism—may well explain much of the shift to dowry. As competition for attractive grooms increased in any community, offering dowry rather than expecting bridewealth was one way to make a bride's family more attractive and more likely to achieve a status-producing match. This transition was likely eased, or perhaps initiated in the first place, because of the prestige associated with the upper-caste and then upper-class practice of dowry. The emulation of higher castes and higher classes makes sense in a society in which status markers are more up for grabs than they were a century ago, and even more so since economic liberalization in 1991. Today there remains some competition for attractive grooms, even as grooms' families are also trying to make an advantageous match—though the pool of potential brides is itself becoming increasingly differentiated as more women achieve higher education and enter salaried occupations. Finally, increasing consumerism, and consumption as a crucial marker of status, make grooms' families more desirous of gaining a bride whose dowry will reflect well on them, just as they make brides' families more desirous of demonstrating their economic and social worth by giving the largest dowry they can manage.

Finally, the increasing *size* of marriage transactions has also had a number of impacts on families. Two are most important for this study. First, the degree of indebtedness caused by marrying daughters has risen dramatically (see, e.g., Bloch, Rao, and Desai 2004, 675; Caplan 1985, 47–48; Mies 1980, 10). Second, marriage has become increasingly important as a site for displaying the wealth and prestige of both families—the wife's family's because of what they give, and the groom's family's because of how attractive the presentations show them to be. Thus the shift to dowry, like that away from murai ideals, reflects a changing moral universe.

In sum, we see that a shift from bridewealth to dowry in South India has attended the growing importance of class considerations in the arrangement and celebration of marriages. Those criteria that are estimated more highly now—including advantageous economic and social matches at the expense of murai obligations; and higher education, sophistication, and earning potential—both reflect and heighten the importance of class in society and in everyday social standing. Several forces have converged to make marriage arrangements much more focused on class-related criteria than they were a hundred, fifty, even thirty years ago. Dowry is only one element of such socioeconomic considerations, but it (like lavish wedding ceremonies) is especially suited to displaying class standing in a consumer-oriented society.

With my arguments in place about the roles of alliances, wedding ceremonies, and dowry in these processes, I now turn to the alliances of Lakshmi and her siblings to illustrate the key ways in which marriage is related to class: the tendency to match family standings in marriage arrangements, and the many calculations made in the matching; the significance of dowry in making alliances; the use of both dowry and the wedding ceremony to reflect and maintain class position; and the role that both parental and spouses' generations play in producing the couple's future class standing. One of Lakshmi's sister's weddings also leads us to consider a point not yet explored at length, viz., the economic, social, and emotional costs of "marriages by choice" (often called love marriages).

The Reproduction and Display of Class through Marriage: Lakshmi and Her Siblings

Lakshmi and her siblings, with one exception, married into increasingly well-to-do families as their natal household's economic circumstances improved over time. Interestingly, however, each of their marriages was non-normative in some way—as indeed many alliances are (though participants rarely represent them as such). Even in their deviations from the ideal—and indeed *because of* those deviations—they reveal a great deal about class considerations in marriage-making as well as the long-term impacts of marriage alliances on class.

Lakshmi's parents, Venkatraman and Kaveri, were Brahmans from small towns in central Tamil Nadu. During my visit in 2011, Lakshmi told me the story of their marriage for the first time. Her mother's family, she said, was well-off for a rural Brahman family. Still, two factors made it difficult to find a spouse for Kaveri in the 1960s: her mother had died young, and Kaveri was well educated, a high school graduate. Venkatraman's family was much poorer but their reputation was highly respectable, and Venkatraman himself had finished high school as well. Kaveri's family not only was willing to make an alliance with them, but offered a sizeable dowry in gold. (Thus matching families' class was less of a concern for Lakshmi's grandparents than it would later be for her parents, at least in Lakshmi's accounts.) On the wedding day the couple was married at 10:00 A.M. Immediately after the ceremony, Kaveri's new mother-in-law took all of Kaveri's jewels and added them to the dowry of Venkatraman's oldest sister, who was married directly afterward at 11:00 A.M.

Venkatraman co-owned a bus company in the town of Pudukkottai, the financial capital for which came primarily from his in-laws. When the business failed, according to Lakshmi, because of mismanagement by his partners several years after his marriage, he moved the family to the fairly distant city of Madurai. There he was employed in another bus company, but this firm too had failed when I met the family in 1985. Venkatraman was unemployed at that time, but before I left he had a new job as manager of another small bus company. Kaveri was a housewife from the time she married.

Recall that, in 2011, Lakshmi described her family as poor at the time I met them in 1985. Her brother Srinivasan had once characterized the family in the same way—"We had one room for all seven of us, and only one straw mat to sleep on," he reminisced in 2000. Thus this family possessed somewhat mixed class factors and signals shortly before they began to arrange the next generation's marriages: parents and children had good educations for the time, the father was trained in a professional occupation, and the family had a very low income, modest housing, and very few consumer goods. Their lack of material resources shaped their own sense of themselves at the time, but their cultural capital—primarily education and the knowledge and skills that it brought them—would be crucial in shaping the parents' and most of their children's future prospects.

When I left Madurai in 1987 after finishing my first fieldwork, I gave all the money I had left to Venkatraman and Kaveri. The sum was Rs. 2,000, a sizeable amount in that neighborhood and in those days. As I remember, it was about two-thirds of what a university professor earned per month, and easily equal to Venkatraman's annual income. The day before I left, I walked down the street to their compound. After entering their home, I showed my respect by kneeling on the floor to touch Venkatraman's and Kaveri's feet, and then I rose and handed them an envelope with the rupees inside. They had taken me in more than any other family, and this was one of the ways I could reciprocate. They would ignore the envelope until I left their home, in the usual way of receiving gifts, and there would be no mention of the money before I departed.

Two and a half years later, when I returned to Madurai in 1989, I visited the family in their new home just south of downtown. The rented house had two full rooms, and my friends had acquired a fan, metal bureau, and television. Kaveri and Venkatraman told me that their increased financial security was due to the money I had given them in 1987. They had invested it—but in a way I hadn't anticipated: Venkatraman and Kaveri had used the money to take a pilgrimage to the Om Sakthi temple in Melmaruvathur, where the goddess Adiparasakthi had blessed them. After completing the pilgrimage, Venkatraman immediately found a partner who provided the capital to open a new bus company. The company had flourished, and his income had grown as he managed the expanding business with skill. But resources were still tight, and marrying four daughters posed a significant challenge.

Kaveri and Venkatraman wished to marry all their daughters to compatible men of good character and family background, with at least a high school education to match the girls' schooling. For their first two daughters, however, they had almost no money put aside for dowry, and they feared taking out large loans with two more daughters still to marry. To find men whose character, reputation, and education were acceptable but who did not require much dowry, Kaveri and Venkatraman made unusual choices. They chose men who had been widowed. Women who are widowed carry too much stigma to remarry among most higher-caste families, but widowed men do not. Nonetheless, widowers have less prestige as potential spouses and command less dowry than never-married men. The other possible strategies for avoiding ruinous dowries would have been to marry their daughters to men with physical or cognitive disabilities or men who were very poor or divorced, or to allow a love marriage; but any of these choices would have produced more stigma than marrying a widower did.

In 1989 Lakshmi, the oldest, was married to a turner (a skilled lathe worker) who had no children but was twenty years older than she. Rajan, I heard, had won state-wide academic prizes in high school, but he could not attend college because his family could not afford the fees. The simple wedding reflected the families' class standing: it was carried out in a temple with only the small gold tāli (a marriage pendant) for jewelry, and only close relatives and neighbors as guests.

The next daughter, Saraswati, was married the following year. She married Lakshmi's husband's first cousin—a widowed temple priest who lived in Kerala and ran a small business cooking for weddings and other auspicious rituals. He was nearer in age to his wife and somewhat better off than Lakshmi's husband, and his occupation carried greater respect. But he had two very young sons from his first marriage, a disadvantage on the marriage market. By this time Venkatraman was starting to build up some savings from his employment, and the third daughter, Bhanu, was contributing to the family income by working in a department store. The family used their improved economic position to provide Saraswati with a somewhat larger dowry and thus a more prosperous husband, and to finance a finer wedding ceremony. As Lakshmi described the situation many years later,

> My father said to me, "Okay, we have put some money aside, so whatever I couldn't do for you, I should do for Saraswati's marriage." He bought a heavy gold chain for her, and he gave her a nice wedding in a wedding hall. For me, he didn't do anything at all. He didn't do even a *tol* [a small measure of gold].[18] We were really suffering then. My marriage was in a temple. For her, a nice wedding hall.

Venkatraman and Kaveri invested their greater resources in a larger dowry for Saraswati and a respectable, honor- and status-producing wedding ceremony. Here again, both wedding and dowry reflected the family's circumstances.

By the time of my third fieldwork trip in 1990, shortly after Saraswati's marriage and the birth of Lakshmi's first son, Venkatraman and Kaveri were looking for a groom for Bhanu. Lakshmi and Saraswati were both staying at their parents' home when I visited, and they pulled me aside and whispered that a groom had been found, but I wasn't to say anything to Bhanu about him because he had a disfigured arm. He was a very good man, they said, but they were still waiting to let Bhanu know about his disability. Venkatraman and Kaveri had again found a means of identifying a groom whose character and whose family reputation they judged to be good, but who would not require a significant dowry.

That marriage did not come to pass, however, and I do not know why. Perhaps Bhanu found out about the young man's disability and used it as a reason to protest the match. By then in any case, though none of the rest of us was yet aware of it, Bhanu had already found her future husband. He worked in the same department store as she—the Lucky Plaza Department Store, she would say without irony. Years later, in 2011, Bhanu told me that she and the young man, who worked in the wristwatch department on the third floor while she worked in the "gift articles" section on the first floor, had loved each other (love *paṇṇatu*) for seven years. They didn't tell anyone about their love for the first six years. How Bhanu managed to avoid having her parents arrange her marriage in all that time, without telling them about her lover, I am unsure, particularly since according to Bhanu's recounting of the history, her younger sister Geeta was married before Bhanu revealed her secret. (To marry daughters out of order is highly unusual, and can create dishonor for the family because it suggests some flaw in the older, still unmarried daughter's physical, mental, or moral being.)

Bhanu's beloved was a Thevar man, and when she did tell her parents about the relationship in 1995 or 1996, they were predictably furious. After months of constant family fighting, Bhanu's parents arranged a different marriage for her, and Bhanu says she acquiesced to the match because she did not know how to avoid one any longer. Her engagement ceremony took place the day before her younger sister Geeta's pregnancy ceremony, a major protective ritual in the seventh month of pregnancy. On the way home from the engagement, which had taken place in a wedding hall, Bhanu's Thevar lover confronted her family on the street. As Bhanu and Lakshmi told the story in 2011, the young man had an altercation with their father, grabbed Bhanu and then drove her to his house in a friend's taxi, where he introduced her to his mother for the first time. That night, Bhanu said, they were married in a simple ceremony—not even a gold-plated tāli, just a silver one. It was many years before Bhanu's parents would speak with her, as I witnessed. At my son's first birthday party in 2000, all of the family except for Saraswati (who was back in Kerala) came to celebrate. Bhanu tried that night to talk with her father, but he refused to speak with her. Bhanu, holding her two-year-old daughter in her arms, cried alone on the staircase. The affective losses and the economic costs that resulted from choosing her own husband are intertwined.

In the meantime Srinivasan, the only son, had completed a bachelor's degree in business. Lakshmi represented the decision to send him to college as a family strategy and a family effort: "There are four daughters and one son, so we only allowed the son to study for a degree." Lakshmi portrayed this as a heavily gendered decision about how to invest their resources most productively. While daughters were given property through their dowries when possible, the largest investment of family resources went into the son, since this would yield a greater benefit for the family as a whole than would spreading those resources across siblings. The girls could not further their own economic prospects or their parents' as directly as the son could. (Moreover, educating daughters further would have made it even more difficult to find affordable husbands.)

Srinivasan himself worked hard to get through college, selling goods in a variety of retail shops while he worked on his degree. After graduation he first moved to Mumbai, where he worked as a sales representative in a textile mill. Two years later he migrated to Sri Lanka to work as an appraiser and an accountant in a jewelry firm. Srinivasan would call me from Colombo in those years, and talk about how he slept on the shop floor at night with other workers in order to save money to send home. After two years there, he moved to Chennai and worked in a larger jewelry shop. His next two positions were as supervisors and clerks in factories—first in Hosur, where Lakshmi was by then living, and then, in 1999, in a Madurai TVS textiles plant. His remittances increased the family income considerably over those years. As he told me in 2001, he was able to help his sister Geeta to marry "in style" in 1995. With Srinivasan's earnings combined with his father's, they were able to ensure a proper display of dowry goods, clothing, food, and rites at Geeta's wedding.

Geeta, the youngest of the five siblings, was the only daughter to marry into a solidly middle-class family. She married a man from their neighborhood when she was nineteen and he was twenty-two. Their wedding was described by family members as "grand," and Srinivasan says that he bore the expenses. (At my son's first birthday party, I remember Geeta wearing a green silk sari, the only sister who looked decidedly middle-class.) Geeta now has two children. She is a housewife, and until recently she spent much of her time caring for her elderly parents-in-law, with whom they lived in a rented four-room house, which was small but well furnished. I met Gopal, Geeta's husband, in 2011, when I saw Geeta for the first time in eleven years. Gopal, who had recently been promoted to general manager of a car showroom in the area, picked me up in a company car. As he drove me to the family's home in a town outside of Madurai, Gopal told me that the price of the car was Rs. 45,000, that his monthly salary was Rs. 37,000, and that his marriage with Geeta in 1995 was "a love marriage for her and an arranged marriage for me." As Geeta later confirmed, she had seen Gopal in their neighborhood and told her mother that she thought he would be a good husband. Gopal's family was Aiyengar Brahman, a different sub-caste than Geeta's Aiyar family, and the two sub-castes do not normally intermarry. But their mothers were friends as well as neighbors, and Kaveri proposed that they arrange their children's marriage. Gopal's mother agreed. (Their friendship may have made her more likely to overlook the fact that Geeta's older sister was not yet married; perhaps the size of the dowry helped as well.) Gopal, however, was willing only on the condition that they delay the marriage for three years until he was well employed.

Srinivasan's marriage was the last. While working in Madurai in 1999, he and a friend volunteered with a charitable organization that supports people who are deaf. Srinivasan says that he met his wife Kavitha, a beautiful and light-skinned Brahman woman, through the organization. Their parents arranged their marriage in 2000. His wife's parents own and run a private elementary school in Madurai, where they also own a large home, and they are decidedly better off than Venkatraman and Kaveri were. When he told me about the wedding a year later, Srinivasan boasted that he had refused to take a dowry from his wife's parents (by which he meant anything other than the cīr, the personal goods that his wife brought). He cast himself as above materialism, motivated by social justice. Yet his eyes sparkled when he recalled the "grand" three-day wedding that his wife's parents put on, with feast after feast, ritual after ritual, display after display of goods lavished on the bride and the couple by the bride's parents and the wedding guests. Because most weddings now take place within the scope of a single day, it was particularly the length of the wedding (implying in part the expenses that it would necessarily entail, but primarily the visual, aural, and culinary extravaganza) that Srinivasan saw as signaling the stature of the family that he was marrying into. The extravagant ceremony they put on reflected well on them, on Srinivasan, and on his parents and siblings.

Kavitha's parents must have been willing to marry their daughter into a poorer family because they knew her deafness would make it difficult to find a husband. Srinivasan was well educated, hard working, and Brahman; he came from a reputable family that by then was lower-middle class; and he would have been seen as a good match. By not requesting a dowry, Srinivasan showed himself to be above material concerns, confirmed his family's reputation, and gained himself honor.

He also married a beautiful woman and became part of a family with significantly more material wealth than he was accustomed to. While Srinivasan would have expected his wife's parents to bestow them both with gold jewelry and to provide their daughter with saris and other items of wealth, it is likely that he made no specific requests for amounts of gold or particular items of other kinds. He could trust that they would want to confirm their wealth in the display of the gold ornaments they gave their daughter.

After the marriage, Srinivasan moved back to Sri Lanka with his wife. At the time, he worked as the accountant for a temple in Colombo. He and Kavitha soon had two daughters, the elder of whom was born two years after my son. (Since all the members of this family and I call each other by kinship terms, I am Srinivasan's older sister and our children are cross cousins, and he often tells me that his older daughter is my son's murai peṇ—that they are each other's rightful spouses.) Once the daughters were both old enough to enter primary school, Kavitha returned to Madurai with them, and they were enrolled in private schools.

When Srinivasan and I were talking in the Madurai home of his parents-in-law in 2011, I reminded him of our conversation ten years earlier when he had bemoaned the difficulty of being in the middle class because of the major expenditures required for family rituals (see chapter 6). This time, without hesitation, he replied that he is doing well. He has a comfortable income, and recently built a new home on the upper floor of his wife's parents' house. He no longer feels the tension of performing a middle-class life with restricted resources.

Lakshmi's and her siblings' marriages confirm the roles of class isogamy, dowry, and display in the reproduction of class through marriage. In the four marriages that were arranged, the children were married to someone matched to the family's current "desirability," a calculation based largely on class (since none of the children was previously married, or had a stigmatized condition), with long-term consequences that I will explore momentarily. The siblings' descriptions of the wedding ceremonies and dowry are precisely in accord with the family's class, and show an increase in public display over time (as demonstrated in both the ceremony and the dowry). Bhanu, whose marriage was not arranged, fared the worst in all ways: because she chose against her parents' wishes, she had no dowry, a "simple ceremony" with no public display, and the greatest financial insecurity over time.

It is especially instructive to look at these five siblings' situations and reflect on the long-term impacts of the cultural and material resources they brought to their marriages, their marital partners' resources, and their marriage alliances. Lakshmi is now a forewoman in a small rubber factory. Her modest three-room home in a "line" in Hosur has a well-stocked kitchen, a television, a large metal bureau, and a metal cot with a thin mattress. As of 2011, her older son had finished high school and was working in a Bangalore factory, and the younger one was studying for a bachelor's degree in electrical and electronic engineering. Lakshmi's husband continued working as a turner until he developed disabling arthritis at the age of fifty, and although he is now retired from lathe operation he continues to work as the head employee in his factory's cafeteria. While their circumstances are noticeably more comfortable than those in which Lakshmi grew up, their mobility has been limited by her husband's occupation and income, and by the meager dowry that Lakshmi brought to the marriage. Because Lakshmi's parents-in-law had died before the marriage, the couple also suffered by not having access to their support or resources.

Saraswati, in contrast, is now well off. Her husband, who has always earned more than Lakshmi's husband, eventually achieved a position as a priest in a renowned Kerala temple. He now earns sizeable sums carrying out rituals for families who travel great distances to have life-cycle rituals performed there (usually death anniversaries). Saraswati is a housewife. Their two sons have graduated from college, and Saraswati's doted-on daughter also attended college and was recently married into a solidly middle-class Tamil Brahman family in Malaysia. When I looked through the girl's engagement album, I was taken aback to see how "modern" she looked—she appeared, to my eyes, to be dressed and groomed like many an American teenager. She had traveled a much greater distance from her mother's childhood than Lakshmi's children had. Saraswati's husband's greater economic and cultural capital have provided them with far greater vacati than Lakshmi and her conjugal family have had.

Bhanu has fared the worst of the five children. Having a love marriage, she was unable to capitalize on her parents' resources. Indeed, she lost access to those resources, and gained very few through her husband's impoverished family. She and her husband had no dowry to use as capital, and no family alliances to build on. After first living on their own, they and their two daughters later moved in with her husband's parents and sisters. Her husband ekes out a small income from his roadside watch repair business. Bhanu has not, however, lost the support of her siblings. While they rarely visit her at home because of the differences in their castes, they provide her with financial and emotional support. When her thirteen-year-old daughter had heart surgery in Bangalore early in 2011, Bhanu and her daughter lived with Lakshmi for three months. Lakshmi and her husband supported them all with food and transportation, and each of the other siblings sent money to help with the medical costs for the successful surgery and follow-up exams. Married women, unlike married men, are not always able to help siblings, but in this family the sisters have been able to support one another just as Srinivasan has.

Geeta, who married into an economically comfortable family and brought a good dowry with her, became well settled. In 2010, she and her husband bought a nearby plot of land on credit, and planned to build their own home. Their daughter and son attended a top private school and were studying English. When I saw them in 2011, they were about to begin laying the foundation for the new house.

Srinivasan is also well settled. Both his education and his wife's family's social and economic resources have allowed him to build up savings and send his two daughters to private schools in Madurai. His wife cares for their children and does part-time work in tailoring. Srinivasan had been learning to become a priest, and in early 2011 he spent two months in training in a temple in Malaysia, where he studied Brahmanical ritual practices and texts. Later that year he received a visa to work in Malaysia, where he has resettled by himself while his wife and children stay in Madurai. Srinivasan's college education had allowed him job opportunities in settings that gave him a much more cosmopolitan sensibility than his sisters have; these positions also provided him with income and experience. All of these he brought to his marriage. After marriage he also used contacts from his parents-in-law—his new social capital, capital that his parents could not provide him—to find potential positions.

These descriptions of Venkatraman and Kaveri's children's marriages, like Miriam's account of meeting potential brides and their families, illustrate standard elements of marriage alliances. They show the calculus of decision making, including the role of dowry and the ways to compensate for its lack (in order to avoid downward economic mobility for daughters). They show the contemporary importance of dowry—and the costs of not having one. Note that none of these marriages was made with kin.

Although none of these five marriages is entirely normative in terms of partner choice, each illustrates clearly the four ways in which marriage is tied to class, perhaps all the more so because the rules that were "broken" were done so in order to marry children into families that were as well off as possible. These marriages reproduced the natal family's class situation at the time of the marriage; and although (with the exception of Bhanu, who made her own marriage, and Geeta, when she later became widowed, as I discuss below) each child has followed the middle-class trend of improved circumstances since liberalization (see chapter 6), they remain tracked by the relative standing of the natal family at the time they married. The alliances that were negotiated ratified the family's current class position. The weddings and dowries—of those children who had arranged marriages—demonstrated the family's class to a relevant public.

And each child entered marriage with a dual set of resources (cultural, social, symbolic, and economic) that shaped their future opportunities as well as the limits on those opportunities.

Marriage and Class Mobility: Anjali

Occasionally, marriage does significantly alter a person's class. This kind of change differs from the pattern we have seen of economic circumstances varying within a single generation, as when unmarried children's employment adds to family income, or when illnesses or major ritual expenditures deplete savings and increase debt, often for many years. Changes like these are usually cyclical. The formal liberalization of the Indian economy in 1991, however, created potentially longer-term social change for some people (though it should be noted that the intergenerational reproduction of class remains largely entrenched, perhaps even increasingly so with liberalization [see, e.g., Radhakrishnan 2011a, 42–43]).

Anjali, as described earlier, had completed a college degree, while continuing to earn money for her family. By the time she was twenty-two she had established a successful business of her own. She had education, a respectable and modern occupation, excellent earning potential, middle-class cultural capital, and some social capital. Given all of this, her parents hoped to marry her into a family that was decidedly better off than theirs. Unlike most other urban residents, Anjali appeared poised to move up in class standing. How might this happen? Although the outcome was narrated in chapter 3, here I discuss her parents' strategies in order to illustrate how marriage might, in rare circumstances, be used for upward mobility.

In 1999, I asked Anjali whether her parents would look for a groom of their own class, or perhaps of a lower or higher class. Unlike most people I interviewed, Anjali replied, "My parents will look for a little higher level. They'll think, 'So far she has lived in hardship. At least her life could be different after her marriage.'" I asked, "Won't it be hard for you to live in such a place?" She answered philosophically, "I will have to change to fit with the way they are. That's all. It will be a bit difficult in the beginning. But I can observe what they are like, and I can change." This is the stock response of young women as they prepare for marriage in an unknown household, but in Anjali's case it also evoked the difficulty of adjusting to the material surroundings, consumption practices, manners, and social assumptions of people raised in a different class. (Witness Miriam's statement that she would have had to "mold" one potential daughter-in-law to fit into their family, given the differences in their cultural capital, even though those two families were much closer in class than Anjali's and her husband's families would be.) As Tamils say, she would have to learn to "move" in such company, speaking and dressing and behaving appropriately.

Anjali's parents hoped to find her a government servant (a member of the civil service or other branches of the government), or at least a business owner. These positions were a large socioeconomic step up from Anjali's father's occupation as a cycle rickshaw driver. Anjali was educated, sophisticated, and personable enough, however, to attract a family with such a son, if she and her family could produce a sufficient dowry. Like Lakshmi's parents, they wanted a groom whose education, occupation, and temperament would be well matched to their daughter, but they too lacked money for the dowry such a groom would typically require. As I described in chapter 3, they hoped that Anjali's business and its income would substitute for a portion of the dowry.

Government servants in India have secure employment for life and are guaranteed a pension. Yet government servants asked for such high dowries—in the Pillai caste that Anjali's family belongs to, the rate was then 20 "sovereigns" of gold jewelry (160g, 5.5 oz.) and Rs. 15,000–20,000 in cash, according to Anjali's mother—that such a groom was likely to be out of reach for her family. Families of young men who have their own businesses asked for about half of these amounts, still a huge expense for a family whose primary wage-earner made Rs. 1,000 per month when he was working, and that had no savings. Yet if Anjali could marry someone with financial security, she would not have to worry about poverty herself, and she might eventually be able to help her parents and her siblings. Given Anjali's skills and the immense security such a marriage could bring her, the step was worth taking if at all possible. Before her father's injuries, with five household members working and her brother about to be married, this goal seemed realizable. After the accident, it seemed further off, but it remained something they might still work toward. Through a combination of joint financial effort, careful strategizing about Anjali's education and career, effective use of social networks, and Anjali's own talents and drive, Anjali's family seemed poised to attain this ideal.

At the same time, the family's own history shows how difficult reaching this point is. As both Anjali's and Kannan's stories have illustrated, simply *maintaining* current resources can become impossible when illness strikes, or when a wage-earner dies or is incapacitated, since there are few "safety nets" of health and disability insurance, retirement plans, or low-interest loans. Such events can immediately wipe out a family's savings in cash and assets, and plunge them into debt. Even sons' marriages can increase financial hardship, since they may remove wage-earners from the household. In addition, while expensive marriages bring honor to a family, they reduce the savings and other financial capital available for making other long-term investments or for providing a financial cushion when tragedies strike.

Anjali's potential gains were also limited by her family's lack of cultural and social, as well as economic, resources. Their lack of experience with higher education, for example, made Anjali's college experience more challenging than many of her peers', and their lack of contacts in prestigious professions and institutions limited Anjali's ability to obtain a high-status and lucrative career.

Later that year, Anjali and her family's efforts to gain her entrance into a higher class proved fruitful against the odds, although not in precisely the way her parents had planned. In 2001, when Anjali was twenty-five, she married a businessman who was the son of a retired civil servant. While Sundaram was just the type of groom her parents had hoped for, he was not of their choosing. Instead, as I have described, Anjali had an "arranged love marriage."[19] Through her marriage, Anjali was indeed able to move up in class—dramatically so—in terms of economic stability, housing, and social and cultural capital. (Her parents had been considering similarly suitable grooms; it is important to keep in mind both that they *aimed* to create such mobility for Anjali, and that such a strategy is always uncertain.)

Although she chose her own husband, her family agreed to the alliance largely because Sundaram's family had the economic security and social standing they had hoped to attain for their daughter; Sundaram's family agreed because of Anjali's education and earning power, and possibly because of the dowry she brought. While Anjali did not bring cash as dowry, her family gave her numerous cooking vessels to take with her, and she had 20 sovereigns of gold. (Anjali said poignantly that her father had saved for her gold over twenty years by "putting aside a small amount of money every day after he finished carrying schoolchildren home from school.") Ultimately, both families were concerned to avoid the disgrace of an elopement. Both families also made sure that the other one had a reputation for responsible behavior among neighbors and kin. After they agreed to the union, Anjali's struggling family put on a wedding that looked as grand as it would have had they arranged her marriage with a middle-class Pillai husband.

The family she married into has been able to use Anjali's resources to further stabilize their own economic position. Her family of origin has benefited as well. Although they lost some "face" because of their daughter's willful behavior and her marriage to a man of a lower caste, they also gained prestige from making an alliance with a middle-class family. In 2011, Anjali's younger brother Kumar married an elementary school teacher whose parents own a small but successful souvenir shop near the

Meenakshi Temple. Anjali and Kumar's mother told me that both Kumar's professional credentials (from working with his sister and then later with Murugan) and the reputation of Anjali's marital family helped her arrange the marriage successfully. And Anjali and Sundaram have continued to consolidate their class standing by expanding their business and enrolling their children in a prestigious school. To do so, however, they have had to take on large loans, often at high interest rates.

Despite the overall rise in income and consumption spending in India, it remains very difficult for people who are poor to make significant improvements in their material and social conditions. Even for those people who have been part of the limited growth in the middle class, mobility like Anjali's is unusual. Her mobility is all the more atypical since she comes from a family with very limited economic means. Her family's success in overcoming these challenges, for at least one child, brings into relief the mutually constitutive roles that economic, cultural, and social capital play in the construction of everyday experience and class-based opportunity.

Marriage, then, is related to class in a number of ways. The increasing practice of dowry has paralleled the increasing emphasis on class in South Indian marriage arrangements. Wedding ceremonies as well as dowry are used to display the two families' claims to class standing. Marriage alliances, which today are built in large part around class-related criteria, are negotiated according to the interests of both families and thus tend to take place between families of similar class, thereby both reproducing and ratifying that class. Alliances also provide resources that contribute to the spouses' economic and social opportunities (and, often, to their natal families' opportunities as well). The significance of such resources can be seen in the contrast between Bhanu's and her siblings' current situations, where Bhanu has suffered not only because of the economic insecurity of her husband's family but also because she cut herself off from her parents' support. (Anjali fared better, both because her husband's family was financially stable and because she was able to maintain her ties with her parents and siblings.) For all of these reasons, marriage is a significant determinant of individuals' and families' class futures.

A focus on the long-term impacts of marriage choices also demonstrates other aspects of the dynamics of class and their impacts on both individuals and groups. The histories of the families discussed in this chapter illustrate repeatedly that one's chances are determined not only by oneself but also by those with whom one is associated.

In addition, these accounts of marriage reveal once again that women and men have different forms of agency in producing class. Others have examined the gendered differences in class production in greater detail (e.g., Agarwal 1994; Kapadia 1995); here I note briefly what the examples in this chapter also demonstrate. Men's and women's agency in determining their own and family members' class differs primarily for three reasons. First, where economic resources are scarce, as they are in most Indian families, boys will usually receive more education than girls; boys will thus be more likely to enter occupations with higher wages or salaries. Srinivasan is a prime example of this pattern (though as Anjali demonstrates there are exceptions, especially for younger daughters). Second, since men generally hold primary control over the family finances, they have more freedom to support parents and siblings than do women. Because Srinivasan was able to enter much better paid employment than his sisters, he was able to finance his youngest sister's dowry and wedding. He has also supported his sisters when their family members have faced medical emergencies, and contributed generously to life-cycle rituals (though brothers cannot be counted on to fulfill such responsibilities, as Jeyamani knows). His sisters have supported each other as well, as Anjali has done for her siblings, but these women's contributions were contingent on their husbands' and sometimes their in-laws' approval. Such approval could not be taken for granted, and in many families it is not forthcoming.

Finally, particularly in middle- and upper-class families, men are more likely to be employed than women. One important long-term consequence of this pattern is that men have a much better chance of retaining their class position if a spouse dies than women do. Geeta, the youngest and most respectably married of Lakshmi's sisters, recently faced this traumatic reality. Her husband Gopal had a fatal heart attack in 2014. Overnight, Geeta and her children lost not only a husband and father, but also most of their economic and social security. Geeta has always worked as a housewife, with no paid employment, and she has no income from investments or pensions. The only material assets she and Gopal owned were consumer items, including jewelry and a treadmill, and selling these goods has not produced enough cash even to pay off the debt they had accrued in purchasing the land on which they were about to build a home. Geeta and her two children left their town immediately after Gopal's funerary rites were completed, going to live in Lakshmi's small home in Hosur. The children will now attend a government school, and despite their early education and the cultural capital they have gained from family habitus and previous schooling, their prospects are significantly different than when their father was alive. Usha, in contrast, was able to maintain a stable life for her children after Raman died, thanks to their financial investments and to the education that qualified her for professional employment. While even Lakshmi and Anjali would both have greater security than Geeta if they were to lose their husbands—because they are steadily employed, because Lakshmi's sons can earn, and because Anjali has significant capital investments in her business—Geeta is more typical of the many women who have few resources to fall back on when they lose husbands, despite their own past contributions to the marital family's class standing.

These last four chapters have focused on the tight interplay of economic, cultural, and social resources. In the case of marriage, potential spouses are judged not only on their families' material assets but also on their tastes in consumer goods, their manners and sophistication, and their social connections. These assets—or their lack—continue to have an effect on the couple's and their families' class position after the marriage is made. While men and women have different forms and amounts of control over the assets that are combined and produced through a marriage, marriage for both women and men is a key determinant of future class, while also contributing to their natal families' class. In the next chapter, we turn to another wedding ceremony, one that is far more dramatic than those described above, but even more remarkable in its bid to unite participants across lines of class.

Food, Hunger, and the Binding of Class Relations

In this chapter, we move from acts of boundary maintenance between classes to efforts to bind people across classes. We do so by looking again at a wedding—but a wedding whose displays far surpass any discussed in the previous chapter. This was a wedding—and in particular a wedding feast—to which everyone in Madurai was invited. The family putting it on combined solicitous use of food and shared imaginations about hunger to tie people together across classes. Employing the emotionally cathected symbols of food and hunger, they aimed not just to display their wealth but also to show their likeness to, and inclusion of, people who were in many other ways *not* like them. The accounts of the event below will complicate the points I have made in previous chapters about boundary drawing and the judgmental moralizing that attends it.

In early 2009, the Kallar industrialist M. Chellasamy—the man who two years later would send a donation to Kannan's daughter's wedding—invited the public to attend the feast at his son's wedding in Madurai. Banners were strung at crossroads during the weeks before the marriage, and simpler posters were put up on walls in many poorer neighborhoods, announcing that anyone who wished to attend was welcome. The announcements stated explicitly that no wedding gifts or donations were to be given. A public wedding feast is a rare occurrence in the city, and it was widely discussed ahead of time. Kannan and his family, who like Chellasamy and his family are Thevars, accepted the invitation, along with thousands of other residents.[1] When I saw Kannan's family soon after, they effused about the event. Over the next month, I was able to interview them, Chellasamy, and several members of his family.

What is the meaning of a meal to which everyone is invited? As Arjun Appadurai has noted, "food in South Asia is prone to be used in social messages of two diametrically opposed sorts. It can serve to indicate and construct social relations characterized by equality, intimacy, or solidarity; or it can serve to sustain relations characterized by rank, distance, or segmentation" (1981, 507). Accepting prepared foods from others signals either the recipient's subservience or an equality between giver and receiver. Superiors do not normally eat cooked food touched by status inferiors, and people who are distant from each other on lines of caste, class, or religion rarely dine together. Abrogating these lines of difference can make a powerful statement about parity and belonging.

As in many cases of gifting in India, different kinds of participants in these events claim different meanings for them. Given the symbolic importance of feeding and eating—acts that encode intimacies, hierarchies, inclusions, and exclusions—the contrasting perspectives of such participants provide a fruitful realm for exploring the contestation and enactment of class relations. Chellasamy saw himself as following in the footsteps of his hero MGR (M. G. Ramachandran), a film-star–politician who built interlocked careers on his reputation as defender of the poor. Both MGR and Chellasamy drew rhetorically on their experiences of hunger (*paci*) and hardship in childhood to explain their motivation to feed the public, and their supporters actively construct these representations, creating a bond between these wealthy individuals and themselves through the trope of feeding and eating. All of the participants in the wedding feast whom I interviewed (like fans and followers who ate at MGR's home) portray the meals in terms of *constructing relations to class others*—although in highly divergent, positioned, and self-interested ways. While I return at the end of this chapter to the forms of value (Munn 1986) that the event produced for the donors, my initial interest lies less in the reciprocity inspired by the gift than in participants' divergent depictions of *what kind of gift it was*.

Public meals are not uncommon in Tamil Nadu. Organizations may sponsor a meal for children as a charitable service, wealthy families put on temple meals for poor people, political parties vie to show their support for the poor by providing well advertised public meals, and celebrities (usually film stars or politicians) invite fans to eat in their homes. Chellasamy's public feast, however, was unusual because it was carried out at a wedding, and with no stipulation about what kinds of people were invited.

We understand the role of weddings in displaying wealth, social ties, and cultural tastes. But Chellasamy was not just looking for recognition of his vast wealth. He was also carrying out a moral act, and he did so in a way that aimed to unite people across lines of class rather than dividing them. To understand the power of this act, we need to grasp two key subjects: first, the weight of the memory of hunger in Tamil Nadu; and second, the symbolic meanings and social imports of certain kinds of gifts. In the following two sections, I discuss hunger discourses and gift-giving in South India. I then turn to the public wedding feast, exploring it from three perspectives: Chellasamy's, his family members', and

Kannan's and his family members'. I conclude the chapter with a consideration of how discourses of paci and the act of feeding can be used intentionally to create identification across lines of class, how the poor substantiate the wealthy as well as vice versa, and how the desire for recognition is expressed among at least some members of the upper class.

First, however, I need to provide an aside about the hero whom Chellasamy cited as his inspiration, MGR, who is indeed a towering precursor for public generosity. MGR was both the most popular film actor of his time and the top politician in Tamil Nadu before he died in 1987. His beginnings, however, were humble. He was sent by his indigent family to join a boys' drama troupe at age seven.[2] Making his first film appearance in 1936, he eventually came to specialize broadly in two kinds of film roles: the underdog—such as a rickshaw driver, farmer, or indigenous healer—who overcomes oppression, and the ruler, warrior, or public servant who fights righteously for the downtrodden. Fans came to see him as someone who enacted his personal and political values in the film roles he chose. Cinema and politics have a long, multi-sided history in Tamil Nadu, and virtually all heads of the state government have come from cinema since 1967, when the screenwriter and Dravida Munnetra Kazhagam (DMK) party leader C. N. Annadurai became the chief minister of Tamil Nadu. Annadurai and his deputy Mu. Karunanidhi, also a screenwriter, recruited MGR to support their party in the 1950s. MGR broke away to create his own party, the Annadurai-DMK, or ADMK, in 1972. In 1977 he became chief minister of Tamil Nadu, a role he held until his death in 1987.

I have heard stories about MGR's generosity since I first arrived in Madurai in 1985. They continue to be powerful today. Fans talk about numerous examples of MGR's love (anpu) for the people, including his (short-lived) price controls on rice and his expansion of a popular welfare program, the Nutritious Meal Programme. Most relevant to this chapter, however, was MGR's habit of feeding his fans in large groups in his home in Madras (Chennai). M.S.S. Pandian contends that after MGR entered office in 1977 (and very likely before), "whosoever went to MGR's home—especially party workers and his film fans—was invariably fed with a meal from a kitchen which worked almost round the clock. They carried the message of MGR's generosity wherever they went" (1992, 104). I began hearing stories of these meals when I interviewed fan club members in the mid- and late 1980s, and even today, fans continue to recount how MGR's house was always open to feed visitors.

Kannan himself often spoke of MGR's generosity, and in 2005, when I carried out research with contemporary fans of MGR, he told me,

"Anyone who comes to his house is always entertained with a fabulous meal. He struggled and labored so hard in his childhood. His mother was a servant, cleaning cooking vessels, and she couldn't educate MGR. They suffered a lot for food, too. When MGR was in the drama troupe, he was not fed properly. So he greets everyone who enters his house with a good meal, then he listens to them or asks them what they have come for. He is a principled man." Kannan's praise was typical of MGR's followers, who frequently pointed out that when MGR became wealthy and powerful, he did not forget his connection to the poor; instead, he used his power to help them (see Dickey 2008). MGR's childhood suffering, they contended, spurred him on to care for them and to provide what they most needed: food and the inclusion that accompanies it. MGR's as well as Chellasamy's public meals were framed in terms that avoided typical representations of hierarchical giving from a superior to inferiors. MGR—and later Chellasamy—was able to blur those lines because both he and his followers promoted the imagination of a shared hunger.

Memories of Hunger, Modes of Address

There are many reasons that feeding is an emotionally laden theme in personal and political discourse in Tamil Nadu. One is its association with nurture in a political system in which many leaders are presumed to be exploitative (an association still foregrounded by current MGR fans). Another is the significant presence of hunger in Tamil Nadu, where scarcity, and the threat of scarcity, have a long history (see, e.g., Raman 2013, 7). Despite the existence of widely praised food distribution programs—such as not only the Nutritious Meal Programme but also the Public Distribution System—the 2008 *India State Hunger Index* shows Tamil Nadu to have the highest percentage of caloric undernourishment, at 29.1 percent, of the seventeen states surveyed. While caloric intake is only a partial measure of hunger (since it is not paired with calories expended), and while the *Hunger Index* shows that Tamil Nadu actually fares *better* than average on measures such as under-five child malnutrition and mortality (Menon, Deolalikar, and Bhaskar 2008, 15), the data nonetheless point to the likelihood of persistent hunger among a notable percentage of the population (see also Harriss-White 2004).

Moreover, not just persistent hunger, but also repeated famines and starvation, have a memorable history in the South, as in the rest of India. Famines have frequently been catastrophic: Ravi Ahuja states that "hundred[s] of thousands and sometimes millions of Indians died in major famines between 1769–70 and 1943" (2004, 147), and David Arnold notes that the official mortality estimate from the 1876–78 famine was at least 3.5 million in the Madras Presidency alone (1984, 68). Arnold explains both the causes of famine and its intensity in the popular imagination:

> In India the perennial problem of subsistence for the poor was intensi-fied by the extreme dependence of agriculture on the arrival of ade-quate monsoon rains. The consequences of even a few weeks' delay or a partial failure of monsoon were well-known from experience. It was not therefore from blind or irrational panic that the prospect of drought and dearth caused alarm and generated such widespread sus-picion, anxiety and fear. . . . The memory of past famines was deeply entrenched in the collective consciousness of the Indian peasantry. (1984, 66–67)

Not surprisingly, then, the subjects of food and hunger have a long history in Tamil literature and oral traditions (see Arnold 1984, 67, 69; Raman 2013). Given the spectacular nature of famine and the more gen-eral regularity of hunger, it makes sense that these topics have been elaborated in narratives, poetry, and proverbs. The responsibility for *addressing* the problem of hunger is also reiterated in such texts. Whereas in the earliest extant Tamil literature it is kings who are assigned this burden, by the time the epic *Manimekalai* was written (between the fifth and the seventh century), Srilata Raman observes, "the duty to feed the hungry shifts from the hands of kings into the hands of others" (2013, 11). And, she notes, "the social and cultural consequences of hunger" con-tinue in more recent texts (2013, 12). Particularly interesting for the sub-ject of this chapter is Raman's discussion of a nineteenth-century Hindu social reformer, Ramalinga Swamigal. This reformer, whose treatises are informed by earlier Tamil literature, established an almshouse for feeding the poor in 1867, and wrote that "the most elemental of sufferings, more basic than all others, is that of hunger" (2013, 24). He also wrote that of all forms of suffering, "the one that should be tackled primarily, which generates the greatest salvific benefit for the practitioner of compassion, is hunger—indeed, one who tackles the hunger of others will tackle all other forms of suffering too" (Raman 2013, 3). Giving food, then, is giving life and relief from deprivation.

In sum, it is not just actual experiences of hunger, but also discursive representations of hunger—what Arjun Appadurai (personal communi-cation) has termed "paci discourse"[3]—that shape the imagination of a shared hunger between certain givers and receivers of food.

Gift-giving in South India

A gift—any gift—both means something and produces something. What meanings did the wedding feast hold for Chellasamy, his family members, and those who accepted his gift? What goods did it generate for all of them? To answer these questions, we must next consider local "categories" of gifts. Different types of gifts create different meanings and different effects—thus we cannot tell what they mean or produce unless we know what kind of gifts they are or are perceived to be. Moreover, as we will see, givers and receivers may disagree about what category a gift falls into, and thus what its meaning is.

Chellasamy's and MGR's meals display elements of three overlapping types of gifts: *dān* (Tamil *tānam*), *īkai*, and philanthropy.[4] Because respondents drew from all of these concepts, both explicitly and implicitly, when making sense of the wedding feast, I introduce each of them briefly.

Types of Gifting

Dān is a special type of gift because it must be given with no expectation of return from the recipient, thereby accruing merit and auspiciousness to the donor. It is thus sometimes called a "free gift." In addition, it must be given only to recipients whose moral character, action, or need qualifies them as "worthy."[5] Dān appears to have originated in Hindu law, and is also included among Buddhist and Jain forms of gifting (Heim 2004). While some argue that true dān occurs only in the absence of expectation of any benefit whatsoever (e.g., Parry 1989, 66; see Heim 2004), dān is frequently seen as benefiting donors in some worldly fashion, as I discuss below. It is crucial, however, that recipients themselves do not reciprocate. Furthermore, dān is also distinctive because it is often understood to remove sin or inauspiciousness from the donor by passing it on via the gift to the recipient (Parry 1989; Raheja 1988, 31–36, 119). This perception, however, may be contested by recipients themselves, who frequently deny that they have taken on any negative substance (see, e.g., Laidlaw 1995, ch. 2 and 294; Mines 2005, 69–71; Osella and Osella 1996).[6] With or without such transmission, dān is understood to create a hierarchy between giver and receiver.

Of the several local Tamil terms for gifts, īkai is most closely related to Chellasamy's feast.[7] Īkai can be glossed as "generous gift," "donation," or "charity." It is similar to dān in that giving and accepting īkai denotes a hierarchy. But in the past īkai was given by kings, warriors, and other patrons in secular contexts, rather than the ritual settings of dān that appear frequently in Hindu scripture (Kailasapathy 1968, 217–219; Meenakshi 1996, 135, 137–138; Raman 2013). Furthermore, while there is evidence that, at least in the recent past, īkai was meant to be given only to "worthy recipients," their "worthiness" was measured by material need rather than moral standing (Meenakshi 1996; Raman 2013, 13). This is one reason that īkai is an important concept for understanding Chellasamy's feast, as we will see; another is that gifts given to alleviate hunger are always referred to as īkai. Raman even notes (referring to a genre of classical Tamil poetry) that "if there is one word in the *Puram* that perhaps stands in greatest contrast to *paci*, it is īkai" (2013, 10).[8]

In contrast to both dān and īkai, philanthropy is often seen as a practice adopted primarily from the West and, at least to some extent, embraced in conjunction with colonial rule (Caplan 1998; Haynes 1987). It is typically intended to "promote human welfare" (Haynes 1987, 339n. 1), drawing on a notion of humanitarian service that appeared only in the nineteenth century. By the late 1800s, social reform movements were shifting from religious gifting to philanthropy, which was seen as an "instrumentally rational" form of giving (Bornstein 2009, 628). In the South, as Lionel Caplan has observed, philanthropy has long secured social and political influence. It also provided new means for enacting class values and ideologies, "introduc[ing] new ways of displaying wealth and gaining public recognition" (1998, 410). Local philanthropy in Madurai today varies widely, and includes temple and educational endowments and other institutional gifts; scholarships; donations of food, clothing, schoolbooks, and tools; funds to cover the costs of weddings; and organ donations, among many others. As with dān, "needy" recipients may disagree with donors' representations of the meaning of the gift, challenging, for example, the depiction of their dependency (Caplan 1998, 426–428).

Despite the differences among these three types of gifts, they also have important similarities. While dān is more likely to be framed in terms of gaining spiritual merit and dispersing inauspiciousness, and philanthropy is often discussed in terms of its strategic outcomes, there is nonetheless a good deal of overlap in the forms taken by, motivations for, and outcomes provided by both. Similarly, although īkai is rarely discussed in explicit contrast with dān or philanthropy, in the relatively recent past it has taken on some of their features. Indeed, as we will see, there is a great deal of hybridity in the models produced of Chellasamy's gift. Furthermore, we need to keep in mind that despite the contrasts made in the literature and everyday dialogues between reciprocated and unreciprocated gifts, and between altruistic and self-interested gifts, virtually all gifts have some elements of both and thus such contrasts are at the least artificial and very often misleading.

Each of these three types of gifting makes an appearance in this chapter. Chellasamy's wedding feast was widely seen in Madurai as philanthropy; Chellasamy viewed it as dān; and it fits the model of īkai as well. On the other hand, for reasons I will explain below, the feast is also a rather atypical example of these forms of gifting (except for īkai), and the actual event's contrasts with these forms are as relevant for the event's meanings as are the similarities.

Personal and Structural Outcomes of Gift-giving

Gifting does typically produce rewards for donors, even when the charitable act is considered to be entirely selfless or unreciprocated. Wealth is, or can be, a moral "problem" in India, even as it is a sign of strength and (sometimes) power. Giving one's wealth to worthy others creates a moral good (Berry 1987, 306; Haynes 1987, 358). "Selfless altruism" also promotes one's name, elevates one's reputation, positions oneself as a leader (or strengthens that position), and can garner other benefits as well (Mines 1994, 42; cf. Bourdieu 1990b). It often suggests concern for the well-being of less wealthy others, a concern sometimes constructed on the basis of empathy born out of donors' own history of poverty (e.g., Caplan 1998, 421, 422; see also Caplan 1985, 174–175). As we will see, all of these elements—the conversion of wealth to moral gifting, the claim of empathy born out of shared hardship, and the potential acquisition of leadership—appear in the discussions surrounding Chellasamy's wedding feast.

Gifting can thus achieve a great deal for the donor who successfully marshals the eye of a relevant public or spiritual audience. It can also, in certain cases, alleviate distress among recipients; this relief may be only sporadic but can also be critical to survival (see Caplan 1998, 423). Gifting produces other outcomes, however, that are less personal and more structural. In particular, philanthropy almost invariably reinforces class relations and ideologies—though, as I will argue, in certain cases it may aim for a contrary egalitarianism.

At the most basic level, philanthropy creates the categories of donors and receivers. As Patricia Caplan points out, in order for donors to avail the potential benefits of gifting, "it is necessary for a class of those in need of social welfare to exist; by being there, by accepting charity, they enable" such benefits. Recipients remain in their dependent position, however, and "social welfare activities thus appear to be very much about defining class relations—a class of givers and one of receivers" (1985, 175). She notes that the ideological import of philanthropy in India is to individualize poverty—to explain it as an "individual failure" rather than the result of "social conditions" (1985, 224; see also Caplan 1998, 414, 425).

Furthermore, philanthropic activities often distinguish between the "deserving" and the "undeserving" poor. Lionel Caplan observed in the 1990s that contemporary charitable organizations still "apply the Victorian notion that only specific categories of poor deserve charitable help"

(1998, 417). Thus the (moral) worthiness of recipients is often a condition for philanthropy as it is for dān (see Bornstein 2009). This worthiness is frequently rooted in class-based values. Charitable activities also include aims at "reform." Here too, donors attempt to remake recipients into proper individuals according to middle- and upper-class values (Caplan 1985).

The Public Wedding Feast

Both weddings and wedding meals are characterized by quite specific social dynamics. Weddings as a whole demonstrate the economic, cultural, and social capital of both families, as we have seen. In this chapter we focus on the meal itself, which plays a crucial role. Appadurai has described the marriage feast as "a quintessentially gastro-political arena . . . because the intimate, private, restricted, and everyday nature of food transactions in the domestic hearth is quite removed from the public, formal, extended, and extraordinary nature of the marriage feast" (1981, 502). Guests, both kin and nonkin, are ranked by, and assert their rank by, negotiating or contesting the mechanisms of the wedding feast. These "mechanisms" include the time it takes to be seated, spatial proximity to the wedding party, amount and quality of food, and servers' levels of generosity (Appadurai 1981, 504–505).

In Chellasamy's case, the complexity of the work done by the ritual of the meal is heightened by the fact that it is a truly *public* meal. Such commensality is rare in domestic spaces, where the likeness of family, caste, and religious community are reproduced (Marriott 1968; Mayer 1970; Osella 2008; Selwyn 1980).[9] Moreover, the public wedding meal's power derives from its demonstration *to* the public of wealth, connections, values, and character.

The symbolic value of the meal is also heightened by the fact that Thevars are not among the Madurai caste communities currently most renowned for philanthropy. (Although they too have a history of "charitable giving"—see Price [2013] and Dirks [1982]—it is not part of their contemporary public image.) "Thevar" is an umbrella term that includes several closely ranked castes sharing some similar history, including classification by the British as "criminal tribes" in the early twentieth century (see Blackburn 1978; Dirks 2001; Pandian 2005, 2009; Shulman 1980). In Madurai today, the communities instead most widely known for philanthropy are Chettiars (of various types) and Nadars. Many of these caste groups' charitable works are large-scale activities such as the endowment of temples, schools, and hospitals. Chellasamy's feast (like the meals eaten at MGR's home) differed significantly from these communities' philanthropy in that it was a single event, not an ongoing service. Yet, as we will see, his act identified him with the giving of these more "honorable" castes, particularly with another Chettiar tradition, that of charitable feeding.

To return, then, to a version of the question I asked at the beginning of this chapter: what is the meaning of a wedding feast to which an urban public is invited? As with other instances of philanthropy or of dān in India, the event may be represented in divergent ways by different participants. Food and feeding can be used to include and enact similarity, or to produce difference and distance. Public meals are typically seen as doing either one or the other. R. S. Khare, for example, has noted that "some give food to assert their social status and privileges while others do so to express equality and nearness" (1986, 278–279). Chellasamy, I will argue, can be seen to be furthering both goals simultaneously.

Considerations of dān, īkai, philanthropy, and wedding meals will be returned to below. For the moment, I will preview the argument to follow by pointing out very briefly the ways that Chellasamy's wedding feast was an atypical example of each. First, although the feast constructs a hierarchical relationship among participants (though in varying ways and degrees, depending on the teller's rhetorical construction), the donors never distinguish between worthy and unworthy recipients (neither in terms of character nor in terms of need). Second, there is no discourse on poverty as individual failure. And finally, there is no publicly apparent attempt to rank wedding guests. Indeed, as I will argue, Chellasamy's feast is represented in many ways—and from multiple perspectives—as dissolving or reducing class difference.

Food, Hunger, and Class Imaginaries: What Kind of Event Was the Public Wedding Feast?

For weeks before his son's wedding in early 2009, Chellasamy used bright banners, posters, and more personal invitations to encourage the public to join the wedding meal. Although I had to be in Chennai during the wedding and could not attend it myself, over the following month I was able to interview Kannan's family, Chellasamy and his older son, and three of Chellasamy's female relatives about the event.

Each set of speakers portrayed the wedding feast according to a different model. Chellasamy and his son represented the feast as *annatānam* (a charitable meal that today is typically put on for the poor by temple donors). His older sister, wife, and daughter-in-law instead portrayed it as *camapanti pōjanam*, a community meal in which diners of diverse castes, classes, and religions sit as equals. Kannan and his family insisted that the feast was neither annatānam nor camapanti pōjanam, arguing instead that they had been invited and honored as guests by the wedding party.

Below I recount the divergent ways in which these three sets of participants represented the wedding feast. Each view reveals a careful positioning in a set of class relationships. The claims draw from a number of sources: kingly models of solidifying followings, patterns of patron–client relations, the cultural performances of anti-caste movements, and weddings as public sites for displaying the standings of guests and hosts alike. In each case, the *relation* between or among participants is key.

CHELLASAMY AND HIS SON

I begin with the story told by the man who sponsored the feast. I became interested in interviewing Chellasamy after seeing the banners announcing the wedding, at a time when I happened to be in Madurai to learn about the kinds of philanthropy carried out by wealthy residents. Talking with Kannan's family about the feast solidified my interest. Arranging a meeting with a major industrialist like Chellasamy, however, was even more complicated and challenging than I anticipated. Using a range of contacts in the city, I tried to reach him, with no success. I then turned to research associate J. Rajasekaran, whose admirable sleuthing and perseverance ultimately proved successful, and gained us access.

The interview took place at Chellasamy's office in the midst of his massive factory. When Rajasekaran and I arrived, we were met by administrators who suspiciously queried our intentions but eventually escorted us to Chellasamy's office, where the industrialist and his older son and an assistant were waiting. There the apparent suspicion vanished, and when Chellasamy learned that I spoke Tamil, he greeted us warmly and proceeded to speak passionately for two hours about his life and his family's most recent wedding. The account that follows is primarily a representation of what Chellasamy conveyed in that oral narrative and in subsequent conversations. Themes of food and hunger were introduced early in the narrative and then repeated frequently.

Chellasamy was born in a Kallar-dominated village west of Madurai. His parents possessed a small amount of land, and his father from time to time owned different businesses, but they made most of their income from moneylending. Chellasamy had two older sisters, one of whom studied to second grade, the other to fifth. He himself studied through the seventh grade, and would have stayed longer if the closing of his school during anti-Hindi violence hadn't coincided with the bankruptcy of his father's small construction company in 1965. His mother, worried about losing her only son, would not let him return to school when the violence ended, and by then they had no funds to pay for school fees in any case because they had sold off her gold to repay the father's debts. From this time Chellasamy recalls his mother telling him every morning, "Just once, before we die, we must see the Meenakshi Amman Temple in Madurai." He commented ruefully, "It was just the Meenakshi Temple—and only 50 km away. That's how things were for someone like me who was born in the village."

In 1968, at age seventeen, Chellasamy was sent to work at a dam construction site for a company owned by his paternal uncle. At first he supervised laborers on the site, but after a year he was moved into the uncle's home to do domestic chores, including taking care of a new baby. This move suggests that Chellasamy was being groomed to marry into the uncle's family, if he proved himself trustworthy, and eventually to be given part of the family property. Chellasamy says that nonetheless he was often treated as a servant, and in particular was given little to eat. Today, he said, he tells his wife that he himself should eat only after their young domestic workers have eaten: "I insist on that [because] I am someone who experienced that hunger as a servant."

In 1974 the uncle bought a large amount of land near Chellasamy's natal village, and installed Chellasamy as the agricultural supervisor of the property. Chellasamy's marriage was arranged by his parents the next year, however, to a nonrelative. In describing his marriage, he anticipated the contrast with his own children's lavish and ceremonious weddings:

> The auspicious time for the marriage was 10:30 A.M. to 12:00 noon. I was working in the fields that morning until 10:00. No shaving or dressing up. I came back, took a pot of water, squatted on the ground, and someone poured the water over me. I bathed and just smoothed my hair with my hand, no comb. I tossed away the hair that came out in my hands while I was walking to the wedding—I didn't even have time to dispose of that. As I got nearer I heard the wedding songs on the records and the percussion instruments, and we went and finished the wedding. After the wedding was over, I had to go visit my father-in-law's house. I went there that night in my boss's car. Then I got up at 4:00 A.M., took a shower, caught the bus back at 5:00, reached here at 6:00, and began my work [in the fields].

Three years later, shortly after his first son was born, Chellasamy was fired from his position as agricultural supervisor. He had recently taken his uncle's son to the cinema in a remote town, traveling by public bus. The uncle's younger brother saw them and told the uncle, "Hey, your son is going out in a town bus like a common laborer. He's gone with another laborer to see a movie." The uncle, furious, said to Chellasamy, "If you stick around here, you will spoil my son, you will spoil my family. You leave tomorrow." Chellasamy, stunned, returned to his parents' home without his uncle's blessing or severance pay, despite his many years of service.

After being treated by his relatives like a "laborer" instead of the "boss's son," and then being cheated by his uncle after almost a decade of painstaking work, Chellasamy says, he set out on his own. Over the next few years he took on different construction-related jobs, and in the 1980s he joined two cousins to establish a construction business, which over the next several years became quite successful. Eventually he struck out on his own again and was looking to diversify his interests. After Chellasamy considered various options that seemed unviable, a relative in the town of Melur suggested he consider the granite business, and by the early 1990s he had established his first quarry.

Telling the story of this new venture, Chellasamy begins not with how he obtained the government permits or extracted the granite, but, strikingly, with how he fed his workers. He had twenty to twenty-five employees, and on the first day that the quarry opened they all ate in a small restaurant in a nearby village. Since Chellasamy was the boss, the others out of respect could not eat until after he had finished, so they then had to hurry their meal and run back to the quarry in the scorching mid-day heat to return to work on time. "This pained me," he says. "Then I thought of an idea. Instead of eating in this little restaurant, we can cook our meals ourselves." So he and one of his workers went down to Madurai, bought all the necessary cooking equipment, purchased a sack of rice and vegetables, and started a canteen on their worksite. He says that he told his worker, "Hey, you are going to cook tomorrow morning. However you cook it, it's okay with me. Even if all you make is rice gruel (kanci), I'll eat it." Everything was cooked in the open air, "and it was good." Soon, Chellasamy built a thatched shed and employed a real cook. It was simple local food, and then "little by little it picked up." The next step was to put up plastic sheeting to provide better shade for workers while they ate, then a tile roof, and eventually a strong concrete roof. Step by step, they had a real canteen.

Today, Chellasamy owns an extensive factory and warehouse in addition to his many quarries. His factory employs thousands of workers. After our interview, Chellasamy's assistants took Rajasekaran and me on an extended tour of the factory. The last stop was the kitchen, at the heart of the complex. All employees receive a free meal each day. That evening, vegetables were being prepared for the next day's cooking. Massive piles of produce were clustered on a cloth on the floor. The vegetables were quite fresh; Chellasamy had said he bought local, in-season produce to keep costs down and quality high. I remember seeing immense piles of beets, green chiles, and bottle gourds, and a mound of garlic that was 10 feet in diameter. Along the walls, enormous stainless steel pots were stacked in shining rows. The kitchen rooms, like the factory sheds, were spotlessly clean. In fact, they were the cleanest kitchens I have ever seen—including the several well maintained institutional kitchens in which I have worked in the United States.

Feeding, already a continuing theme in Chellasamy's description of his life, was an important element of his children's weddings. For each, he invited the public to eat at the marriage. For his daughter's recent wedding, he had booked three large marriage halls to accommodate the crowd. For the younger son's wedding in 2009, Chellasamy rented an expansive exhibition ground and erected temporary structures for the wedding rituals and meals. Large banners bearing an image of Chellasamy and announcing the wedding were placed at major crossroads around the city, and posters were plastered on walls in many lower-income neighborhoods. The banners announced free performances by actors, dancers, and musicians at one of the city's largest stadiums for the two days prior to the wedding. Banners and posters also invited the public to eat at the wedding, and, as with all the individual wedding invitations Chellasamy sent out to relatives, friends, employees, and acquaintances, they stated, "Please no gifts [*tayavuceytu anpaḷippu vēṇṭām*]." In a restaging of standard gift practices at marriages, the gift was meant to come from Chellasamy to his guests—including the people at large.

When I asked Chellasamy what led him to feed the public at his children's weddings, he replied, "God has given so much to this ordinary laborer, and we [our family] are well off. Our act of annatānam should allow many people to eat well." The idea of doing annatānam, he said, developed from his own early experience of hunger. It also came from practices of feeding employees at the granite factory, where workers receive coffee at 10:00, lunch at 1:00, tea at 4:00, and a packet of milk or biscuits to take home. One day while he was at work in the factory, Chellasamy recalled, the idea of doing annatānam at his children's weddings "just came. That is, we have to live well . . . I am happy, and [I did this] thinking everyone should become happy." Then he expanded, "We should be remembered after our death. Our name must be remembered."

Annatānam is the dān of food, often stated to be the best of all dān. It is a gift of "sustaining substance" (Copeman 2011, 1068), a gift that "facilitate[s] the cycle of life" (Ramanujan 1992, 244). In Tamil Nadu this act of charitable feeding is typically carried out in Hindu temples by high-caste temple donors for the sake of the poor. In Madurai, the Nattukottai Chettiars have a well-documented, centuries-long history of performing dān in the surrounding region (Rudner 1987), and they have been called the "great performers" of annatānam (Moreno 1992, 162). In recent years, politicians too have sponsored annatānam feasts, in a widening range of venues, including mosques, churches, and railway stations.[10]

While most scholarly discussions of annatānam's outcomes focus on the karmic merit that donors accrue (see, e.g., Khare 1992, 208; Ramanujan 1992, 244–249), this element was absent from Chellasamy's discourse. Instead, Chellasamy spoke openly about what he hoped to achieve in this world—for himself as well as for the recipients. He hoped for his own posterity, using the Tamil word *pēr* that literally means "name" but also signifies reputation and renown. He also desired, he said, to alleviate the hunger of people whose suffering he himself has experienced, and to share his current happiness with the "common people" from whom he has come. He appeared to derive significant personal satisfaction from accomplishing these goals.

Like other forms of individual philanthropy, the feast may also produce additional returns for the donor. Without question it demonstrates Chellasamy's wealth. In a society where philanthropy is a sign of personal character, it creates a "name" for Chellasamy in the present, not merely in the future, enhancing his reputation among peers and others alike. (The honorable character that it demonstrates is, I believe, especially significant for a Thevar/Kallar donor whose caste is not now associated with the high-status gifting of annatānam.) In so doing, it may also create a political or quasi-political following for Chellasamy, utilizing both historical and contemporary Tamil models of political patronage. Finally—and in this respect it is crucially distinct from the type of feast described below by Chellasamy's female family members and by Kannan's family—as a type of dān, it by definition creates a hierarchy between donor and recipients.

In sum, Chellasamy's representation of the feast-as-gift and of its benefits reveals expectations of this-worldly benefits for himself and for recipients, employing a hierarchical model of the relationship between donor and recipients. Interestingly, however, it also contains strong elements of identification and sameness with recipients, emphasizing a common history of hunger and hardship, and a desire to share his current good fortune with those who still suffer.

CHELLASAMY'S SISTER, WIFE, AND DAUGHTER-IN-LAW

At the end of our interview, Chellasamy invited me to come to his house the following day and meet "the women in my family." Arriving at Chellasamy's grand home the next evening, I found each of his three children and their spouses there, along with Chellasamy's wife and one of his older sisters. After touring the lavishly designed and decorated house, I sat down to talk about the wedding with Chellasamy's older sister, his wife, and his first daughter-in-law. His sister Devakiammal still lives near the village home in which she and her brother grew up, but she visits Chellasamy frequently; both Chellasamy's account from the previous day and his actions that evening suggested a tight and affectionate bond between them. His more urbanized wife, Selvi, comes from a village near Chellasamy's, and studied through the sixth grade. Their daughter-in-law Meena grew up in a nearby city, and like Chellasamy's own daughter and the new daughter-in-law, she had studied through the tenth grade.

Intriguingly, when I asked these three women to talk about "the annatānam," adopting the term that Chellasamy had used to describe the feast, all of them objected immediately. Meena, the daughter-in-law, adamantly protested that the meal was not annatānam because calling it that would denote charity. She argued, "We have embraced them [the diners] as a member of our family and we are sharing with them. If it were annatānam, it would create a division, so we embraced them as family members."

Devakiammal, whose presence dominated the group, stoutly agreed. Rather than annatānam, she said, this was camapanti pōjanam, a meal in which people of different statuses and groups eat together as equals and are seated without ranked differentiation. "In the village, at a wedding," she explained, "you invite everyone, even the people you have conflicts with. They come, and you can't tell them to go away, and you forget the conflicts for as long as the wedding lasts. You make peace by sharing food. It's a village tradition. You invite people from all the groups in the village, and whatever is going on, the good and the bad, they take part in it."

Camapanti pōjanam is indeed used as a way of healing rifts in communities.[11] It is also used as a means of asserting equality across lines of difference or in the face of discrimination. "Inter-caste dining" was employed from the 1890s onward by several sections of the Dravidian Movement, especially (beginning in the 1920s) by the Self-Respect Movement (Baker 1976, 86; Paulraj 1995, 109, 113; Ram 1979). The movement was led by E. V. Ramasamy, who promoted rationalist, atheist, anti-caste, and feminist principles and practices. N. Ram has argued that activities such as camapanti pōjanam are representative of "the assertion of democratic cultural elements in Tamil society" with which Ramasamy and his followers identified themselves (Ram 1979, 393). Like annatānam, camapanti meals are still used by contemporary political leaders to build or solidify their followings.[12]

Why, I wondered, did they want to hold camapanti pōjanam at the wedding? Devakiammal replied, "We hope that good [*nallatu*] will come to us. If we feed all the poor and destitute people, we hope that some good will happen to us. When we don't see people as either poor or rich, when we treat them all the same as equals, when we have them sit together and eat, those people will talk about it, right? So good will come to us." Her brother's wife Selvi quietly but firmly agreed.

Thus all three women resisted the model of annatānam because it is inherently hierarchical. Even in those cases of dān where recipients are not intended to take on troublesome inauspiciousness, they are always structurally poised as inferior. Hosting camapanti pōjanam, on the other hand, is a way of including diverse others in a meal without formally marking distinctions among the diners or between the host and other diners. Because of the power of commensality, those who partake of the feast signal that they are willing to overcome any conflicts among individuals or communities, at least for the period of the meal. The camapanti also states unequivocally that all diners are equal despite their differences in rank.

Furthermore, annatānam today is commonly perceived to carry the stigma of poverty. In insisting that this meal was not a form of charity but an egalitarian community gathering, Meena refused either to distance herself and her affines from co-diners or to characterize those diners as poor. Indeed, she stated that the diners became part of her family. Devakiammal, who is of a different generation and has a very different habitus, was more (candidly?) willing to refer to recipients as poor, but she too emphasized the significance of treating people of different classes equally. In sum, these women positioned themselves as members of a community on par with all other members.

Interestingly, however, even though these women and Chellasamy represented the feast using quite different models, they all identified two similar outcomes: creating positive impacts for other people, and building renown for themselves. In addition to constructing a harmonious community, the women expected to create a good name for the family, and to garner the praise not only of those who attended but of other Madurai residents as well. Such a meal, they believed, demonstrates the family's wealth, civic-mindedness, and inclusive, egalitarian ethos.

KANNAN AND HIS FAMILY

One of the people who responded to the banners and posters put up by Chellasamy was Kannan. He and his two daughters, son-in-law, and two older grandchildren attended the wedding feast. I interviewed them about the feast a few weeks later, before I had spoken with Chellasamy and his family.

Kannan grew up in a similar caste and in roughly similar economic circumstances to Chellasamy's. He had left his lower-middle-class family (whose income appears to have been more stable than Chellasamy's parents') when he married at age fourteen. His first work as a bicycle rickshaw driver was significantly lower in status than that of an agricultural supervisor, though within a few years he had left manual labor behind by gaining the skills and license to drive an autorickshaw.

Kannan had attended both of the previous Chellasamy family wedding feasts on his own (and he reported that they were less elaborate). Before this final wedding, he had noticed the posters in his neighborhood and in other parts of the city, but he decided to take his entire family to the wedding only after an event that occurred one week before the marriage. Kannan recounted this event with some wonder. He had been sitting outside a wedding hall with other auto drivers, he said, all of them waiting on that hot afternoon for guests to exit the marriage hall. Another auto, lavishly decorated with garlands and equipped with double loudspeakers, drove by announcing the upcoming wedding feast of Chellasamy's son. The vehicle stopped near the drivers, and all of a sudden Chellasamy himself stepped down and said, "All of you auto drivers, please come [to the wedding]. Everyone come. It is our [*namma*] wedding.[13] Please don't think you shouldn't come just because I invited you at your auto stand, and I haven't given you a [printed] invitation. You all belong to my family. Bring all of your people." Then, Kannan said, Chellasamy called over a tea vendor riding by on a bicycle, and "he bought himself a tea and drank it." During our interview, Kannan's daughter Prema explained the import of this act: "Look at how natural and humble he was. Right? He drank his tea right along with us [i.e., people like us], didn't he? He is a very unassuming person." Kannan added, "I have never gone to any event like this before and I had never taken my family to such a wedding. He is such a gentleman. He personally invited each of us to come. That was a shock."

After the personal invitation, Kannan's whole family was eager to attend. His daughter Bhumati had heard her co-workers telling stories of Chellasamy's wealth and generosity, talking with great anticipation about the wedding, making her family even more eager. On the day of the wedding, the family dressed in their best clothes. Excited, but uncertain of how they would be treated, they arrived at the exhibition grounds at 11:00 A.M., just as the priests completed the wedding rituals. They described with pleasure the "super" decorations at the grounds. They were welcomed, escorted into the dining area, and immediately shown to a table, where servers began to place a sequence of dishes on banana leaves. The meal included, in order, peanut candy, soup with "a large piece of meat," a chicken leg and thigh, a bottle of mineral water, mutton curry, mutton biriyani with a boiled egg and condiments, chicken biriyani, plain rice, another mutton curry (this one with bone sauce), goat intestine sauce, rasam, buttermilk, and sambar. (They reported additional options for vegetarians.) This rich meal finally ended with ice cream. Bhumati said, "They told us, 'You can eat as much as you want.' The servers kept coming back and asking what we wanted." Prema added, "It's not just serving some sambar [spiced lentil sauce] and mixing up some payasam [milk-and-tapioca pudding]. If *we* had to cook this kind of food, it would cost at least 300 rupees. Even middle-class families like ours can only afford to spend that much on meat at Deepavali,[14] but these people have served such expensive food for the entire day, for [so many] families." Kannan's daughters emphasized that all of this was given without expectation of return. The posters, they recalled, had insisted on "no gifts" and "no moy."

Amazed as Kannan's family was by the feast, however, they effused most about the treatment they received. When they arrived at the venue, they were greeted warmly by Chellasamy's representatives, and welcomed "just like the closest family members usually are." Kannan described the scene: "Everyone ate together. They treated all their guests alike [*avaṅka kesṭu orē mātiri*]. There were no segregated spaces for VIPs, for company employees; everyone was absolutely equal [*carikku camamā*]. All the people who don't have enough to eat, rich people, people adorned with jewelry, the family's own relatives, the company employees . . . all were equal. All the well-to-do people can sit at this table, and all the poor people can sit here too. Everyone has the same standing." Bhumati interjected, "They acted like, 'You are as important to me as all the other people. . . . Because you have come, we see you as our guest. We have invited you. Come and eat your fill. . . . All we wish is your heartfelt blessings' . . . We didn't expect that in a million years."

While Kannan's family attended the feast with an air of having been accorded respect simply by being invited, they would also have expected the usual "gastro-politics." That is, they understood that they would receive less honor than other guests who were wealthier or more closely related to the hosts. They were surprised and pleased, therefore, to find that they observed no distinctions in how guests were treated, and that all were embraced—as Chellasamy and his daughter-in-law also claimed—as family members.[15]

This sameness despite the differences of class was key to the family's description of and response to the feast. So too was their representation of themselves as guests—and insistently not as recipients of charity. When I first saw them a few days after the wedding and asked them about the annatānam, they swiftly responded that they hadn't attended any annatānam; instead, they had been guests at a wedding (*"annatānam ille, kalyānam. namma keṣṭu-tān"*). Whereas receiving tānam or charity is stigmatized, being invited as a guest is a position of honor. Such an invitation demonstrates worth, standing, and a relationship to the host. Thus we can understand Kannan's pleasure at Chellasamy's personal invitation to the auto drivers, and his family's repeated description of themselves as guests accorded the same respect as all other guests.

The family had several explanations for why they thought Chellasamy had sponsored such a feast, including both tangible and intangible benefits. These had to do with his character, life experiences, and potential economic and political gains. First and foremost, Kannan said, Chellasamy is a good man, a *nallavar*. "He is good to the public. Isn't he doing good things for the common people?" Kannan speculated that it made most sense to carry out such public philanthropy at a wedding. If Chellasamy had simply offered a public feast in the absence of such an occasion, "without a reason" or "just to show off" his wealth, income tax officials might become suspicious about where the money originated. But "since this is his own family function, he could do anything there without warranting attention." (Kannan may also have been implying that the largesse was a way of disposing of black money. But he never said this directly, and emphasized only the goodness of the act.) He immediately added, "This will look like something good. People will praise him and they will bless him for having a good heart. He will keep a good reputation." Kannan also pointed out that such spending could gain Chellasamy public support should he later run for office.

Most of all, they emphasized the childhood experiences that made Chellasamy care for the common people today. Bhumati, for example, said, "He suffered since childhood. He struggled, and then became successful. So [he wonders], what can he do to help the struggling people? . . . Material gifts won't reach everyone, and food in a temple would feed only about ten [people]. But for him this was a long-held dream. What is the most important part of a wedding? It is the feast. We get the biggest satisfaction from feeding our stomachs. Annatānam is the best of all the tānam." Her mother Vellaiamma added, "When he was young, he was breaking stones for only 50 paise a day. Today he has advanced to where he can give a feast to 50,000 people. You can see how hard he has worked to make it here." Kannan capped off the narrative, stating, "He was hungry growing up. That's why he understands poor people's hardships really well."[16] They went on to praise Chellasamy's extensive factory and warehouses, his equipment and trucks, and his palatial home. All of this wealth they learned about, they said, at the wedding. (It was only later that Kannan would visit Chellasamy's home—first when he drove me there to meet and interview Chellasamy's family, and two years later when he and his wife delivered an invitation to Prema's wedding.)

Why were Kannan, Bhumati, and Prema determined to portray themselves as guests rather than as recipients of annatānam (with the striking exception of Bhumati's final comment, which I will address shortly)? To accept annatānam is to accept a depiction of oneself as in need, but to be a guest implies recognition as something definitively other than poor. Indeed, they felt affirmingly recognized as human beings, as people of social and moral worth. Even beyond this was the honor of being invited to a wedding. Kannan and his family describe— with wonder and "shock"—how Chellasamy has put himself at their level, and how his family has made them feel equal with all other guests. They explain this move toward equivalence as a product of Chellasamy's own childhood poverty and hunger, and of the desire rooted in this to share his wealth with others who know hunger. Here, Bhumati's reference to annatānam makes sense when we remember the rhetorical history of hunger as the greatest of all forms of suffering, and that gifts that alleviate hunger—annatānam—are life-giving because they "tackle all other forms of suffering too" (Raman 2013, 3). Both Chellasamy's and Kannan's family's versions of Chellasamy's life are stories of advancement—from semi-impoverished rurality to wealthy urbanity, from hard childhood labor to adult mega-wealth—and both intentionally demonstrate how he still identifies with the poor. Kannan's family, like Chellasamy himself, constructs identification through hard work, poverty, and especially that greatest of hardships, hunger (just as Kannan had done with MGR, when talking with me years earlier).

What does their account of the feast tell us about the outcomes for the donors? Kannan's family members believe Chellasamy may receive material gains, such as support for political office, in line with longstanding models of gift-giving to followers/constituents (see note 4 in this chapter) (though they pointed out correctly that Chellasamy has so far turned down requests to stand for elected positions). Most of all, however, they believe he gains personal satisfaction from feeding people. They tie both the desire to feed the public and the satisfaction that Chellasamy feels to a childhood of putative poverty and hunger, experiences of hardship that create an identification between Chellasamy and illātavaṅka (as in Prema's description of his drinking tea at the auto stand). Judging by this family's response (and by the friends', neighbors', and co-workers' responses they described), Chellasamy indeed acquires significant praise, fame, and "name" from his gift, and his own representation of his motivation for giving is narrated very similarly by those who praise him.

What the Meal Did

We have here three vitally different representations of a public meal. In the abstract, annatānam expresses hierarchy and difference; camapanti pōjanam, equality and sameness; and guests invited by a host, degrees of respect and honor. Intriguingly, however, the ways in which the three parties use these terms demonstrate that the models are not entirely distinct from one another. There are in fact notable overlaps among them. Annatānam and camapanti pōjanam bring "good" to the family. Camapanti pōjanam and the host/guest model are both described as creating equality among participants, who receive equal treatment despite the differences that rank them as superior and inferior in other contexts; both are also said to enfold diners into the family. The descriptions in this chapter of annatānam and of host/guest emphasize the donor's/host's desire for participants to gain happiness, the personal satisfaction gained by the donor/host, and the creation of a following for the generous giver. Finally, all three models of a public meal are said to create name and renown for the giver, and all three sets of speakers emphasize the meal as a gift given without desire for reciprocity.

As I noted at the outset, food and feeding can be used to include others and enact similarity, or to produce difference, distance, and hierarchy. While public meals are generally regarded as doing one or the other, Chellasamy's feast seems to have accomplished both, and I believe Chellasamy's success in this is unusual. This industrialist could have demonstrated his wealth and generosity, gained renown, and developed himself as a patron through any number of standard philanthropic acts, such as endowing a hospital, sponsoring a temple or church festival, or donating books to schoolchildren. But because he used *food*, he was able to connect himself with diners through a mutually imagined shared hunger, create an egalitarian setting by mixing diners and treating them equivalently, and simultaneously heighten his own prestige.

At one level, this account is yet another example of an act of philanthropy or dān whose meaning is contested by the donor and the recipients (though it is also a case in which the sponsors disagree *among themselves* about the meaning of the event). Most interesting to me, however, are the unusual messages about class that the feast communicates. Unlike most forms of Indian philanthropy, there is no hint here of reproducing the standard dominant class values. There are no patronizing lessons about hygiene or money management, and in particular Chellasamy makes no distinction between the deserving and undeserving poor (points that also, from what I can gather, were true of MGR's meals for his fans). Instead, Chellasamy asserts values he claims from childhood of the valorization of common people, including those who are poor and hungry. Both his words and his acts show him trying to give back to people like him. Gifting, as Haynes observes, "generate[s] moral relationships" (1987, 339n. 1). The morality of Chellasamy's act is, in the most basic terms, to feed and perform identity with those who need food. Likewise, his family's evocation of camapanti pōjanam creates an identification with participants at the feast. And Kannan's family's response shows the success of the enacted ethos of egalitarianism, even as it re-interprets the event in an idiom of honor. Each set of participants has created somewhat hybrid models of gifting, and their strategies in doing so have produced recognition, regard, and dignity for all participants—givers and receivers alike.

The Impulse to Bind across Boundaries

Chellasamy's gift of food, like MGR's in the past, creates inclusion across lines of class difference. The sameness derives from highly successful representations of shared histories of hardship and hunger. Both Chellasamy's own version of his life history and Kannan's family's account of it are stories of dramatic upward mobility, from rural semi-servitude to massive urban wealth. MGR's political organs and his fans also constructed fairly similar stories (with some disavowal, however, of the wealth that MGR accrued). The key to the glorification accomplished by these stories is that each man remains identified with the poor even after achieving power and position, and this identification is located in memories of deprivation and struggle, focused especially on hunger. The gifts of food, accepted by recipients, produce value for Chellasamy in the form of renown (Munn 1986) not only for his wealth but also for his inclusive and egalitarian impulses.

This paci discourse not only provides legitimacy for donors and their wealth. It also allows recipients—guests—to feel included rather than "aided." In each of the three sets of participants' models of these events, recipients are given a form of parity. They are included in the family of Chellasamy. Ignoring or breaking boundaries between people enacts love and intimacy (Trawick 1990), and no sign of this is more powerful than commensality. Here, this mixing (kalattal) creates a sense of sameness, of similarity, of oneness in the memory (or reality) of paci. The forms of īkai, dān, and philanthropy that characterized these gifts are especially striking because they were (intentionally) enacted and received in ways that provided recognition of worth and bestowed dignity on those who received the gifts.

Here, then, we have an impulse, and a process, in direct contradistinction to the creation of exclusion described in chapter 6. It is also, in fact, a process that differs from much formal gifting. Rather than setting themselves off from class others, all those who discursively create the gifting by Chellasamy are constructing inclusion through an idiom of sameness despite the acknowledgment of difference. Moreover, they do so without any negative moralizing in these relationships, either up or down the hierarchy. Of course these accounts and events also produce distinction and value for the donors—and not just as an unintended, undesired byproduct; it seems inarguable that public philanthropy is not used intentionally as both a striking form of cultural capital and a demonstration of economic capital—but it does so with a rhetoric and, I would contend, even a goal that is far different from that of the policing of class boundaries. And while Chellasamy's gift enacts different class dynamics than do most philanthropic gifts, the fact that it draws from significant historical models, and coexists with contemporary political examples, demonstrates that it is neither idiosyncratic nor unique.

It also returns us to a point I made in chapter 1, that just as the poor are who they are because of their relation to the wealthy, the reverse is also necessarily true. Here, Chellasamy and his family define themselves in relation to those they help. Not only are they wealthy because they control the labor of others and extract a profit from that labor; they also gain pēr and, at least in some quarters, mariyātai because of their gift to the poor. The different classes substantiate each other.

This brings us to a final point. The value Chellasamy and his family receive from their gift of food is not only the display of wealth. They are also recognized as moral people despite their wealth and their caste. Because Kannan and other guests praise the feast, the honor of attending it, and the egalitarian treatment they observed there, the inclusive elements in both of the models put forth by the family members (annatānam and camapanti pōjanam) are borne out. By "tak[ing] on the role of equal," Kannan and other guests like him allow "the person extending the offer the satisfaction of adequate recognition" (Sayer 2005b, 171). Dignity, then, is important not only to the guests who are recognized as guests, but also to the donors who feel recognized as the wealthy givers they wish to be seen as: here, a moral wealthy man (and his family) who cares about people who struggled as he did.

9 Conclusions

When Anjali introduced me to Murugan in 1999, both young people were working in the same office building. Each would soon establish an independent business. Murugan created a partnership with a still photographer, and within a decade he had set up his own business with three employees. I hired him myself to record my son's first and tenth birthday parties in Madurai (in 2000 and in 2009). The two recordings, the first a video and the second a DVD, demonstrate a deft flair with both technologies. Murugan's success as a videographer—his sense of style, his growing clientele, and most of all his expertise with the technologies themselves—marked him as a "modern" person.

It was several years before I watched the tenth birthday party DVD. (I had shared it with relatives, but having been at the party myself, I didn't think to watch the recording until writing the conclusion of this book.) To my surprise, the DVD included footage of *two* events. Murugan had presented me a gift by adding a recording of his family's *kula teyvam* (ancestral deity) festival procession, held in a village outside Madurai in February 2009, a ceremony that my family and I had attended with him. Murugan had appended, to the modern birthday party, a village festival that he would later describe to me as the antithesis of modernity, and one that would soon raise his own fears of being seen as unmodern and unworthy of middle-class standing. This concluding chapter is the story of how Murugan became a fierce god's dancer and yet remained middle class. It is also a reflection on how this accomplishment complicates our understanding of class boundaries, categories, and moralizing; and on how tight the connection between dignity and capital may sometimes be.

The God and His Ritual Dancer

Rajan, Murugan's father, had been the hereditary cāmiyāṭi or "god dancer" for their lineage's kula teyvam since 1974. The *āṭṭam*, the "dance" of possession, serves both dancer and audience as "the medium for an intimate knowledge of divinity" (Ram 2013, 112). Ritual possession provides the cāmiyāṭi "a way of reaching out to a deity and making him or her come alive to all who are gathered to witness the power" (Ram 2012, 204).

It also allows worshippers direct access to the deity's knowledge during rituals in which they individually ask about the future (*kuri kēḷu*) and the god provides answers and guidance (*kuri collu*).

The deity, Sudalai Madan (*Cuṭalai Māṭan*), sometimes called Madasamy, is one of the powerful "fierce gods" (*māṭans*) of the region. Madasamy resides in many Tamil-speaking areas, and is sometimes said to be the "head" or "chief" of the māṭans in a particular area (e.g., John 2008, 125). Fierce gods often serve as guardians for *amman* mother goddesses (like Karumariamman, whose festival I attended with Lakshmi), their images situated immediately outside the goddess's shrine or temple (Mines 2005, 131). In Murugan's kula teyvam temple, however, Sudalai Madan is the presiding deity, ensconced at the center of the temple and flanked by numerous other fierce gods *and* by the local goddess. Fierce gods inhere in the soil of a village, and this Sudalai Madan had been carried by Murugan's ancestors in a handful of earth when they migrated "centuries ago" from Thiruchendur in southern Tamil Nadu (a region that many Nadars, including Murugan's family, consider their homeland). Virtually all the 100 or so families of the *uravinmurai* (the lineage) have moved away from this village, in search of "better jobs" and "modern work," according to Anjali, and they return only for annual temple festivals. In much of Tamil Nadu, such festivals are called *koṭais*, a Tamil word for gift (see note 7 in chapter 8), in this case a gift to the deity.

Sudalai Madan's origin myths usually describe him as a son of Shiva and Parvati (see Bonta 2005; John 2008),[1] but he hardly bears the upright comportment that their sons Ganesh and Murugan generally do. Cuṭalai means "cremation ground," and this son feasts on the bones and ashes of burned corpses. Like other māṭans he is "as unpredictable and unstable as anger itself," and may either "protect or attack" those who propitiate him (Mines 2005, 131; see also Masilamani-Meyer 2004, 29; Ram 2013, 227). Eveline Masilamani-Meyer contends that a god like Madasamy "has two aspects: the negative and the positive, while at the same time also transcending the duality . . . he or she is the malignant spirit and the force that counteracts it. As a malignant spirit the deity is feared, as a force that can deal with the negative powers, the deity is worshipped" (2004, 68).

Māṭans are worshipped almost entirely by people of lower castes, though feared by almost all. The same continuum of coolness/passivity and heatedness/activity that distinguishes humans along caste and class lines (see chapter 6) correlates closely with the primary deities that families worship. Thus the more respectably conformist deities worshipped by the upper castes are calm, contained, and vegetarian (they include, in addition to Shiva and Parvati, deities such as Vishnu and his avatars, Lakshmi, and Saraswati). In contrast, the deities of the lower castes—such as māṭans and most ammans—are often quick to anger, and their heated character may require animal sacrifices in appeasement (see also Blackburn 1981; Inglis 1985). Yet while māṭans may have less orthodox genealogies—some upper-caste Hindus contend they are not "real" Hindu gods at all, and many refer to them as pēys, "demons"—they tend to be much more active and powerful in everyday affairs than are the more reserved deities (Mines 2005).

Generally, only lower-caste bodies can withstand the heat of the fierce gods' possession. Indeed, possession by any deity or other supernatural being is associated more with lower- and middle-caste people than with upper-caste people, given its association with loss of control, dissolution of the self, and internal heat. (Nonetheless, people of higher castes—especially women—do sometimes become possessed; see, e.g., Hancock [1995, 62]; Harper [1963]. Furthermore, recall that not just Lakshmi but also her sons had been possessed by the goddess when they walked the fire in Hosur; and Anjali recently told me that two of her older brothers are cāmiyāṭis for their kula teyvam.) During a māṭan festival, the god inhabits his human vessel in order to carry out his work. He demonstrates his strength and ferocity; answers worshippers' questions about the future, giving them guidance about what to do in their lives; and vigilantly guards the village borders, protecting against the incursions of demons and other maleficent forces.

Murugan's father, Rajan, a retired truck and car driver, had been cāmiyāṭi for this Sudalai Madan for thirty-six years. To be accepted as cāmiyāṭi by a god confers great prestige within the rural and/or lineal community because it "indicates the superior moral virtue and 'purity' of the person who is possessed" (Kapadia 1996, 426). The role normally passes from father to eldest son, but Rajan inherited the position from his uncle (his periyappā, father's older brother). Rajan told me that the god did not "grab" or possess (piṭikkalle) his uncle's son, implying that the uncle's son was not "clean" enough. Rajan explained that he himself never smoked, drank, or lied, and therefore the deity accepted him as cāmiyāṭi. The 2009 koṭai was expected to be Rajan's last turn in this role. He was then sixty-eight years old, and he hoped that Murugan, his only son, would soon replace him.

The 2009 *Koṭai* Procession

Like most kula teyvam festivals, the Sudalai Madan koṭai lasts for three days (beginning, in this case, on the evening of Shivarattiri, an annual Hindu festival in honor of Shiva). While certain koṭai rituals are attended only by the cāmiyāṭis, most are open to all members of the uravinmurai and their guests. During the final day, affinal relatives from outside the lineage often attend the temple rituals as well, and the gods' grace is also extended to residents of the village during the final circumambulatory procession.

In 2009, I had the chance to watch the final procession, an important protective ritual (*pātukāppu*) during which the god inspects the borders of the village and drives away any demonic pēys (a term that, as I noted, some people in Tamil Nadu would apply to Sudalai Madan as well) and any other threats to the village. Murugan invited Anjali's family, my family, and some visiting friends. He drove us all to his lineage temple, in a village about an hour south of Madurai, using a borrowed van. As soon as we drove into the village we could see that, unlike most Madasamy temples, this one stands in a densely settled part of the village, rather than on the far perimeter or in a wasteland area.

We had brought with us a garland (*mālai*) of marigolds as an offering to the deity. Heading immediately into the temple, we added our mālai to the many already placed on the fearsome black image of Madasamy, adorned with his festival finery—gleaming silver eyes, eyebrows, forehead "ash" stripes, mustache, and fangs. Murugan then led us to the adjoining hall to sit with other diners and eat a delicious meal of mutton curry (made from goats sacrificed the previous night), rice, yogurt with raw onions, and buttermilk. Touring the temple after the meal, we threaded around the outside of the temple to a large covered area in the back, where several additional shrines had been decorated (including a simpler, nonanthropomorphic shrine for Madasamy).

When we came back into the temple proper, we found Rajan and five other cāmiyāṭis (each the dancer for a specific deity) donning their *vēcam*, ceremonial clothing consisting primarily of embroidered and appliqued red or black pants, and muslin strips crossed diagonally over the dancers' torso and shoulders. Rajan, as the lead cāmiyāṭi, also wore a shimmering red hat. The temple soon filled with incense, and as the pitch of the nagaswaram reed instruments heightened and the udukkai drum was pounded with increasing intensity, the cāmiyāṭis and other vow-takers became possessed. The god dancer for Karuppusamy ("Black God") swayed so violently that he had to be supported upright. An old man among the onlookers suddenly screamed and jutted through the crowd with his arms angled rigidly in front of him. The Karuppusamy cāmiyāṭi let out a guttural yell and danced around the crowded enclosure, arms stretched overhead and an *aruval* (a sickle-type knife) gripped at both ends. Most of the other cāmiyāṭis followed quickly.

Rajan's possession was slower. As the audience leaned in toward the tall black statue of Madasamy, we watched as the god began to descend (*eranku*) on his cāmiyāṭi. Rajan's body stayed very still for a time, then

Photo 6. Garlanded Madasamy image and ritual attendant, 2015. Photo credit: Sara Dickey.

became more animated, swaying and hopping, eyes far away. Bells were rung, loudly and irregularly, ramping up the pulsing sound in the temple. Around Rajan, the younger cāmiyāṭis were already lunging frenetically, many waving sickles or stakes. Then, as Madasamy's aruval was placed in Rajan's hand, the god descended fully. Rajan's eyes closed, then opened

Photo 7. Rajan as Madasamy giving ash during the procession, 2009. Photo credit: Pamelia Edgerton.

and rolled back; he gave one brief stretch of the arms and a sharp yell, and from that moment Rajan was the god.

All those who were possessed now filed out (in a rather rambunctious file) to begin circumambulating the scrub fields outside the village. By this time it was very hot, over 100 degrees Fahrenheit, and they had a long procession ahead. Music played on loudspeakers, and I recognized one song from an old MGR movie. But rather than following the crowd this day, I retired with my son, Daniel, who was sick with a cough, to a nearby shop for a cool drink. My partner, Punnie, continued with the procession.

Years later, watching the DVD, I would observe that all the possessed participants became placid as soon as they entered the road. A streaming tail of villagers and uravinmurai members followed them. Rajan/Madasamy led the procession, stately and calm, stopping at the temple of every deity on the route. Periodically the cāmiyāṭis would also halt in other places where villagers had gathered. At each stop, women ran out and poured cooling turmeric water on the feet of all those who were possessed, while other women ululated. Women, girls, and boys touched the feet of the cāmiyāṭis as they asked for guidance on urgent matters and requested predictions (kuri) about the future.[2] They were thus able, as Edward Harper observed years earlier, "to speak to the deity personally and to receive an immediate reply" (1963, 166). Rajan rubbed sacred ash on the foreheads of all. There was little sound, other than the villagers' requests and brief ululations, murmured answers from the cāmiyāṭis, and an occasional hoot from Rajan.

The cāmiyāṭis and vow-takers became wildly active again as they returned to the temple, passing Daniel and me on their way. Some had to be held as they entered to avoid falling or striking onlookers. Inside, they crouched on the ground as dozens of women poured pot after pot of turmeric water over their bodies. They remained possessed, however, and became relinquished by their deities only as they walked clockwise around Madasamy's central shrine.

The Videographer Possessed

In March 2009, a few weeks after the procession, Murugan talked to me about watching the festival as a child. He described what it had been like to watch his father as cāmiyāṭi.

> MURUGAN: Back then, when we were young, we got scared if we saw him. We wouldn't go near the dancers. They would put on costumes [vēcam]. Even if someone told us, "Hey, that's just your father," we'd refuse to get close and we'd run away. Later, we got used to it bit by bit, and it became normal.

SARA: Did you tell your classmates?

MURUGAN: Yes.

SARA: How did they react?

MURUGAN: They respected it [*mariyātai varum*]. Even now, that's how people respond about my father.

Yet Murugan anticipated neither respect nor prestige for himself if he inherited his father's position. Murugan—a dutiful son who had continued to live with his parents after his marriage, and had contributed willingly to his six sisters' dowries—was reluctant to take on this family responsibility. "Now that my father has retired as the cāmiyāṭi, our entire lineage wants me to be the next one. But I can't imagine it," he said somewhat sheepishly. "I am too modern, so how can I take on that wild village practice? And I don't like to put on those costumes, it's embarrassing [*caṅkaṭam*]." Murugan was dreading the loss of dignity that would come from having people outside his lineage think of him as a backward, disorderly god dancer. After a pause, he reflected, "But if the god chooses me, I can't refuse."

Murugan explained that "all the relatives" in the uravinmurai would soon gather to select the next cāmiyāṭi. Since he did not want the position, they would first consider other members of the patriline. If someone else agreed to take it on, Murugan would be asked for his opinion of that person's suitability. But even if no one else stepped forward and his relatives insisted that he become cāmiyāṭi, he said, "It's still not certain. The other issue is that the person must have the power to get possessed. Sometimes the god won't possess him. Only one out of ten can get possessed. If I am the one who gets possessed [i.e., whom the god chooses], though, then there's nothing I can do. I'll have to take on this old village life." He told me that if that happened, he would not tell anyone in Madurai that he had become a cāmiyāṭi. "Only other cāmiyāṭis will know. The rest of the time, I will just be like an ordinary person. There's no urgency for me to tell everyone, right? It doesn't *fit me* to be a cāmiyāṭi."

What precisely was Murugan's concern? Fierce gods like Madasamy are wild and difficult to control; they demand the "heat" of animal sacrifice. Possession itself is seen as an act of losing control. Being a cāmiyāṭi for a dangerous fierce god, then, requires not only moral virtue according to caste rules, but also an association with frenzy and with excess (cf. Seizer 2005, 77–79). As Karin Kapadia observed during her fieldwork in a Tamil Nadu village, "the lower castes saw their 'abandonment' as a surrendering of self to possession by God, but to the Chettiars and Brahmins this was dangerously close to 'mere' abandonment and 'mere' freedom from restraint. It was dangerously close to anarchy" (1996, 437–438). Moreover,

Kalpana Ram notes, "*all* forms of possession are devalued and margin-alised in the wider context of Indian modernity" (2012, 204).

As I have argued in previous chapters, "decent" qualities that in the past were associated with the upper castes—cleanliness, neatness, moderation, restraint, and modesty—are today seen as critical signs of middle-class standing and modernity. And while those values of decency have become adopted by many lower-class people as well, stereotyped lower-caste attributes such as dirtiness, disorder, violence, and other "backward" practices are now ascribed, by people of *all* castes, to the lower *classes*. Thus the Nadar caste's religious practice would be read by others as a lower-class behavior. Compounding this, as Murugan keenly felt, was the understanding that possession is a quintessentially anti-modern village practice, in a time when cosmopolitanism and modernity are key signs of the middle class in Indian cities (Srinivas 2010, 196).

Murugan thus was not only worried about losing dignity and recognition from an urban audience; he also worried that if his position as cāmiyāṭi became known outside of his family and close friends, the positive cultural capital he has gained in adulthood, including through his work as a videographer, would be undercut by the negative cultural capital of being possessed by a fierce god (even though it serves as *positive* cultural capital in some circles, including his lineage). He feared that others would perceive his body—which now merges with a dangerous god of the cremation grounds—as uncontrolled, uncontained, unhygienic, and unmodern—in short, not decent. His most visceral worry was that others would disdain him, making it hard for him to be recognized as the person he sees himself and has built himself to be, and to maintain the dignity of others' regard. He also worried that this shift in others' perception of his cultural capital would affect both his economic and social capital, most directly because some people would no longer want to hire a person of ambiguous modernity to document their lives in a way that should reflect their own stylish modernity, using the photo albums and videos as part of their own "showcase."

All these concerns condensed in his anxiety that he would no longer be seen as modern and middle class. In fact, concerns about dignity and capital were almost impossible to disentangle from one another in this case. How could the same person be both videographer and cāmiyāṭi, he asked? But two months later, after his father persuaded him that the family, lineage, and deity would lose both strength and mariyātai if Murugan declined this responsibility, he reluctantly agreed. When the lineage members gathered soon after at the village temple, Sudalai Madan did possess Murugan. Later that year, having been confirmed by the uravin-murai and accepted by Madasamy, he became what he did not want to be. Knowing his foreboding, I waited to see how he would grapple with this new role.

The 2015 *Koṭai*

It would be several years until I could return at the time of the annual festival, but in February 2015 I was at last able to attend all three days of the annual koṭai. Mindful during the intervening years of my friend's distress at becoming cāmiyāṭi, I hoped to learn whether he had reconciled his disparate identities, and if so, how. I also wanted to see his family because of important recent events. Rajan had died in 2012, leaving Murugan as the male head of this family, and Murugan's first child, a girl, was born in late 2014.

In the years between the festivals I attended, I had taken the time to learn more about māṭans, koṭais, and possession. Back in Madurai again, I was also able to ask Murugan questions about the festival during the few days beforehand. One subject he explained was how the festival is funded: each family in the uravinmurai is required to pay annual dues, which go toward the temple, and certain elements of the festival—such as each day's meals, or the gods' vestments or the cāmiyāṭis' vēcam—are sponsored and paid for by individual families, who are named at the events. One reason that lineage members, all related through a common male ancestor, are willing to pay annual dues (which have risen in recent years as lineage members' average wealth has risen) is that the kula teyvam is seen as a representation of the lineage, a "highly idiosyncratic expression of the lineage and its history" (Kjaersholm 1990, 73). The success of the festival reflects, and publicly communicates, the success of the lineage members—it does for the uravinmurai much of what wedding ceremonies do for families.

Anjali, her husband, and children had attended the festival twice since Murugan first performed as cāmiyāṭi. Anjali was eager to attend again, and she joined me for the full three days. Her husband, Sundaram, and their children were also able to attend for the first two days, and on the first evening, we all drove to the village in a car with Ilango, one of Murugan's employees. We arrived at 10:00 P.M. Murugan—who had been on the phone with Anjali off and on during the evening as he kept postponing the ritual's estimated start time—was waiting for us in front of the temple, wearing an orange veshti. Just as we had six years earlier, we viewed the deities inside and behind the temple, marveling at their decorations and adding our own garland to those already wreathing Madasamy's main image, and ate a (vegetarian) meal in the hall. We then gossiped with Murugan's relatives while ritual preparations continued.

Around midnight, young boys started to clang the bronze bells hung around Madasamy's platform. Two drummers began to play, and the air filled with incense. Four cāmiyāṭis, all dressed simply in orange veshtis, followed the young priest as he did *pujas* (rituals of worship) at the three shrines inside the temple, then followed him to the space behind the temple. There, as the strident pitch of the nagaswaram was added and the rhythm and speed of the drums increased, the gods descended. They would alight partially, then retreat, then return and descend fully. In addition to the cāmiyāṭis, many women of all ages became spontaneously possessed. The space soon churned as those who were possessed wove and tumbled through the rest of us. Murugan, much more animated than his elderly father had been, was dramatic: screeching and growling, plunging into the crowd, grabbing the aruval from an assistant, charging around the Madasamy platform. Watching him was a shock. I simply had not anticipated how it would feel to see my gentle laughing friend become another being entirely, ferocious and god-filled.

Soon we all left the temple and proceeded behind the cāmiyāṭis to a dry riverbed half a kilometer away. There, under an extremely bright tubelight, we crowded around the cāmiyāṭis as they came out of their possession. When they were fully released, Murugan looked over and smiled at me. Once again my solicitous friend, he later came to tell me that we would be there for an hour. I joined his mother to sit on the riverbank with all the other women watching the rituals, while Anjali and her children rested in Ilango's car. Eventually the crowd headed back to

Photo 8. Dancers possessed (Madasamy on the left, Karuppusamy on the right), 2015. Photo credit: Sara Dickey.

the temple, Madasamy in the lead. Murugan, while visibly possessed, was now staid compared to the other cāmiyāṭis. He held his arms rigidly overhead, gripping the knife as he led us.

Reentering the temple, the cāmiyāṭis took up positions in front of different shrines. Lineage members clustered around them, asking advice of the gods. One of Murugan's younger sisters tearfully asked Madasamy about a problem she was facing. As Madasamy listened and told kuri to each person, Murugan's eyes lolled in his head, and he made a "fff" sound—it made me think of contained energy, fittingly reminding me of a pressure cooker with a slight valve release. He pushed ash onto people's heads roughly, without Murugan's usual coordination. Madasamy's voice, however, was the same as Murugan's.

The kuri sessions lasted for hours. Eventually our group of guests all left around 3:00 A.M. to rest in a room in a nearby lodge. The children and men fell asleep quickly, but Anjali and I were awake until after 5:00 A.M. Shortly after 6:00, Ilango's phone rang. It was Murugan, calling to instruct his colleague to go relieve another videographer who had covered a different all-night temple festival in the neighboring village.

The rest of us then rose quickly and returned to the Madasamy temple for the morning rituals, which began in the covered space behind the temple. Pujas were done to all of the twenty-one gods residing there (many of them coresident in a single towering stake, the *kaḻu maram*). We shifted to the main temple, where the pujas continued; the cāmiyāṭis, again in vēcam, began to become possessed once more. The primary ritual that morning was walking the fire, the coals of which glowed in a narrow pit dug into the temple floor. Murugan again became possessed more slowly than the others, but soon was animated, and like the others he crossed the burning coals multiple times. At the Karumariamman temple festival in Hosur in 2011, the dozens of devotees had processed in a steady walk across the long fire pit. These men, however, all dancing for the gods, lunged and lurched, and the Karuppusamy dancer dramatically plunged his knees into the coals with each step.

I watched few other rituals that day, since most were attended only by cāmiyāṭis. Anjali and I stayed in Madurai that night, and returned to the village the next morning at 6:00 A.M. Murugan again greeted us as we drove up, having again remained awake all night (often possessed) during the sacrifices of goats and chickens. This was the day of the mutton feast, and the meal was larger than in 2009, reflecting the lineage members' and the temple's growing prosperity over the past six years. In addition to the curry, rice, yogurt, and buttermilk, this year it included lentils with mutton parts, a fried sweet, and peppery rasam water.

This was also the day of the procession outside the village. Around 8:00 A.M., pujas were again offered to the deities inside and behind the temple. Next the cāmiyāṭis put on their vēcam, and as soon as the musicians began to play, many women in the audience became possessed (I learned later that they were Murugan's mother's relatives). The procession began as soon as the gods had finishing descending. Madasamy and the other gods made seven stops as they wound around a path outside the village. In a repeat of what I had seen on the 2009 recording, villagers approached them at each step, pouring turmeric water on cāmiyāṭis' feet, touching their feet to receive a blessing, asking kuri and receiving sacred ash. Women around them ululated. Then, rather abruptly, the cāmiyāṭis would head forward. During most of the procession they were fairly restrained, though breathing heavily with that "fff" sound, but occasionally they shrieked or hooted.

After half an hour, as they completed the protective loop, the cāmiyāṭis became invigorated again and whooped as they ran toward the temple. There they huddled in front of the temple and, as before, were doused with turmeric water. Cooled but still possessed, the cāmiyāṭis then entered the temple and a priest placed *vibhuti* (sacred ash) on their foreheads and told the māṭans, *"mālaikku ēri"* ("go up into the mountains," where the gods reside). Only then, Murugan later told me, did the gods depart. From what I saw, this final possession was especially difficult to come out of. When I called Murugan at his home that night, I asked how he was. "Exhausted," he answered, but he also sounded satisfied.

The Modern *Cāmiyāṭi*

The day after the Sudalai Madan festival ended, I left to visit Lakshmi in Hosur (for the first time since we had attended the goddess festival four years previously), which meant it would be several days before I could see Murugan again. I was eager to talk with him about the festival ceremonies, and when I returned he asked me to meet at his home since his office would not be private. The first thing he told me when I arrived was that his wife, a mathematics teacher in a private primary school, had been accepted into an M.Ed. program. He was proud of her, and made it clear that he had encouraged and supported her application (which he saw as noteworthy, since many of his male peers would not do so). We all talked and played with the baby for a while. Then I showed Murugan the photos I had taken during the ceremonies. I had asked once before whether he was comfortable seeing images of himself when he was dancing—that is, when he was Madasamy—and I asked him again when I arrived at his house. Each time he gave a firm yes (and at the end of this visit he would ask me to send him the photos and videos, since "I've never seen myself in this part of the festival"). Showing him the photos allowed me to clear up some details, and enabled Murugan to point out others that I had missed. He explained how each of the different dancers is related to him (all are his first cousins, the sons of his father's brothers), noted the tiny statue of Shiva ("Madasamy's father") on the base of the image of Madasamy behind the temple, and asked if I had spotted the cigars among the offerings given to Madasamy (I hadn't, though I knew they were likely to be there).

The last thing we discussed that day was what it is like for him to be a cāmiyāṭi, and how it compared with his expectations in 2009. He described a process of adjustment. His dominant memory from the first year as cāmiyāṭi was surprise at being given so much mariyātai at the temple. Everyone touched his feet, he said, and worshipped him. Despite having seen his father receive such respect over the years, it came as a visceral shock. Perhaps this is explained by what he told me of his second year as cāmiyāṭi. In the first year, Murugan said, he had not taken the role all that seriously, breaking the rules about austerity before the festival. "For example," he told me, "I'm not supposed to have meat for thirty days, but I ate meat on at least ten of those days." (He was also supposed to refrain from wearing shoes, cutting or shaving hair, and lying on mattresses, just as Lakshmi does.) As a result, the āṭṭam "didn't come right." By the second year, however, he feared the god. His fear allowed a true union (*bhakti*) with Madasamy, and the god now possesses him fully.

I asked Murugan to think about the discomfort he had originally felt about becoming a cāmiyāṭi. He recalled how nervous he had been about other people's judgments at the time. At first, he said, he was anxious about telling other people that he was a cāmiyāṭi, but their reactions were not as he expected. Instead, he was surprised to find that people were respectful (although in a less demonstrative way than the festival-goers), including the people he knows professionally in Madurai. Now "everyone" knows, he said, and he was "mistaken" when he worried that they would dismiss or mock him. He explains to his customers, for example, why he himself cannot be the videographer for events that coincide with his kula teyvam festivals (in these cases, his employees do the filming), and they still continue to request that he film other special events. Indeed, his business and clientele have grown. Murugan reported that fellow videographers treat him as they did before, as do the other people he interacts with, and he no longer feels caṅkaṭam, embarrassment, when he tells them about his ritual role. He did note that the one change with his work is that he has to delegate the filming of Hindu religious ceremonies to his employees, so that he does not become possessed while filming. But he was not eager to relive his feelings from those early days—which must be especially uncomfortable now that he is more invested in promoting his uravinmurai—and I did not push him further. What is most clear is that Murugan says he has found a comfortable way to combine two roles that he once found antithetical. Previously happy to maintain his reserve as the technological recorder of the god, he now unites directly with Madasamy, a porous vessel rather than a distanced technician.

Conclusions

Murugan's story illustrates the processes of class performance and of class relations—and the attitudes and assumptions that underlie them—that make up, and make possible, the politics of class inequality: in short, the main themes of this book. His dilemma, however, has an unexpected and instructive outcome. Before continuing to the lessons it holds, I will reflect on the ways in which his experience of class is typical.

By 2009, Murugan had been economically secure for close to two decades, but when faced with the possibility of becoming a god dancer, his class position suddenly felt fragile. The most immediate threat to his standing that he articulated was not loss of income but loss of cultural capital in the eyes of his class peers and his clients. He worried that this one sphere of his life, performed only a few times a year, could undo the class project he has carried out for so long. Almost everyone has something to lose, and indeed "falling" in class is a frequent enough event, sometimes simply because of domestic cycles, and often because of death and illness; there is an empirical material basis to this fear. There is also the subjective awareness that one's class position is a negotiation with others and must be ratified in order to be real, and as we have seen this position feels especially precarious to members of the middle class.

In Murugan's case, the threat to his cultural capital (with potential repercussions for economic and social capital) was the dominant disdain for people whose bodies or desires are uncontrolled. As we have seen, the emphasis on self-control and self-discipline is one of the most pervasive features of class discourse and relations in Madurai, and these qualities are required for being seen as decent and modern. The value placed on self-control shapes a myriad of practices covered in this book, from the everyday—consumption choices, presentation of the body, hygiene, savings and debt—as well as longer-term or more singular enactments and outcomes of class, such as access to education and occupations, marriage arrangements, and decisions about worthy recipients of charity. The concern with discipline and order is, I have argued, in part a result of the absorption of caste prejudices into class prejudices, which now bear the common-sense stamp of the former and the rational patina of the latter. Like other class judgments, they carry a tremendous moral weight.

We have also seen the presence of such "imaginaries" in discourses about not only possession and debt but also dowry and wedding ceremonies, the nature of the middle class, and shared histories of hunger. Each of these examples underscores the importance of understanding local values and their integration into class categories for comprehending the workings of class, including the class relations that they produce.

Finally, while Murugan's worry about his loss of cultural capital was ultimately an economic fear as well, a concern that others' disdain would hurt his economic enterprises, it was most painfully a concern about dignity. His fear of nonrecognition was more visceral than any concern about a potential long-term decrease in capital. He thought he would no longer be recognized as a person of worth if his colleagues came to know that he was not only a videographer, a responsible husband, and a dutiful son and brother, but also a god dancer for a fearsome deity. In this case, concerns for dignity and class standing were inextricably linked since both were tied to the same source.

Yet Murugan insists that neither his class nor his dignity have been altered, and in my observations, his business success and social regard support this claim. I offer Murugan's story not only because it condenses many of the themes of the book into one dense example, but also because it reminds us that things can happen differently: that people are not always defined, as they may fear, by the definitions of categories or by others' moral judgments. Indeed, at times those moral judgments fail to appear.

In short, it complicates our understanding of the power of class categories. Murugan's experience *may* support Ian Hacking's contention that "classifying changes people, but the changed people cause classifications themselves to be redrawn" (2004, 279). If so, he has done this not by resisting a discriminatory practice nor by insisting that a category's criteria be stretched to allow him entry, but instead by retaining his existing class despite incorporating a socially devalued practice into his sense of self and his public persona. To clarify this distinction, consider Susan Seizer's instructive discussion of Special Drama actresses' response to stigma. Special Drama is a largely rural form of theater in which artists are booked individually for each drama, rather than working together as an ongoing troupe. Actresses who perform in this dramatic genre are stigmatized for the public and sometimes sexualized nature of their acting and the general "excess" of their profession, among other reasons. Seizer argues that Special Drama actresses strive to create a place for themselves within the category of the "good woman" by enacting the norms of proper womanhood and thereby claiming membership in that category for themselves. In doing so, she contends, "they effectively stretch those norms, even alter them somewhat in the process" (2005, 304).

Murugan, on the other hand, is already successfully established in the middle class, and has taken on a different stigmatized practice (also disdained for its excess)—one that he feared would disqualify him for recognition in that class—and yet to all appearances his class standing has not been diminished. He has both kept his class and honored his family heritage, practices that previously appeared incompatible to him. In so doing he has made a form of cultural capital devalued in one sphere seem more valued, or at least less devaluing, within his segment of the middle class. Perhaps, with his exemplary self-discipline in both professional and family spheres, Murugan is in a prime position to mediate the oppositions he now embodies. If so, I suggest that he is not entirely idiosyncratic, given the other examples of possession I have noted in this chapter. His experience, while both individual and anecdotal, suggests that the categories that underlie and inform class difference might at times become more capacious. In any case, Murugan has expanded (or at least confounded) class boundaries for himself and for his family.

It is also instructive to compare Murugan's challenge to class boundaries with Chellasamy's. Both are acts of inclusion. These acts again are highly individual but surely not unique. They remind us that while most individuals' class projects involve drawing lines of exclusion, potent pushes for egalitarianism and inclusiveness also exist. Both cases illustrate an unexpected absence of the policing of class borders, and an unusual lack of moralizing judgment. Chellasamy's wedding feast welcomes an undifferentiated "public" and avoids stigmatizing the poor (even as it legitimates his wealth). It is not category-based in either its discourse or in the representations made by (at least some) participants. Similarly, Murugan's success argues for the ability of a middle-class person to take on (some) practices defined as lower-class and yet retain his class. A key difference between their practices is that while Chellasamy crosses boundaries, Murugan and his onlookers make the categories more commodious. Sustained attention to such alterations of categories, I argue, may lead us to recognize changes in the processes of class relations over time.

Murugan's story reflects the threads of the subjective experience of class—and of its power—that I have explored in this book. Understanding subjective aspects of class is critical for a number of reasons. For those who care about the quality of other people's lives, even those they simply read about in books but whose existence they can imagine, it is important at face value. For those who wish to understand the processes of the production of class identities and relations, I have argued that these aspects shape access to resources for entire categories of people, while in the final two chapters we have observed ways that individuals may also challenge the power of those categories in potentially significant ways. And finally, those who desire to address or deconstruct the politics of class inequality must attend to the subjective, discursive, intangible aspects of class that mold class relations, because they make the politics of class and capitalism possible.

Notes

CHAPTER 1 — INTRODUCTION: THE EVERYDAY LIFE OF CLASS

1. The concept of class as a process (rather than a static structure or series of categories) has a long if sporadic presence in class studies. Marx, for instance, arguably viewed class identities as processual, given his focus on the relational nature of class; more recent discussions of the concept are found for example in Donner and De Neve (2011), Liechty (2003), Rapp (1982), Säävälä (2010), and Tilly (1998).

2. Raka Ray and Seemin Qayum describe, for example, the rationalization of caste prejudices that shape domestic service relationships in Calcutta: employers' "concerns about contamination of bathrooms, clothes washed together, or dirty dishes [are] consciously or unconsciously disguised as the ideology of hygiene" (2009, 155). See also Qayum and Ray (2011, 248).

3. But see Don Kalb's "material relational approach" (1997, 2005), which is wider in scope. So too is the symbolic interactionist school in sociology, the aims of which overlap a great deal with the relational approach to inequality (on the latter point, see Schwalbe et al. 2000).

4. See Ray and Qayum (2009) and Srivastava (2015) for some exceptions.

5. Sources that have been particularly helpful to developing my use and understanding of these concepts, in addition to Bourdieu (1984, 1986, and 1990b), include Bennett and Silva (2011); Deshpande (2003); Sayer (1999); and Smart (1993).

6. John Fiske (1992) and Sarah Thornton (1996) make related points. Fiske labels subaltern cultural capital "popular cultural capital," and Thornton calls it "subcultural capital." I prefer to retain the unmarked term "cultural capital" for all such capital, since the logic of its workings is the same regardless of class origin.

7. Bourdieu's treatment of the valuation of capital is complex. While Bourdieu often portrayed cultural capital as the "legitimate" capital valorized by the bourgeoisie, he also saw it as operating within a specific field and he recognized variability across fields (though not across classes). Some have thus written of a "relative" rather than an "absolute" sense of cultural capital in Bourdieu's work (e.g., Bennett and Silva 2011; Lamont and Lareau 1988; Lareau and Weininger 2003; Prieur and Savage 2011). Many analysts recognize that there are historical and cross-cultural differences in what "counts" as cultural capital, including shifts to more "lowbrow" sources of cultural capital among the contemporary bourgeoisie or middle classes (on the latter,

see, e.g., Bennett et al. 2009; Prieur and Savage 2011). But even this view fails to acknowledge intra-class and, particularly, subaltern forms of cultural capital. At the same time, Bourdieu himself paid attention to the tastes of subordinated classes, but he did not see their tastes as cultural capital. Instead he discussed them in terms of symbolic violence. In this assessment I concur with Fiske that Bourdieu failed "to accord the culture of the subordinate the same sophisticated analysis as that of the dominant" (1992, 32).

8. This distinction between acquired and essential dignity parallels Charles Taylor's distinction between conditional and unconditional respect (1994).

9. Cf. Castleman (2011, 5, 13) and Sayer (2005a, 959) on the utilitarian effects of recognition, and Narayan, Nikitin, and Richard (2009) on the material benefits of "intangible assets."

10. As Geoffrey Brennan and Philip Pettit note: "Esteem cannot be given away or traded in the ordinary manner, for there is no way that I can buy the good opinion of another or sell to others my good opinion of them. . . . But though it is non-tradable in that sense, esteem is still a good that is allocated in society according to more or less systematic determinants; and it is a good whose allocation has an interactive, aggregative aspect" (2004, 3; see also p. 13).

11. Offer says similarly of regard, that it "is a good in its own right, quite apart from its instrumental value" (1997, 472).

CHAPTER 2 — WHAT IS CLASS IN MADURAI?

1. Even today, in my observations, the study of India in U.S. elementary and secondary education typically highlights caste and Hinduism, as though these are what make India "distinctive." Class difference, seen perhaps as either more universal (and therefore less interesting) or more modern (and therefore inapplicable), receives much less attention in standard American curricula on India.

2. Some contemporary authors evince nostalgia for the period of the 1950s through 1980s, seeing it as the heyday of class analysis in South Asia. (See, e.g., Herring and Agarwala [2006], and to some extent Deshpande [2003, 125] and Donner and De Neve [2011, 1–2]. Also see Chibber [2006], though the author argues that class analysis was never entrenched in India other than in agrarian studies.) While materialist class analysis did decline, it did not disappear; more to the point, class analysis understood more broadly *has* continued fairly robustly since then, as even this brief overview demonstrates.

3. See Chibber (2006) for a detailed and compelling discussion of the influence of international political and intellectual trends, and domestic trends as well, on the study of class in India since the 1960s.

4. For a much more thorough account, see Dickey (n.d.a). More narrowly focused, but also more detailed, examinations of portions of that history can be found in

Bhattacharya (2006); Chibber (2006); Ludden (2002); and Thorner (1982). In addition, Kate Currie (1992) discusses class within her overview of Indian stratification literature, and Tirthankar Roy (2004) reviews scholarship on modern Indian economic history since 1983.

5. The introduction of and subsequent fascination with the other dominant paradigm of Indian inequality, Louis Dumont's *Homo Hierarchicus*, took place over the same time period (the book appeared in 1966 in French, 1970 in English). As Ludden notes succinctly, "opposing theories served opposing schools" in the 1960s and 1970s (2002, 8–9).

6. For different takes on this intellectual history, see Bhattacharya (2006, 13–14); Chakrabarty (1993, 1995); Chaturvedi (2007); Chibber (2006); Ludden (2002); Mannathukkaren (2011); Sarkar (1997).

7. A third concept, *māṇam*, which both scholars and laypeople often discuss in tandem with mariyātai, is generally less related to concepts of class, and I do not include it in this overview. While mariyātai is bestowed by others, māṇam is a form of honor more likely to be seen as inhering within a person. As Richard Scherl observes in his sociolinguistic analysis of mariyātai, "the core meaning of *māṇam* is 'honor' in terms of the qualities of an individual, while the meaning of mariyātai is honor in terms of the respect or regard given by others" (1996, 122–123). Or as John Harriss explains, mānam is "personal honour," while in contrast, mariyātai is "the transitive aspect of individual prestige" (1982, 242).

8. For linguistic precision, the Tamil terms in this paragraph are transcribed in their literary Tamil forms. In most of this book, however, speech is transcribed with the colloquial Tamil forms used by the speakers. Paṇakkārarkaḷ, for example, is usually spoken in Madurai as *paṇakkāraṅka*.

9. Minna Säävälä describes a similar set of local class categories in Hyderabad, albeit one in which the middle group is designated less precisely by residents (2001, 302–303). The most frequent class categories that Kathinka Frøystad found used by upper-caste middle-class people in Kanpur are also fairly similar to the Madurai model: *chote log* (small people), *acche log* (good people), and (more rarely) *bare log* (big people). Frøystad, critiquing my accounts of Madurai class categories in the 1990s, makes the important point that these are not simply three parts ranked on the same scale, "given that the 'big' category was of a different order from the 'good' and 'small' categories" (2006, 163) and that thus "class was not merely construed by positioning others below, on a par with, or above themselves" (2005, 99), a point with which I agree.

10. But again see Frøystad (2006), who argues that class judgments in Kanpur are highly informed by unarticulated assumptions about the correlation of caste and class, and that "the distinction between markers based on economic means and genetic heritage was not as clear-cut as it may seem" (2006, 170).

11. For a more extensive analysis of the narrative in which this discussion appeared, see Dickey (2000a, 38–40).

CHAPTER 3 — FOUR RESIDENTS, AS I KNOW THEM

1. Odd numbers suggest the possibility of continuation and increase, and thus are auspicious (unlike even numbers, which signify closure). Monetary gifts such as these are normally given in an odd amount.

CHAPTER 4 — CONSUMPTION AND APPREHENSION:
CLASS IN THE EVERYDAY

1. The 2001 Census of India Housing Profile for Tamil Nadu listed the availability of specified assets in urban households as follows: transistor radio, 50.5 percent; television, 60.7 percent; telephone, 19.9 percent; bicycle, 46 percent; scooter, motorcycle, or moped, 23.6 percent; car, jeep, or van, 3.7 percent; and "none of the specified assets," 21.6 percent (Government of India 2003). Figures from the 2011 census show notable changes. Urban households listed as having a radio totaled 26.9 percent ; television, 88.7 percent; telephone, 84.1 percent; computer/laptop with internet, 7.6 percent; computer/laptop without internet, 9.3 percent; bicycle, 44.3 percent; scooter, motorcycle, or moped, 39.7 percent; car, jeep, or van, 6.9 percent; and "none of the specified assets," 3.6 percent (Government of India 2012).

2. These assertions about the relative significance of caste and money (class) are important as a form of contemporary discourse, but they cannot necessarily be taken at face value.

3. On related gendered qualities of "containment" and demureness, see Lukose (2009, 76–80).

4. This situation is quite different from that in Hyderabad, a larger and more cosmopolitan city, where adherence to norms of decency marks women as lower-middle-class, while fashionable modernity—which exceeds the modest norms of decency—distinguishes women of higher middle-class segments. These norms are not straightforward, however, and "it becomes near impossible for women to be simultaneously fashionable and respectable" (Gilbertson 2014a, 146; see also Lukose 2009, 75–77, 86–90). Male college students in Madurai also see decent clothing as unfashionable, but for them decency is defined in terms of formality, adult maturity, and lack of "style" rather than sexual modesty (Nakassis n.d.).

5. Cf. Steffen Hermann, who cites the practice of *misrecognition* as a means of social exclusion (2011, 134–135). Charles Taylor makes the point even more starkly, arguing that denying a person recognition "can inflict harm, can be a form of oppression, imprisoning someone in a false, distorted, and reduced mode of being" (1994, 25).

6. They draw from data published by the Indian Department of Telecommunications and the Telecom Regulatory Authority of India (TRAI). Also see Jeffrey and Doron (2012, 64, 69).

7. Marcus Banks (2001, 81, 86–87) applies the phrase "material presence" to television sets in India and elsewhere.

8. These roles go well beyond those I focus on in this chapter. They include, to cite a small sample of possibilities, sending a signal through "'missed calls,' taking pictures, checking prices, downloading screen savers, doing pujas" (Jeffrey and Doron 2011, 398). See also Doron (2010). Jeffrey and Doron's recent book (2013) explores an extraordinary wealth of social processes that involve cell phones.

9. Recall that mobile phones had nonetheless been important in Anjali and Sundaram's history. The couple was able to keep their developing "love relationship" secret from their families, and avoid the risk of meeting in person, for a number of years by communicating over their friends' mobile phones. (See Donner et al. [2008] for a discussion of cell phones' place in maintaining "romantic relationships" in Bangalore, and Jeffrey and Doron [2013, 178–182] for Varanasi.) By 2009, Sundaram and Anjali both owned cell phones.

10. More recently, Doron, writing with Jeffrey, has argued that while mobile phone usages "appeared to reaffirm established domestic structures and gender relations," they were nonetheless creating "incremental" change (Jeffrey and Doron 2013, 172). Sirpa Tenhunen (2014) found less restriction on women's usage in rural Rajasthan, but still observed gendered differences in the purposes, frequency, and physical settings of mobile phone usage.

11. There are other gendered patterns linking cell phone use and concerns for decency. One example is men's use of cell phones to share pornography, which must not take place in the presence of women and elders.

CHAPTER 5 — DEBT: THE MATERIAL CONSEQUENCES OF MORAL CONSTRUCTS

1. For more finely distinguished and detailed descriptions of loan sources in South Indian locales, see Guérin et al. (2012); Harriss-White and Colatei (2004); and Rutherford (2006, 2009). One of the most consequential forms of debt in *rural* areas is long-term indebtedness to employers, which is used as a way of securing the debtor's long-term labor (see De Neve 1999). This type of debt never appeared in my conversations and interviews with urban informants.

2. See Austin (1999, 209–220); Frankel (2005, 417–422).

3. By 1980, when six additional banks were nationalized, 92 percent of deposits came under the public sector (Shah, Rao, and Shankar 2007, 1362n. 13).

4. Granville Austin, using Ministry of Finance survey data, reports that "the fourteen nationalized banks increased the number of their offices, overall, between 1969 and June 1993 by 21,898 and, in centres with under 10,000 population, by 12,226" (1999, 220n. 30). This growth, along with targeted loans and limits on interest, did result in increased access to banks and to credit for rural residents (see, e.g., Shah, Rao, and Shankar 2007). For a variety of reasons, however, the policies fell significantly short of original goals (see, e.g., Harriss-White and Colatei 2004, 253–255; Shah, Rao, and Shankar 2007, 1356, 1358).

5. In this system, members periodically pool fixed sums and then immediately auction the rights to the pool, and repeat this process as many times as there are members in the cooperative. At each auction, the member who bids the lowest sum—that is, the member willing to take the smallest amount of the total pool for his or her turn—receives that sum. Each member wins the bid once (and must continue to contribute to the pool after doing so), and those willing to wait the longest generally get the largest amounts (see Rutherford 2009, 45–50).

6. One of the few other analyses of debt in an Indian city found that in Hyderabad, "households living below $2 a day primarily borrow from moneylenders (52 percent), friends or neighbors (24 percent), and family members (13 percent), and only 5 percent of the loans are with commercial banks" (Banerjee and Duflo 2007, 155).

7. In 2008 the Reserve Bank of India felt it necessary to issue a cautionary circular to its member banks titled "Recovery Agents Engaged by Banks." It noted in part: "It is understood that some banks set very stiff recovery targets or offer high incentives to recovery agents. These have, in turn, induced the recovery agents to use intimidatory and questionable methods for recovery of dues. Banks are, therefore, advised to ensure that the contracts with the recovery agents do not induce adoption of uncivilized, unlawful and questionable behaviour or recovery process" (http://www.rbi.org.in/scripts/NotificationUser.aspx?Id=4141&Mode=0, last accessed August 23, 2015). The RBI continues to send an annual circular to member banks repeating this and other injunctions of the 2008 circular, in which it enjoins lenders not to "resort to undue harassment viz. persistently bothering the borrowers at odd hours, use of muscle power for recovery of loans, etc." (e.g., http://www.rbi.org.in/scripts/BS_ViewMasCirculardetails.aspx?id=8135, last accessed August 23, 2015).

8. Cf. Gregory (2012, 385): "We use the word 'credit' when we want to say money lending is a good thing and the word 'debt' when we want to say that money lending is a bad thing."

9. One of the reasons that the poor must borrow for everyday consumption and life-cycle events is not simply that their income is low, but because maintaining savings is extremely difficult under the material and social conditions of poverty. Without access to a bank or cooperative association, they have almost no safe or truly hidden places to sequester saved-up cash; and families face daily demands that, while not about immediate survival, are difficult to refuse. Abhijit Banerjee and Esther Duflo explain that for the poor, "saving at home is hard. The money may be stolen (especially if you live in a house that cannot be locked) or grabbed by your spouse or your son. Also, if you have money at hand, you are constantly resisting temptation to spend: to buy something, to help someone to whom you find it difficult to say 'no,' to give your child a treat. Such temptations may be especially hard for the poor, because many of the temptations they are resisting are things that everyone else might take for granted" (2007, 164; see also Rutherford 2009, 2).

10. One of the few sympathetic depictions of moneylenders, scarce even in scholarly literature, is found in Ramachandran and Swaminathan (2005a, 173–176). Also see Kar

(2013) for an extended discussion of the experiences of microfinance loan officers, who were criticized during the 2010 Indian "subprime crisis" as "no better than a money-lender" (2013, 482). See Gregory (1997, 218ff.) for an unusually even-handed description of "village money lending" practices.

11. See also Barbara Harriss-White and Diego Colatei, who note, "We find general reputation (scheduled castes as drunkards; women as docile and biddable) powerful in the segmentation and fracturing of 'markets' in money" (2004, 260).

CHAPTER 6 — PERFORMING THE MIDDLE

1. For consonant approaches to the category and study of the "middle class," see Derné (2005), Donner and De Neve (2011), Srivastava (2015), and Upadhya (2011).

2. This is not, for example, Judith Butler's sense of performativity, in which identities are naturalized and made real by reiteratively acting them out (see especially Butler 1993), nor Victor Turner's sense of the reflexive self-observation occasioned by social dramas (e.g., Turner 1984).

3. Carol Upadhya finds an even broader swathe of people self-identifying as middle class, and notes that "people who regard themselves as middle-class include the poor as well as the rich" (2011, 168n. 1). See also De Neve (2011), Lemanski and Tawa Lama-Rewal (2013, 91–92), Radhakrishnan (2011b, 195), and Srivastava (2011, 364).

4. A limited number of policies and inputs began to shape the contemporary middle class even earlier. William Mazzarella cites, for example, "Indira Gandhi's 1973 Pay Commission, the long-term effects of the green revolution, [and] remittances from Indian migrant labourers in the Gulf" (2005, 1–2).

5. For the difficulties of measuring the middle classes in India with existing data, see Desai (2007, 345), Deshpande (2003, 132–133), Mazzarella (2005, 2–3), Meyer and Birdsall (2012), and Sridharan (2004, 410).

6. For a range of approaches to defining the middle class in South Asia, see Appadurai and Breckenridge (1995), Bardhan (1984), Béteille (2001), Chakrabarti and Cullenberg (2003), Dwyer (2000), Fernandes and Heller (2006), Fuller and Narasimhan (2014), Liechty (2003), McCarthy (1994), Shah (1987), Sridharan (2004, 2008), Vanaik (2002), van Wessel (2004), and Waldrop (2012).

7. By 2008 there was also an increasing tendency to differentiate between paṇakkāraṅka as those who have established wealth in property (usually land and/or gold), and vacatiyāṉavaṅka as those who own significant consumer goods—often acquired with loans—but do not have durable wealth.

8. For other work on the moral boundary-drawing that characterizes middle classes in South Asia, see Liechty (2003), Säävälä (2010), and Srivastava (2015).

9. Individual Tamil speakers' lexical incorporation of terms that originated in English is in part a form of cultural capital tied to modernity and class. The use of these terms rather than Tamil semi-equivalents may also, as Laura Ring argues for Karachi,

suggest that the English terms capture and represent concepts that were less prevalent or salient before the terms' use became common. See Ring (2006, 83–85).

10. Ordinariness does not mean the majority or even the mode, however. My own observations strongly suggest that people who identify as middle class remain in the minority of Madurai's population. Nonetheless, when I asked middle-class people what percentage of the population their class comprised, they routinely estimated between 30 percent and 70 percent. Thus their sense of "ordinariness" also includes an assumption of themselves as a norm.

11. Nicholas Nisbett (2007) also notes the confluence of relational and moralizing aspects of middle-class identities among young men in Bangalore.

12. Their education, parents' occupations, and (where applicable) spouse's occupation were as follows: Amu had recently completed a B.Sc. in chemistry and was planning to enter an M.Sc. program in agriculture. Her parents owned a jewelry store. Janaki, Amu's sister-in-law, had a bachelor's degree in business. Her father had been a small businessman, her mother was a housewife, and her husband worked in his father's business. Priya, whose father is a travel agent and her mother an accountant, had a B.A. in English. Kumarasamy, the son of a retired teacher and a housewife, had a B.Sc. in chemistry and an M.A. in English. Lalitha, the daughter of a building contractor and a housewife, had a bachelor's degree in education and was married to a contractor. Rajendran, whose family owned a stationery store and other enterprises, had a B.A. in English and a postgraduate degree in computer applications. Except for Rajendran, who was a Nadar Christian, all were Hindu and members of middle to upper castes: Amu and Janaki were Chettiar; Priya, Acari; Kumarasamy, Yadava; and Lalitha, Naidu.

13. A year later, Lalitha was the only one of these students to have attained a related position, teaching medical transcription in a women's college. By 2008, none of the former students had become employed as transcribers. Lalitha had by then entered the civil service in Delhi—but she attained the position because of her English skills and her brother-in-law's connections, not because of her postbaccalaureate credentials.

14. See van Wessel (2004, 114) and Liechty (2003) for similar views in Baroda and Kathmandu, respectively.

15. Interestingly, these assumptions coexist with the belief that poor people irresponsibly spend *beyond* their limits and thus must go into debt unnecessarily.

16. See Dean (2013), Dwyer (2000), Fernandes (2006), Liechty (2003), Mankekar (1999), Säävälä (2010).

17. Säävälä provides powerful examples of the enactment of this attitude toward the poor, and observes, "The poor have only an instrumental role in middle-class classification struggles; they are not considered as social actors in any sense" (2010, 118).

18. See Säävälä (2001) for a detailed discussion of the risks encountered by one family in using domestic rituals for upward mobility.

CHAPTER 7 — MARRIAGE: DRAMA, DISPLAY,
AND THE REPRODUCTION OF CLASS

1. A married person is someone who has "achieved marriage" (*kalyāṇam āyiṭuccu*).

2. Only 1 percent to 2 percent of men and women remain unmarried, according to 2001 Indian Census data, and Sonalde Desai and Lester Andrist report that only 5 percent of women responding to the 2005 Indian Human Development Survey "had a primary role in choosing their husbands" (2010, 675).

3. Reputation refers to publicly perceived moral character, as well as to factors such as lineage and, in rural areas, ancestral standing within the community.

4. For discussions of the normative criteria used in different South Indian communities, see Caplan (1984), Dickey (2010), Kapadia (1995), and Meinzen (1980).

5. See Beck (1972, 237ff.), Caldwell, Reddy, and Caldwell (1983, 347), Clark-Decès (2014), Good (1980, 474), Gough (1956, 844), Kapadia (1993, 26–34), Nishimura (1998), Srinivas (1976, 143–144), and Trawick (1990, 118ff.).

6. See Caldwell, Reddy, and Caldwell (1983, 347), Krishnamoorthy and Audinarayana (2001, 192), and Ramesh, Srikumari, and Sukumar (1989, 251).

7. Although caste and religious communities often have preferential rules for or pre-scriptive rules against a specific type of close-kin marriage, studies of marriage patterns show that both parallel and cross-cousin marriages, patrilateral as well as matrilateral, occur in virtually all communities in South India (see, e.g., Rao and Inbaraj 1977; Ramesh, Srikumari, and Sukumar 1989). This is largely true of matrilateral uncle–niece marriages as well (e.g., Ramesh, Srikumari, and Sukumar 1989, 250–251). On Muslim cross-cousin and parallel-cousin marriage, see also Kalam (2004); on Muslim consanguinity, see Bittles and Hussain (2000).

8. For a more recent overview of changing marriage patterns in South India, based on survey data rather than ethnographic studies, see Krishnamoorthy and Audinarayana (2001), which includes a discussion of the declining incidence of close-kin marriage.

9. See Caldwell, Reddy, and Caldwell (1983, 347, 357), Fuller and Narasimhan (2008a, 742), Gough (1956, 834), Rogers (2008, 82, 84), and Srinivasan (2005, 602).

10. For discussion of the widely documented shift from bridewealth to dowry in different South Indian communities, see Bloch and Rao (2002, 1030), Bradford (1985), Caldwell, Reddy, and Caldwell (1983, 345–347), Caplan (1984, 218), Dean (2011, 251), Epstein (1973, 194–199), Gough (1956), Heyer (1992), Iyer (2002, 96, 111), Kapadia (1993, 34), Meinzen (1980, 1140), Srinivas (1962, 1984), Srinivasan (2005, 596–600), and Upadhya (1990, 37–38).

11. The mean age at marriage in Tamil Nadu is nineteen (Desai and Andrist 2010, 676).

12. Those few studies that explicitly explore the groom's family's perspective support this contention that less anxiety attends a son's marriage than a daughter's. See Epstein (1973, 196), Heyer (2000, 21), and Iyer (2002, 111); for North India, see Donner (2008).

13. A *ghagra-choli* is a combination of blouse, embroidered skirt, and dupatta, associated with northern and western India. Unlike the salwar kamiz, a northern import that has become commonplace in urban South India, ghagra choli is considered neither local nor everyday wear.

14. The mean expenditure for weddings alone in Tamil Nadu in 2005 was reported to be Rs. 102,349 (Desai and Andrist 2010, 676).

15. Cīr has a broader meaning than the other terms; it refers to a long sequence of gifts from the bride's family, which begins with the "engagement" ceremony (*nicciyatārttam*) and continues on ritual occasions for years (see Dean 2011; Srinivasan 2005; van Hollen 2003).

16. This distinction is a broad generalization, and the components that make up what is now broadly referred to as "dowry" are divided differently in some communities than others.

17. The fourth standard explanation, the need to compensate in-laws for taking on an unproductive woman in a situation in which women are being removed from productive labor (Epstein 1973; Kapadia 1995, 66–67; Rajaraman 1983), is not supported by quantitative studies (Rao 1993), and ignores the explicit value of women's other labor to the conjugal family (Srinivas 1989, 110). For a detailed discussion of all these points, see Dickey (n.d.b).

18. A tol is an old Indian measure of weight, equivalent to about 12 grams, or less than ½ ounce.

19. See Mody (2008) for a discussion of the intricate meanings of arranged love marriages, their permutations and impulsions.

CHAPTER 8 — FOOD, HUNGER, AND THE BINDING OF CLASS RELATIONS

1. "Thevar" is actually a cluster of closely ranked castes. Members of these individual castes sometimes refer to themselves by this umbrella term, as we have seen in previous chapters, and sometimes by their specific caste name. Chellasamy's more precise jāti identity is Piramalai Kallar; Kannan's, Maravar; and Kannan's wife Vellaiamma, Agamudayar. All three of these people and their families alternate, depending on context, in identifying themselves as Thevar or as a member of their specific jāti.

2. MGR's year of birth is disputed. While official biographies list it as 1917, some analysts and fans believe MGR was born five to ten years earlier.

3. Appadurai suggested this term in his remarks as a discussant at the Global South Asia conference, New York University, in February 2014.

4. They also display potential elements of a fourth type, political patronage. From medieval times to the present, leaders have given material gifts to forge or reinforce relations with followers, and followers have acknowledged loyalty by accepting those gifts (see Dickey 1993). Because in Chellasamy's case this form of gifting was rarely mentioned and never actualized, I have omitted it here for reasons of space.

5. Dān appears frequently in the literature in part because it appears to contravene Marcel Mauss's (1990) classic contention that there are no "free gifts."

6. For overarching discussions of the perceived outcomes of dān, see Copeman (2011), Heim (2004), Laidlaw (1995), Parry (1986), and Raheja (1988, 1994).

7. I thank Ravi Sriramachandran, personal communication, for pointing out the importance of īkai and of koṭai, another Tamil concept of gifting. Koṭai can be glossed as "gift" or "munificence." In recent centuries, the two terms appear to have been used similarly, though īkai tends (not entirely consistently) to connote a more sizeable gift. (In addition, koṭai can refer to a gift for a god, as well as for a festival in honor of a deity, as in the following chapter.) The standard Tamil gloss for philanthropist or charitable donor is koṭaiyāḷar or koṭaiyāḷi.

See Meenakshi (1996) for a discussion of various Tamil concepts of gifts—including paricil, as well as īkai and koṭai—in the context of Sangam poetry; a briefer discussion is also found in Kailasapathy (1968, 218).

8. This usage of īkai in reference to gifts of food meant to allay hunger also appears in *Manimekalai* and in religious treatises of the eighteenth and nineteenth centuries (Raman 2013).

9. But see Caplan (2008), who observes a conscious attempt to relax rules of commensality among women friends of different castes and religions in Chennai.

10. In 2006, for example, the Election Manifesto of the AIADMK party (All India Anna Dravida Munnetra Kazhagam) listed "Annadhanam Scheme in Temples, Darghas and Churches to Feed Hungry Mouths" as one of Chief Minister J. Jayalalithaa's accomplishments from her 2001–2006 term (Palanithurai and Nanda 2007, 60).

11. After the famous mass conversion of Dalits to Islam in the village of Meenakshipuram in 1981, for example, Hindu leaders concerned about Dalits' disaffection held a camapanti pōjanam to reconcile low- and high-caste residents of the village (Samartha 1982).

12. While Jayalalitha and the AIADMK have sponsored annatānam, officials of the competing DMK party (Dravida Munnetra Kazhagam) have sponsored camapanti pōjanam. Both these parties have roots in the Dravidian Movement.

13. Tamil includes two forms of we/our, one of which (*namma*) includes listeners while the other excludes them. In Kannan's recounting, Chellasamy used the inclusive form when he said "our wedding," thus including the auto drivers with his family.

14. Deepavali, or Diwali, is the most important religious holiday of the year for most Hindus.

15. Nonetheless, it is extremely likely that some distinctions were created that might not have been visible to Kannan's family, such as directing different kinds of guests to different halls for dining.

16. Cf. De Neve (2011) on discourses of poverty, simple beginnings, and hard toil.

CHAPTER 9 — CONCLUSIONS: NUANCING CLASS BOUNDARIES

1. See Masilimani-Meyer (2004, 28–29) for alternate origin stories.

2. I have glossed kuri here as "predictions," but kuri function as a more complicated sign than this may suggest. The most fitting description I have found is Isabelle Nabokov's: she explains kuri as "the invisible 'marks' that encode the meaning of the past, present, and future" (2000, 20), marks that are seen and interpreted by the possessed person.

References

Agarwal, Bina. 1994. *A Field of One's Own*. Cambridge: Cambridge University Press.

Ahuja, Ravi. 2004. "State Formations and Famine Policy in Early Colonial South India." In *Land, Politics, and Trade in South Asia*, edited by Sanjay Subrahmanyam, 147–185. New Delhi: Oxford University Press.

Appadurai, Arjun. 1981. "Gastro-Politics in Hindu South Asia." *American Ethnologist* 8 (3): 494–511.

———. 2004. "The Capacity to Aspire: Culture and the Terms of Recognition." In *Culture and Public Action*, edited by Michael Walton and Vijayendra Rao, 59–84. Washington, DC: World Bank Publications.

Appadurai, Arjun and Carol A. Breckenridge. 1976. "The South Indian Temple: Authority, Honour, and Redistribution." *Contributions to Indian Sociology*, n.s., 10 (2): 187–211.

———. 1995. "Public Modernity in India." In *Consuming Modernity*, edited by Carol A. Breckenridge, 1–20. Minneapolis: University of Minnesota Press.

Arnold, David. 1984. "Famine in Peasant Consciousness and Peasant Action: Madras 1876–8." In *Subaltern Studies III*, edited by Ranajit Guha, 62–115. Delhi: Oxford University Press.

Austin, Granville. 1999. *Working a Democratic Constitution*. New Delhi: Oxford University Press.

Baker, Christopher John. 1976. *The Politics of South India, 1920–1937*. New Delhi: Vikas.

———. 1984. *An Indian Rural Economy 1880–1955*. Oxford: Clarendon.

Banerjee, Abhijit V. and Esther Duflo. 2007. "The Economic Lives of the Poor." *Journal of Economic Perspectives* 21 (1): 141–168.

Banerjee, Mukulika and Daniel Miller. 2003. *The Sari*. Oxford: Berg.

Banks, Marcus. 2001. *Visual Methods in Social Research*. London: Sage.

Bardhan, Pranab. 1984. *The Political Economy of Development in India*. London: Oxford University Press.

Basile, Elisabetta and Barbara Harriss-White. 2003. "Corporatist Capitalism: The Politics of Accumulation in South India." In *Asian Politics in Development*, edited by Robert Benewick, Mark Blecher, and Sarah Cook, 109–122. London: Routledge.

Baskaran, S. T. 1981. *The Message Bearers*. Madras: Cre-A.

Basu, Alaka Malwade. 1999. "Fertility Decline and Increasing Gender Imbalance in India, Including a Possible South Indian Turnaround." *Development and Change* 30 (2): 237–263.

Bayly, C. A. 1983. *Rulers, Townsmen, and Bazaars*. Cambridge: Cambridge University Press.

Beck, Brenda E. F. 1972. *Peasant Society in Koṅku*. Vancouver: University of British Columbia Press.

Bennett, Tony and Elizabeth Silva. 2011. "Introduction: Cultural Capital—Histories, Limits, Prospects." *Poetics* 39 (6): 427–443.

Bennett, Tony, Mike Savage, Elizabeth Silva, Alan Warde, Modesto Gayo-Cal, and David Wright. 2009. *Culture, Class, Distinction*. London: Routledge.

Berry, Mary Elizabeth. 1987. "Giving in Asia—A Symposium." *Journal of Asian Studies* 46 (2): 305–308.

Béteille, André. 1974. *Studies in Agrarian Social Structure*. Delhi: Oxford University Press.

———. 1991. "The Reproduction of Inequality: Occupation, Caste, and Family." *Contributions to Indian Sociology*, n.s., 25 (1): 3–28.

———. 2001. "The Social Character of the Indian Middle Class." In *Middle Class Values in India and Western Europe*, edited by Imtiaz Ahmad and Helmut Reifeld, 73–85. New Delhi: Social Science.

Bhattacharya, Sabyasachi. 2006. "Introduction." In *Coolies, Capital, and Colonialism*, edited by Rana P. Behal and Marcel van der Linden, 7–19. Cambridge: Cambridge University Press.

Biehl, João. 2009. *Will to Live*. Princeton: Princeton University Press.

Billig, Michael S. 1992. "The Marriage Squeeze and the Rise of Groomprice in India's Kerala State." *Journal of Comparative Family Studies* 23 (2): 197–216.

Bittles, A. H. and R. Hussain. 2000. "An Analysis of Consanguineous Marriage in the Muslim Population of India at Regional and State Levels." *Annals of Human Biology* 27 (2): 163–171.

Blackburn, Stuart H. 1978. "The Folk Hero and Class Interests in Tamil Heroic Ballads." *Asian Folklore Studies* 37 (1): 131–149.

———. 1981. "Oral Performance: Narrative and Ritual in a Tamil Tradition." *Journal of American Folklore* 94 (372): 207–227.

Bloch, Francis and Vijayendra Rao. 2002. "Terror as a Bargaining Instrument: A Case Study of Dowry Violence in Rural India." *American Economic Review* 92 (4): 1029–1043.

Bloch, Francis, Vijayendra Rao, and Sonalde Desai. 2004. "Wedding Celebrations as Conspicuous Consumption: Signaling Social Status in Rural India." *Journal of Human Resources* 39 (3): 675–695.

Blok, Anton. 2001. *Honour and Violence*. Cambridge: Polity.

Bonta, Steven. 2005. "In the Still of the Night." *Via Negativa*. Accessed January 31, 2015, http://www.vianegativa.us/author/steven.

Bornstein, Erica. 2009. "The Impulse of Philanthropy." *Cultural Anthropology* 24 (4): 622–651.

Bourdieu, Pierre. 1984. *Distinction*. Translated by Richard Nice. Cambridge, MA: Harvard University Press.

———. 1986. "The Forms of Capital." In *Handbook of Theory and Research for the Sociology of Education*, edited by John G. Richardson, 241–258. Westport, CT: Greenwood.

———. 1990a. *In Other Words: Essays towards a Reflexive Sociology*. Translated by Matthew Adamson. Cambridge: Polity.

———. 1990b. *The Logic of Practice*. Translated by Richard Nice. Stanford, CA: Stanford University Press.

Bradford, Nicholas J. 1985. "From Bridewealth to Groom-fee: Transformed Marriage Customs and Socio-economic Polarisation amongst Lingayats." *Contributions to Indian Sociology*, n.s., 19 (2): 269–302.

Brennan, Geoffrey and Philip Pettit. 2004. *The Economy of Esteem*. Oxford: Oxford University Press.

Brosius, Christiane. 2010. *India's Middle Class*. London: Routledge.

Butler, Judith. 1993. *Bodies That Matter*. New York: Routledge.

Caldwell, J. C., P. H. Reddy, and Pat Caldwell. 1983. "The Causes of Marriage Change in South India." *Population Studies* 37 (3): 343–361.

Caplan, Lionel. 1984. "Bridegroom Price in Urban India: Class, Caste, and 'Dowry Evil' among Christians in Madras." *Man* 19 (2): 216–233.

———. 1987. *Class and Culture in Urban India*. Oxford: Clarendon.

———. 1998. "Gifting and Receiving: Anglo-Indian Charity and Its Beneficiaries in Madras." *Contributions to Indian Sociology*, n.s., 32 (2): 409–431.

Caplan, Patricia. 1985. *Class and Gender in India*. London: Tavistock.

———. 2008. "Crossing the Veg/Non-Veg Divide: Commensality and Sociality among the Middle Classes in Madras/Chennai." *South Asia* 31 (1): 118–142.

Carswell, Grace and Geert De Neve. 2014. "T-shirts and Tumblers: Caste, Politics, and Industrial Work in Tiruppur's Textile Belt, South India." *Contributions to Indian Sociology*, n.s., 48 (1): 103–131.

Castleman, Tony. 2011. "Human Recognition and Its Role in Economic Development: A Descriptive Review." Institute for International Economic Policy Working Paper Series. George Washington University.

Chakrabarti, Anjan and Stephen Cullenberg. 2003. *Transition and Development in India.* New York: Routledge.

Chakrabarti, Rajesh. 2005 "Banking in India—Reforms and Reorganization." *Social Science Research Network.* Accessed January 31, 2015, http://papers.ssrn.com/sof3/papers.cfm?abstract_id=649855.

Chakrabarty, Dipesh. 1993. "Marx after Marxism: A Subaltern Historian's Perspective." *Economic and Political Weekly* 28 (2): 1094–1086.

———. 1995. "Radical Histories and Question of Enlightenment Rationalism: Some Recent Critiques of *Subaltern Studies.*" *Economic and Political Weekly* 30 (14): 751–759.

Chambers, Robert. 1992. "Poverty in India: Concepts, Research, and Reality." In *Poverty in India*, edited by Barbara Harriss, S. Guhan, and R. H. Cassen, 301–332. New Delhi: Oxford University Press.

Chandavarkar, Rajnarayan. 1998. *Imperial Power and Popular Politics.* Cambridge: Cambridge University Press.

Chaturvedi, Vinayak. 2007. "A Critical Theory of Subalternity: Rethinking Class in Indian Historiography." *Left History* 12 (1): 9–28.

Chavan, Pallavi. 2007. "Access to Bank Credit: Implications for Dalit Rural Households." *Economic and Political Weekly* 42 (31): 3219–3224.

Chibber, Vivek. 2006. "On the Decline of Class Analysis in South Asian Studies." *Critical Asian Studies* 38 (4): 357–387.

Clark-Decès [Nabokov], Isabelle. 2014. *The Right Spouse.* Stanford, CA: Stanford University Press.

Constable, Nicole. 2003. *Romance on a Global Stage.* Berkeley: University of California Press.

Copeman, Jacob. 2011. "The Gift and Its Forms of Life in Contemporary India." *Modern Asian Studies* 45 (5): 1051–1094.

Currie, Kate. 1992. "The Indian Stratification Debate: A Discursive Exposition of Problems and Issues in the Analysis of Caste, Class and Gender." *Dialectical Anthropology* 17 (2): 115–139.

Da Costa, Dia. 2008. "'Spoiled Sons' and 'Sincere Daughters': Schooling, Security, and Empowerment in Rural West Bengal, India." *Signs* 33 (2): 283–308.

Daniel, E. Valentine. 1984. *Fluid Signs.* Berkeley: University of California Press.

Dean, Melanie. 2011. "From Darśan to Tiruṣṭi: 'Evil Eye' and the Politics of Visibility in Contemporary South India." Ph.D. diss., University of Pennsylvania.

———. 2013. "From 'Evil Eye' Anxiety to the Desirability of Envy: Status, Consumption, and the Politics of Visibility in Urban South India." *Contributions to Indian Sociology*, n.s., 47 (2): 185–216.

De Neve, Geert. 1999. "Asking for and Giving Baki: Neo-bondage, or the Interplay of Bondage and Resistance in the Tamilnadu Power-Loom Industry." *Contributions to Indian Sociology*, n.s., 33 (1–2): 379.

———. 2005. *The Everyday Politics of Labour.* New Delhi: Social Science Press.

———. 2006. "Economic Liberalisation, Class Restructuring, and Social Space in Provincial South India." In *The Meaning of the Local*, edited by Geert De Neve and Henrike Donner, 21–43. London: Routledge.

———. 2011. "'Keeping It in the Family': Work, Education, and Gender Hierarchies among Tiruppur's Industrial Capitalists." In *Being Middle Class in India*, edited by Henrike Donner, 73–99. London: Routledge.

Department of Telecommunications. 2015. "Annual Report 2014–15." Accessed December 13, 2015, http://www.dot.gov.in/sites/default/files/u10/English%20AR%202015.pdf.

Derné, Steve. 2005. "Globalization and the Making of a Transnational Middle Class: Implications for Class Analysis." In *Critical Globalization Studies*, edited by Richard P. Applebaum and William I. Robinson, 177–186. New York: Routledge.

Desai, Sonalde. 2007. "The Middle Class." In *The Oxford Companion to Economics in India*, edited by Kaushik Basu, 345–347. New Delhi: Oxford University Press.

Desai, Sonalde and Lester Andrist. 2010. "Gender Scripts and Age at Marriage in India." *Demography* 47 (3): 667–687.

Desai, Sonalde and Amaresh Dubey. 2011. "Caste in 21st Century India: Competing Narratives." *Economic and Political Weekly* 46 (11): 40–49.

Desai, Sonalde and Veena Kulkarni. 2008. "Changing Educational Inequalities in India in the Context of Affirmative Action." *Demography* 45 (2): 245–270.

Deshpande, Satish. 2003. *Contemporary India.* New Delhi: Penguin.

Dickey, Sara. 1993. "The Politics of Adulation: Cinema and the Production of Politicians in South India." *Journal of Asian Studies* 52 (2): 340–372.

———. 2000a. "Mutual Exclusions: Domestic Workers and Employers on Labor, Class, and Character in South India." In *Home and Hegemony*, edited by Kathleen M. Adams and Sara Dickey, 31–62. Ann Arbor: University of Michigan Press.

———. 2000b. "Permeable Homes: Domestic Service, Household Space, and the Vulnerability of Class Boundaries in Urban India." *American Ethnologist* 27 (2): 462–489.

———. 2001. "Opposing Faces: Film Star Fan Clubs and the Construction of Class Identity in South India." In *Pleasure and the Nation*, edited by Christopher Pinney and Rachel Dwyer, 212–246. Delhi: Oxford University Press.

———. 2005. "Still 'One Man in a Thousand.'" In *Living Pictures*, edited by David Blamey and Robert E. D'Souza, 69–78. London: Open Editions.

———. 2008. "The Nurturing Hero: Changing Images of MGR." In *Tamil Cinema*, edited by Selvaraj Velayutham. London: RoutledgeCurzon.

———. 2010. "Anjali's Alliance: Class Mobility in Urban India." In *Everyday Life in South Asia*, edited by Diane P. Mines and Sarah Lamb, 2nd ed., 192–205. Bloomington: Indiana University Press.

———. 2012. "The Pleasures and Anxieties of Being in the Middle: Emerging Middle Class Identities in Urban South India." *Modern Asian Studies* 46 (3): 559–599.

———. 2013. "Apprehensions: On Gaining Recognition as Middle-Class in Madurai," *Contributions to Indian Sociology*, n.s., 47 (2): 217–243.

———. n.d.a. "A Century of Class Analysis in India." Unpublished ms.

———. n.d.b. "Scarce Grooms, Unproductive Women, Sanskritizing Castes, and . . . Hypergamy? Problems with the Literature on Dowry in South India." Unpublished ms.

Dirks, Nicholas. 1982. "The Pasts of a *Pāḷaiyakārar*: The Ethnohistory of a South Indian Little King." *Journal of Asian Studies* 41 (4): 655–683.

———. 1987. *The Hollow Crown*. Cambridge: Cambridge University Press.

———. 2001. *Castes of Mind*. Princeton: Princeton University Press.

Donner, Henrike. 2008. *Domestic Goddesses*. Hampshire: Ashgate.

Donner, Henrike and Geert De Neve. 2011. "Introduction." In *Being Middle Class in India*, edited by Henrike Donner, 1–22. London: Routledge.

Donner, Jonathan, Nimmi Rangaswamy, Molly Wright Steenson, and Carolyn Wei. 2008. "'Express Yourself' and 'Stay Together': The Middle Class Indian Family." In *Handbook of Mobile Communication Studies*, edited by James E. Katz, 325–337. Cambridge, MA: MIT.

Doron, Assa. 2010. "India's Mobile Revolution: A View from Below." *Inside Story*. Accessed May 3, 2010, http://inside.org.au/india-mobile-revolution.

———. 2012. "Mobile Persons: Cell Phones, Gender, and the Self in North India." *Asia Pacific Journal of Anthropology* 13 (5): 414–433.

Dumont, Louis. 1980. *Homo Hierarchicus*. Rev. ed. Translated by Mark Sainsbury, Louis Dumont, and Basia Gulati. London: Weidenfeld and Nicholson.

———. 1983. *Affinity as a Value*. Chicago: University of Chicago Press.

Dutt, Ashok K., Allen G. Noble, and Zeenat Hasan. 1994. "Spatial Pattern of Commercial Establishments in Two South Asian City Centers: Rajshahi and Madurai." In *The Asian City*, edited by Ashok K. Dutt, Frank J. Costa, Surinder Aggarwal, and Allen G. Noble, 99–118. Dordrecht: Kluwer.

Dwyer, Rachel. 2000. *All You Want Is Money, All You Need Is Love*. New York: Cassell.

Eck, Diana L. 1981. *Darśan*. Chambersburg, PA: Anima.

Ehouman, Lydie, Sandra Fried, Theresa Mann, and Haroon Ullah. 2002. "Tamil Nadu: The Path to Becoming India's Leading State." Strategy Paper. Center for International Development, Kennedy School of Government, Harvard University. Accessed September 5, 2015, http://www.cid.harvard.edu/archive/india/pdfs/tamilnadu_leadingstate.pdf.

Epstein, T. Scarlett. 1973. *South India*. New York: Holmes & Meier.

Fernandes, Leela. 2000a. "Nationalizing 'The Global': Media Images, Cultural Politics, and the Middle Class in India." *Media, Culture & Society* 22 (5): 611–628.

———. 2000b. "Restructuring the New Middle Class in Liberalizing India." *Comparative Studies of South Asia, Africa, and the Middle East* 20 (1/2): 88–104.

———. 2006. *India's New Middle Class*. Minneapolis: University of Minnesota Press.

Fernandes, Leela and Patrick Heller. 2006. "Hegemonic Aspirations: New Middle Class Politics and India's Democracy in Comparative Perspective." *Critical Asian Studies* 38 (4): 495–522.

Fiske, John. 1992. "The Cultural Economy of Fandom." In *The Adoring Audience*, edited by Lisa A. Lewis, 30–49. London: Routledge.

Foucault, Michel. 1978. *The History of Sexuality*, Vol. 1. Translated by Robert Hurley. New York: Pantheon.

———. 1980. *Power/Knowledge*. Translated and edited by Colin Gordon. New York: Pantheon.

Frankel, Francine. 2005. *India's Political Economy, 1947–2004*. 2nd ed. New Delhi: Oxford University Press.

Frøystad, Kathinka. 2005. *Blended Boundaries*. New Delhi: Oxford University Press.

———. 2006. "Anonymous Encounters: Class Categorisation and Social Distancing in Public Places." In *The Meaning of the Local*, edited by Geert De Neve and Henrike Donner, 159–181. London: Routledge.

Fujita Koichi and Sato Keiko. 2011. "Self-Help Groups and the Rural Financial Market in South India: A Case of a Tamil Nadu Village." *Southeast Asian Studies* 49 (1): 74–92.

Fuller, C. J. 1973. "Caste and Class, or the Anthropology of Underdevelopment." *Cambridge Anthropology* 1 (1): 1–9.

———. 1996. "Introduction: Caste Today." In *Caste Today*, edited by C. J. Fuller, 1–31. New York: Oxford University Press.

Fuller, C. J. and Haripriya Narasimhan. 2007. "Information Technology Professionals and the New-Rich Middle Class in Chennai (Madras)." *Modern Asian Studies* 41 (1): 121–150.

———. 2008a. "Companionate Marriage in India: The Changing Marriage System in a Middle-Class Brahman Subcaste." *Journal of the Royal Anthropological Institute*, n.s., 14 (4): 736–754.

———. 2008b. "From Landlords to Software Engineers: Migration and Urbanization among Tamil Brahmins." *Comparative Studies in Society and History* 50 (1): 170–196.

———. 2014. *Tamil Brahmans*. Chicago: University of Chicago Press.

Ganguly-Scrase, Ruchira and Timothy J. Scrase. 2008. "Hegemony, Globalisation, and Neoliberalism: The Case of West Bengal, India." In *Hegemony*, edited by Richard Howson and Kylie Smith, 184–200. New York: Routledge.

———. 2009. *Globalization and the Middle Classes in India*. London: Routledge.

Gaulin, Steven J. C. and James S. Boster. 1990. "Dowry as Female Competition." *American Anthropologist* 92 (4): 994–1005.

Ghosh, Jayati. 1994. "Gender Concerns in Macro-Economic Policy." *Economic and Political Weekly* 29 (18): WS2–WS4.

Gilbertson, Amanda. 2014a. "A Fine Balance: Negotiating Fashion and Respectable Femininity in Middle-Class Hyderabad, India." *Modern Asian Studies* 48 (1): 120–158.

———. 2014b. "From Respect to Friendship? Companionate Marriage and Conjugal Power Negotiation in Middle-Class Hyderabad." *South Asia* 37 (2): 225–238.

Ginsburg, Faye. 1993. "The Case of Mistaken Identity: Problems in Representing Women on the Right." In *When They Read What We Write: The Politics of Ethnography*, edited by Caroline B. Brettell, 163–176. Westport, CT: Bergin & Garvey.

Goffman, Erving. 1959. *The Presentation of Self in Everyday Life*. Rev. ed. Garden City, NY: Doubleday.

Good, Anthony. 1980. "Elder Sister's Daughter Marriage in South Asia." *Journal of Anthropological Research* 36 (4): 474–500.

———. 1981. "Prescription, Preference, and Practice: Marriage Patterns among the Kondaiyankottai Maravar of South India." *Man*, n.s., 16 (1): 108–129.

Gorringe, Hugo. 2006. "'Banal Violence'? The Everyday Underpinnings of Collective Violence." *Identities* 13 (2): 237–260.

———. 2010. "Shifting the 'Grindstone of Caste'? Decreasing Dependency among Dalit Labourers in Tamil Nadu." In *The Comparative Political Economy of Development*, edited by Barbara Harriss-White and Judith Heyer, 248–266. London: Routledge.

Gough, Kathleen. 1956. "Brahman Kinship in a Tamil Village." *American Anthropologist*, n.s., 58 (5): 826–853.

Government of India. 2003. "Housing Profile, Tamil Nadu." *Census of India 2001*. Accessed February 5, 2004, http://www.censusindia.net/state_index.html.

———. 2012. "Tamil Nadu Houses Household Amenities and Assets Figures at a Glance." *Census of India 2011*. Accessed August 25, 2015, http://censusindia.gov.in/2011census/hlo/Data_sheet/TN/Figures_at_a_glance.pdf.

Graeber, David. 2011. *Debt*. Brooklyn, NY: Melville House.

Green, Maia. 2006. "Representing Poverty and Attacking Representations: Perspectives on Poverty from Social Anthropology." *Journal of Development Studies* 42 (7): 1108–1129.

Greenough, Paul. 1995. "Nation, Economy, and Tradition Displayed: The Crafts Museum, New Delhi." In *Consuming Modernity*, edited by Carol A. Breckenridge, 216–248. Minneapolis: University of Minnesota Press.

Gregory, Chris A. 1997. *Savage Money*. Amsterdam: Harwood Academic.

———. 2012. "On Money Debt and Morality: Some Reflections on the Contribution of Economic Anthropology." *Social Anthropology* 20 (4): 380–396.

Guérin, Isabelle, Bert D'Espallier, Marc Roesch, and G. Venkatasubramanian. 2011. "Debt in Rural South India: Fragmentation, Social Regulation, and Discrimination." RUME Working Paper Series 2011-3.

Guérin, Isabelle, Marc Roesch, Govindan Venkatasubramanian, and Bert D'Espallier. 2012. "Credit from Whom and for What? The Diversity of Borrowing Sources and Uses in Rural Southern India." *Journal of International Development* 24 (Supplement S1): S122–S137.

Guérin, Isabelle, Marc Roesch, Govindan Venkatasubramanian, and Santosh Kumar. 2011. "The Social Meaning of Over-Indebtedness and Creditworthiness in the Context of Poor Rural South India Households (Tamil Nadu)." RUME Working Paper Series 2011-1.

Hacking, Ian. 2004. "Between Michel Foucault and Erving Goffman: Between Discourse in the Abstract and Face-to-Face Interaction." *Economy and Society* 33 (3): 277–302.

Hancock, Mary. 1995. "Hindu Culture for an Indian Nation: Gender, Politics, and Elite Identity in Urban South India." *American Ethnologist* 22 (4): 907–926.

———. 1999. *Womanhood in the Making.* Boulder, CO: Westview.

Hardgrave, Robert L., Jr. 1969. *The Nadars of Tamilnad.* Berkeley: University of California Press.

Harper, Edward. 1963. "Spirit Possession and Social Structure." In *Anthropology on the March*, edited by L. K. Bala Ratnam, 165–177. Madras: Book Centre and Social Sciences Association.

Harriss, John. 1982. *Capitalism and Peasant Farming.* Bombay: Oxford University Press.

———. 1991. "A Review of Rural Society and Agrarian Change in South Asia." *South Asia Research* 11 (1): 16–39.

———. 2006. "Middle-Class Activism and the Politics of the Informal Working Class: A Perspective on Class Relations and Civil Society in Indian Cities." *Critical Asian Studies* 38 (4): 445–465.

———. 2009. "Bringing Politics Back into Poverty Analysis: Why Understanding of Social Relations Matters More for Policy on Chronic Poverty than Measurement." In *Poverty Dynamics*, edited by Tony Addison, David Hulme, and Ravi Kanbur, 205–224. Oxford: Oxford University Press.

Harriss-White, Barbara. 2003. *India Working.* Cambridge: Cambridge University Press.

———. 2004. "Food, Nutrition, and the State in Northern Tamil Nadu." In *Rural India Facing the 21st Century*, edited by Barbara Harriss-White and S. Janakarajan, 373–410. London: Anthem.

Harriss-White, Barbara and Diego Colatei. 2004. "Rural Credit and the Collateral Question." In *Rural India Facing the 21st Century*, edited by Barbara Harriss-White and S. Janakarajan, 252–283. London: Anthem.

Haynes, Douglas E. 1987. "From Tribute to Philanthropy: The Politics of Gift Giving in a Western Indian City." *Journal of Asian Studies* 46 (2): 339–360.

———. 1991. *Rhetoric and Ritual in Colonial India*. Berkeley: University of California Press.

Haynes, Douglas E. and Abigail McGowan. 2010. "Introduction." In *Towards a History of Consumption in South Asia*, edited by Douglas E. Haynes, Abigail McGowan, Tirthankar Roy, and Haruka Yanagisawa, 1–25. New Delhi: Oxford University Press.

Heim, Maria. 2004. *Theories of the Gift in South Asia*. London: Routledge.

Hermann, Steffen K. 2011. "Social Exclusion: Practices of Misrecognition." In *Humiliation, Degradation, Dehumanization: Human Dignity Violated*, edited by Paulus Kaufmann, Hannes Kuch, Christian Neuhäeuser, and Elaine Webster, 133–149. New York: Springer.

Herring, Ronald J. and Rina Agarwala. 2006. "Restoring Agency to Class: Puzzles from the Subcontinent." *Critical Asian Studies* 38 (4): 323–356.

Heyer, Judith. 1992. "The Role of Dowries and Daughters' Marriages in the Accumulation and Distribution of Capital in a South Indian Community." *Journal of International Development* 4 (4): 419–436.

———. 2000. "The Changing Position of *Thottam Farmers* in Villages in Rural Coimbatore, Tamil Nadu, between 1981/2 and 1996." Working Paper Number 59. QEH Working Paper Series.

———. 2012. "Labour Standards and Social Policy: A South Indian Case Study." *Global Labour Journal* 3 (1): 91–117.

Holmström, Mark. 1972. "Caste and Status in an Indian City." *Economic and Political Weekly* 7 (15): 769–744.

Honneth, A. 1995. *The Struggle for Recognition*. Cambridge: Polity.

Ifeka, Caroline. 1989. "Hierarchical Woman: The 'Dowry' System and Its Implications among Christians in Goa, India." *Contributions to Indian Sociology*, n.s., 23 (2): 261–284.

Inden, Ronald. 2000. *Imagining India*. Bloomington: Indiana University Press.

Inglis, Stephen. 1985. "Possession and Poverty: Serving the Divine in a South Indian Community." In *Gods of Flesh, Gods of Stone*, edited by Joanne Punzo Waghorne and Norman Cutler, with Vasudha Narayanan, 89–102. Chambersburg, PA: Anima.

Iyer, Sriya. 2002. *Demography and Religion in India*. Oxford: Oxford University Press.

Jackson, Michael. 1998. *Minima Ethnographica*. Chicago: University of Chicago Press.

Jeffery, Patricia. 2014. "Supply-and-Demand Demographics: Dowry, Daughter Aversion, and Marriage Markets in Contemporary North India." *Contemporary South Asia* 22 (2): 171–188.

Jeffery, Roger, Patricia Jeffery, and Craig Jeffrey. 2011. "Are Rich Rural Jats Middle-Class?" In *Elite and Everyman*, edited by Amita Baviskar and Raka Ray, 140–163. London: Routledge.

Jeffrey, Craig. 2001. "'A Fist Is Stronger Than Five Fingers': Caste and Dominance in Rural North India." *Transactions of the Institute of British Geographers* 26 (2): 217–236.

Jeffrey, Robin and Assa Doron. 2011. "Celling India: Exploring a Society's Embrace of the Mobile Phone." *South Asian History and Culture* 2 (3): 397–416.

———. 2012. "Mobile-izing: Democracy, Organization and India's First 'Mass Mobile Phone Elections.'" *Journal of Asian Studies* 71 (1): 63–80.

———. 2013. *The Great Indian Phone Book*. Cambridge, MA: Harvard University Press.

Jenkins, Richard. 2008. *Social Identity*. 3rd ed. New York: Routledge.

Jeromi, P. D. 2007. "Regulation of Informal Financial Institutions: A Study of Money Lenders in Kerala." *Reserve Bank of India Occasional Papers* 28 (1): 1–31.

John, S. Simon. 2008. "Kaniyan: Ritual Performers of Tamil Nadu, South India." *Asian Ethnology* 67 (1): 123–135.

Joshi, Vijay and I.M.D. Little. 1996. *India's Economic Reforms: 1991–2001*. Oxford: Clarendon.

Jouhki, Jukka. 2013. "A Phone of One's Own? Social Value, Cultural Meaning, and Gendered Use of the Mobile Phone in South India." *Suomen Antropologi: Journal of the Finnish Anthropological Society* 38 (1): 37–58.

Kailasapathy, K. 1968. *Tamil Heroic Poetry*. Oxford: Clarendon.

Kalam, M. S. 2004. "Language, Ethnicity, and Identity among the Muslims of the Palar Valley." In *Industrialisation and Socio-Cultural Change in the Tannery Belt of the Palar Valley (Tamil Nadu)*, edited by Loraine Kennedy. Pondicherry: French Institute of Pondicherry. Accessed June 28, 2014, http://www.palar.cnrs.fr/PUB%20WORD/Kalam2004.pdf.

Kalb, Don. 1997. *Expanding Class*. Durham, NC: Duke University Press.

———. 2005. "'Bare Legs Like Ice': Recasting Class for Local/Global Inquiry." In *Critical Junctions*, edited by Don Kalb and Herman Tak, 109–136. New York: Berghahn.

Kapadia, Karin. 1993. "Marrying Money: Changing Preference and Practice in Tamil Marriage." *Contributions to Indian Sociology*, n.s., 27 (1): 25–51.

———. 1995. *Siva and Her Sisters*. Boulder, CO: Westview.

———. 1996. "Dancing the Goddess: Possession and Class in Tamil South India." *Modern Asian Studies* 30 (2): 423–445.

———. 1999. "Gender Ideologies and the Formation of Rural Industrial Classes in South India Today." *Contributions to Indian Sociology*, n.s., 33 (1/2): 329–352.

Kar, Sohini. 2013. "Recovering Debt: Microfinance Loan Officers and the Work of 'Proxy-Creditors' in India." *American Ethnologist* 40 (3): 480–493.

Kaufmann, Paulus, Hannes Kuch, Christian Neuehäuser, and Elaine Webster. 2011. *Humiliation, Degradation, Dehumanization*. New York: Springer.

Khare, R. S. 1986. "Hospitality, Charity, and Rationing: Three Channels of Food Distribution in India." In *Food, Society & Culture*, edited by R. S. Khare and M.S.A. Rao, 277–296. Durham, NC: Carolina Academic.

———. 1992. "*Annabrahman*: Cultural Models, Meanings, and Aesthetics of Hindu Food." In *The Eternal Food*, edited by R. S. Khare, 201–220. Albany: SUNY Press.

Kjaersholm, Lars. 1990. "Kula Teyvam Worship in Tamilnadu: A Link between Past and Present." In *Rites and Beliefs in Modern India*, edited by Gabriella Eichinger Ferro-Luzzi, 67–87. Delhi: Manohar.

Kodoth, Praveena. 2006. "Producing a Rationale for Dowry?" Working Paper 16, London School of Economics, Asia Research Centre.

Kohli, Atul. 1990. *Democracy and Discontent*. Cambridge: Cambridge University Press.

Kolenda, Pauline. 2003. *Caste, Marriage, and Inequality*. Jaipur: Rawat.

Kothari, Rajni. 1995. *Poverty*. Atlantic Highlands, NJ: Zed.

Kretzmer, David and Eckart Klein, eds. 2002. *The Concept of Human Dignity in Human Rights Discourse*. The Hague: Kluwer Law International.

Krishnamoorthy, S. and N. Audinarayana. 2001. "Trends in Consanguinity in South India." *Journal of Biosocial Science* 33 (2): 185–197.

Kumar, Dharma. 1983. "South India." In *The Cambridge Economic History of India*, edited by Dharma Kumar, with Meghnad Desai, vol. 2, 207–241. Cambridge: Cambridge University Press.

Laidlaw, James. 1995. *Riches and Renunciation*. Oxford: Clarendon.

Lakha, Salim. 1999. "The State, Globalisation, and Indian Middle-Class Identity." In *Culture and Privilege in Capitalist Asia*, edited by Michael Pinches, 251–274. New York: Routledge.

Lakshmi, C. S. 1989. "On Kidneys and Dowry." *Economic and Political Weekly* 24 (4): 189–190.

Lamont, Michele. 1992. *Money, Morals, and Manners*. Chicago: University of Chicago Press.

Lamont, Michele and Annette Lareau. 1988. "Cultural Capital: Allusions, Gaps, and Glissandos in Recent Theoretical Developments." *Sociological Theory* 6 (2): 153–168.

Lareau, Annette and Elliot B. Weininger. 2003. "Cultural Capital in Educational Research: A Critical Assessment." *Theory and Society* 32 (5/6): 567–606.

Lemanski, Charlotte and Stéphanie Tawa Lama-Rewal. 2013. "The 'Missing Middle': Class and Urban Governance in Delhi's Unauthorised Colonies." *Transactions* 38 (1): 91–105.

Liechty, Mark. 2003. *Suitably Modern*. Princeton: Princeton University Press.

Ludden, David. 1985. *Peasant History in South India*. Princeton: Princeton University Press.

———. 2002. "Introduction: A Brief History of Subalternity." In *Reading Subaltern Studies*, edited by David Ludden, 1–39. London: Anthem.

Lukose, Ritty. 2009. *Liberalization's Children*. Durham, NC: Duke University Press.

Mankekar, Purnima. 1999. *Screening Culture, Viewing Politics*. Durham, NC: Duke University Press.

Mannathukkaren, Nissim. 2011. "Redistribution and Recognition: Land Reforms in Kerala and the Limits of Culturalism." *Journal of Peasant Studies* 38 (2): 379–411.

Marriott, McKim. 1968. "Caste Ranking and Food Transactions: A Matrix Analysis." In *Structure and Change in Indian Society*, edited by Milton Singer and Bernard S. Cohn, 133–171. Chicago: Aldine.

Masilamani-Meyer, Eveline. 2004. *Guardians of Tamilnadu*. Halle: Verlag der Franckeschen Stiftungen zu Halle.

Mauss, Marcel. 1990. *The Gift*. Translated by W. D. Halls. New York: W. W. Norton.

Mayer, Adrian C. 1970. *Caste and Kinship in an Indian Village*. Berkeley: University of California Press.

Mazzarella, William. 2003. *Shoveling Smoke*. Durham, NC: Duke University Press.

———. 2005. "Middle Class." In *Keywords in South Asian Studies*, edited by Rachel Dwyer. Accessed January 31, 2015, https://www.soas.ac.uk/south-asia-institute/keywords/file24808.pdf.

McCarthy, Paul. 1994. *Postmodern Desire*. New Delhi: Promilla and Co.

McGilvray, Dennis B. 1998. *Symbolic Heat*. Middletown, N.J.: Grantha.

McGowan, Abigail. 2009. *Crafting the Nation in Colonial India*. New York: Palgrave Macmillan.

Meenakshi, K. 1996. "Guidance Poems (Āṟṟupaṭai) and the Dānastutis (RV): A Comparative Study." *Journal of Tamil Studies* 49–50: 103–139.

Meinzen, Ruth Suneela. 1980. "Norms and Realities of Marriage Arrangements in a South Indian Town." *Economic & Political Weekly* 15 (27): 1137–1144.

Menon, Purnima, Anil Deolalikar, and Anjor Bhaskar. 2008. *India State Hunger Index*. Washington, DC: International Food Policy Research Institute.

Meyer, Christian and Nancy Birdsall. 2012. "New Estimates of India's Middle Class: Technical Note." Washington, DC: Center for Global Development.

Meyer, Michael J. 2002. "Dignity as a (Modern) Virtue." In *The Concept of Human Dignity in Human Rights Discourse*, edited by David Kretzmer and Eckart Klein, 195–208. The Hague: Kluwer Law International.

Mies, Maria. 1980. "Capitalist Development and Subsistence Reproduction; Rural Women in India." *Bulletin of Concerned Asian Scholars* 12 (1): 2–14.

Miller, Daniel. 1987. *Material Culture and Mass Consumption*. Oxford: Blackwell.

———. 2010. *Stuff*. Cambridge: Polity.

Mines, Diane P. 2005. *Fierce Gods*. Bloomington: Indiana University Press.

Mines, Mattison. 1994. *Public Faces, Private Voices*. Berkeley: University of California Press.

Mody, Perveez. 2008. *The Intimate State*. New Delhi: Routledge.

Moreno, Manuel. 1992. "Pañcāmirtam: God's Washings as Food." In *The Eternal Food*, edited by R. S. Khare, 147–178. New York: SUNY Press.

Mosse, David. 1994. "Idioms of Subordination and Styles of Protest among Christian and Hindu Harijan Castes in Tamil Nadu." *Contributions to Indian Sociology*, n.s., 28 (1): 67–106.

———. 2010. "A Relational Approach to Durable Poverty, Inequality and Power." *Journal of Development Studies* 46 (7): 1156–1178.

Motiram, Sripad and Nayantara Sarma. 2011. "Polarization, Inequality, and Growth: The Indian Experience." Working paper, Mumbai: Indira Gandhi Institute of Development Research.

Mukund, Kanakalatha. 1999a. *The Trading World of the Tamil Merchant*. Hyderabad: Orient Longman.

———. 1999b. "Women's Property Rights: A Review." *Economic and Political Weekly* 34 (22): 1352–1358.

Munn, Nancy D. 1986. *The Fame of Gawa*. Cambridge: Cambridge University Press.

Myers, Fred R. 2001. "Introduction: The Empire of Things." In *The Empire of Things*, edited by Fred Myers, 3–61. Santa Fe: School of American Research.

Nabokov, Isabelle [Clark-Decès]. 2000. *Religion against the Self*. Oxford: Oxford University Press.

Nair, Janaki. 2005. *The Promise of the Metropolis*. Delhi: Oxford University Press.

Nakassis, Constantine. 2013. "Youth Masculinity, 'Style,' and the Peer Group in Tamil Nadu, India." *Contributions to Indian Sociology* 47 (2): 245–269.

———. n.d. "Brand and Brandedness in Tamil Nadu, India." Unpublished ms. in author's possession.

Narayan, Deepa, Denis Nikitin, and Brice Richard. 2009. "Communities Where Poor People Prosper." In *Moving Out of Poverty*, edited by Deepa Narayan, vol. 3, 64–111. New York: Palgrave Macmillan and The World Bank.

Narayana Rao, Velcheru, David Shulman, and S. Subrahmanyam. 1992. *Symbols of Substance*. Delhi: Oxford University Press.

Nisbett, Nicholas. 2007. "Friendship, Consumption, Morality: Practising Identity, Negotiating Hierarchy in Middle-Class Bangalore." *Journal of the Royal Anthropological Institute*, n.s., 13 (4): 935–950.

Nishimura, Yuko. 1994. "Marriage Payments among the Nagarattars in South India." *Contributions to Indian Sociology*, n.s., 28 (2): 243–272.

———. 1998. *Gender, Kinship, and Property Rights*. Delhi: Oxford University Press.

Offer, Avner. 1997. "Between the Gift and the Market: The Economy of Regard." *Economic History Review* 50 (3): 450–476.

———. 2006. *The Challenge of Affluence*. Oxford: Oxford University Press.

Ortner, Sherry L. 2003. *New Jersey Dreaming*. Durham, NC: Duke University Press.

Osella, Caroline. 2008. "Introduction." *South Asia* 31 (1): 1–9.

Osella, Filippo and Caroline Osella. 1996. "Articulation of Physical and Social Bodies in Kerala." *Contributions to Indian Sociology*, n.s., 30 (1): 37–68.

———. 1999. "From Transience to Immanence: Consumption, Life-Cycle and Social Mobility in Kerala, South India." *Modern Asian Studies* 33 (4): 989–1020.

Pal, Parthapratim and Jayati Ghosh. 2007. "Inequality in India: A Survey of Recent Trends." UN/DESA Working Paper No. 45.

Palanithurai, G. and Swati Sucharita Nanda, eds. 2007. *Voters Expectation and the Reasoning of Participation in Electoral Process*. New Delhi: Concept Publishing Company.

Palumbo-Liu, David. 1997. "Introduction: Unhabituated Habituses." In *Streams of Cultural Capital*, edited by David Palumbo-Liu and Hans Ulrich Gumbrecht, 1–21. Stanford, CA: Stanford University Press.

Pandian, Anand. 2005. "Securing the Rural Citizen: The Anti-Kallar Movement of 1896." *Indian Economic and Social History Review* 42 (1): 1–39.

———. 2009. *Crooked Stalks*. Durham, NC: Duke University Press.

Pandian, M.S.S. 1992. *The Image Trap*. New Delhi: Sage.

Parry, Jonathan. 1986. "The Gift, the Indian Gift, and the 'Indian Gift.'" *Man* 21 (3): 453–473.

———. 1989. "On the Moral Perils of Exchange." In *Money and the Morality of Exchange*, edited by Jonathan Parry and Maurice Bloch, 64–93. Cambridge: Cambridge University Press.

———. 2014. "Company and Contract Labour in a Central Indian Steel Plant." *Economy and Society* 42 (3): 348–374.

Paulraj, Rajamanickam. 1995. "A Theological Reappraisal of the Mission of the Christian Church in Tamilnadu in the Light of the Challenge Presented by the Dravida Kazhagam Movement (a Secular Humanistic Movement)." Ph.D. diss., University of Durham. Accessed October 10, 2013, http://etheses.dur.ac.uk/1033.

Peace, Adrian. 1984. "Constructions of Class, Images of Inequality: The Middle Class and the Urban Poor in a North Indian City." *Urban Anthropology* 13 (2/3): 261–294.

Peebles, Gustav. 2010. "The Anthropology of Credit and Debt." *Annual Review of Anthropology* 39: 225–240.

Pinney, Christopher. 2002. "The Indian Work of Art in the Age of Mechanical Reproduction: Or, What Happens When Peasants 'Get Hold' of Images." In *Media Worlds*, edited by Faye D. Ginsburg, Lila Abu-Lughod, and Brian Larkin, 355–369. Berkeley: University of California Press.

Pocock, David F. 1992. "The Evil Eye." In *Religion in India*, edited by T. N. Madan, 50–62. Delhi: Oxford University Press.

Portes, Alejandro. 1998. "Social Capital: Its Origins and Applications in Modern Sociology." *Annual Review of Sociology* 24: 1–24.

Prakash, Gyan. 2002. "The Urban Turn." *Sarai Reader 02*: 2–7.

Price, Pamela G. 1996a. *Kingship and Political Practice in Colonial India*. Cambridge: Cambridge University Press.

———. 1996b. "Revolution and Rank in Tamil Nationalism." *Journal of Asian Studies* 55 (2): 359–383.

———. 2006. "Changing Meanings of Authority in Contemporary Rural India." *Qualitative Sociology* 29 (3): 301–316.

———. 2013. "Raja-Dharma in Nineteenth-Century South India: Land, Litigation, and Largesse in Ramnad Zamindari." In *The Writings of Pamela Price*, 19–58. New Delhi: Orient BlackSwan.

Prieur, Annick and Mike Savage. 2011. "Updating Cultural Capital Theory: A Discussion Based on Studies in Denmark and in Britain." *Poetics* 39 (6): 566–580.

Qayum, Seemin and Raka Ray. 2011. "The Middle Classes at Home." In *Elite and Everyman*, edited by Amita Baviskar and Raka Ray, 246–270. London: Routledge.

Radhakrishnan, Smitha. 2011a. *Appropriately Indian*. Durham, NC: Duke University Press.

———. 2011b. "Gender, the IT Revolution, and the Making of a Middle-Class India." In *Elite and Everyman*, edited by Amita Baviskar and Raka Ray, 193–219. London: Routledge.

Raffles, Hugh. 2010. *Insectopedia*. New York: Pantheon.

Raheja, Gloria. 1988. *The Poison in the Gift*. Chicago: University of Chicago Press.

———. 1994. "On the Uses of Irony and Ambiguity: Shifting Perspectives on Patriliny and Women's Ties to Natal Kin." In *Listen to the Heron's Words*, edited by Gloria Goodwin Raheja and Ann Grodzins Gold, 73–120. Berkeley: University of California Press.

Rajagopal, Arvind. 2001. "Thinking About the New Indian Middle Class: Gender, Advertising, and Politics in an Age of Globalisation." In *Signposts: Gender Issues in Post-Independence India*, edited by Raji Sunder Rajan, 57–99. New Brunswick, NJ: Rutgers University Press.

Rajaraman, Indira. 1983. "Economics of Bride-Price and Dowry." *Economic and Political Weekly* 18 (8): 275–279.

Ram, Kalpana. 1992. *Mukkuvar Women*. New Delhi: Kali for Women.

———. 2009. "Modernity as a 'Rain of Words': Tracing the Flows of 'Rain' between Dalit Women and Intellectuals in Tamil Nadu." *Asian Studies Review* 33 (4): 501–516.

———. 2012. "How is Afflictive Possession 'Learned'? Gender and Motility in South India." *Ethnos* 77 (2): 203–226.

———. 2013. *Fertile Disorder*. Honolulu: University of Hawaii Press.

Ram, N. 1979. "Dravidian Movement in Its Pre-Independence Phases." *Economic and Political Weekly* 14 (7/8): 377–402.

Ramachandran, V. K. and Madhura Swaminathan. 2005a. "Financial Liberalization, Rural Credit, and Landless Labour Households: Evidence from a Tamil Nadu Village, 1977, 1985 and 1999." In *Financial Liberalization and Rural Credit in India*, edited by V. K. Ramachandran and Madhura Swaminathan, 157–177. New Delhi: Tulika Books.

———. 2005b. "Introduction." In *Financial Liberalization and Rural Credit in India*, edited by V. K. Ramachandran and Madhura Swaminathan, xxi–xliii. New Delhi: Tulika Books.

Raman, Srilata. 2013. "The Spaces in Between: Ramalinga Swamigal (1823–1874), Hunger, and Religion in Colonial India." *History of Religions* 53 (1): 1–27.

Ramanujan, A. K. 1992. "Food for Thought: Toward an Anthology of Food Images." In *The Eternal Food*, edited by R. S. Khare, 221–250. Albany: SUNY Press.

Ramesh, A., C. R. Srikumari, and S. Sukumar. 1989. "Parallel Cousin Marriages in Madras, Tamil Nadu: New Trends in Dravidian Kinship." *Social Biology* 36 (3/4): 248–254.

Rao, P.S.S. and S. G. Inbaraj. 1977. "Inbreeding in Tamil Nadu, South India." *Social Biology* 24 (4): 281–288.

Rao, Vijayendra. 1993. "The Rising Price of Husbands: A Hedonic Analysis of Dowry Increases in Rural India." *Journal of Political Economy* 101 (4): 666–677.

———. 2001a. "Celebrations as Social Investments: Festival Expenditures, Unit Price Variation, and Social Status in South India." *Journal of Development Studies* 38 (1): 71–97.

———. 2001b. "Poverty and Public Celebrations in Rural India." *Annals of the American Academy of Political and Social Science* 573: 85–104.

Rao, Vijayendra and Paromita Sanyal. 2010. "Dignity through Discourse: Poverty and the Culture of Deliberation in Indian Village Democracies." *Annals of the American Academy of Political and Social Science* 629: 146–172.

Rapp, Rayna. 1982. "Family and Class in Contemporary America: Notes Toward an Understanding of Ideology." In *Rethinking the Family*, edited by Barrie Thorne and Marilyn Yalom, 168–187. New York: Longman.

Ray, Raka and Seemin Qayum. 2009. *Cultures of Servitude*. Stanford, CA: Stanford University Press.

Ring, Laura A. 2006. *Zenana*. Bloomington: Indiana University Press.

Robinson, Jennifer. 2006. *Ordinary Cities*. London: Routledge.

Rogers, Martyn. 2008. "Modernity, 'Authenticity,' and Ambivalence: Subaltern Masculinities on a South Indian College Campus." *Journal of the Royal Anthropological Institute*, n.s., 14 (1): 79–95.

Roulet, Marguerite. 1996. "Dowry and Prestige in North India." *Contributions to Indian Sociology*, n.s., 30 (1): 89–107.

Roy, Tirthankar. 1997. "Capitalism and Community: A Study of the Madurai Sourashtras." *Indian Economic and Political History* 34 (4): 437–463.

———. 2004. "Flourishing Branches, Wilting Core: Research in Modern Indian Economic History." *Australian Economic History Review* 44 (3): 221–240.

Rudner, David West. 1987. "Religious Gifting and Inland Commerce in Seventeenth-Century South India." *Journal of Asian Studies* 46 (2): 361–379.

———. 1989. "Banker's Trust and the Culture of Banking among the Nattukottai Chettiars of Colonial India." *Modern Asian Studies* 23 (3): 417–458.

———. 1994. *Caste and Capitalism in Colonial India*. Berkeley: University of California Press.

Rutherford, Stuart. 2006. "A Critical Typology of Financial Services for the Poor." Accessed February 5, 2015, http://media.microfinancelessons.com/resources/Critical_Typology_Section1.pdf.

Rutherford, Stuart. 2009. *The Poor and Their Money*. 2nd ed. With Sukhwinder Arora. Warwickshire: Practical Action Publishing.

Säävälä, Minna. 2001. "Low Caste but Middle-Class: Some Religious Strategies for Middle-Class Identification in Hyderabad." *Contributions to Indian Sociology*, n.s., 35 (3): 293–318.

———. 2010. *Middle-Class Moralities*. Delhi: Orient BlackSwan.

Samartha, S. J. 1982. "Indian Realities and the Wholeness of Christ." *Missiology* 10 (3): 301–317.

Sarkar, Sumit. 1997. "The Decline of the Subaltern in *Subaltern Studies*." In *Writing Social History*, 82–108. Delhi: Oxford University Press.

Sayer, Andrew. 1999. "Bourdieu, Smith, and Disinterested Judgement." *Sociological Review* 47 (3): 403–431.

———. 2005a. "Class, Moral Worth and Recognition." *Sociology* 39 (5): 947–963.

———. 2005b. *The Moral Significance of Class*. Cambridge: Cambridge University Press.

———. 2007. "Dignity at Work: Broadening the Agenda." *Organization* 14 (4): 565–581.

Schaber, Peter. 2011. "Absolute Poverty: Human Dignity, Self-Respect, and Dependency." In *Humiliation, Degradation, Dehumanization: Human Dignity Violated*, edited by

Paulus Kaufmann, Hannes Kuch, Christian Neuhäeuser, and Elaine Webster, 151–158. New York: Springer.

Scherl, Richard. 1996. "Speaking with Mariyātai: A Linguistic and Cultural Analysis of Markers of Plurality in Tamil, Vol. 1." Ph.D. diss., University of Chicago.

Schrader, Heiko. 1992. "The Socioeconomic Function of Moneylenders in Expanding Economies: The Case of the Chettiars." *Savings and Development* 16 (1): 69–82.

Schwalbe, Michael, Sandra Godwin, Daphne Holden, Douglas Schrock, Shealy Thompson, and Michele Wolkomir. 2000. "Generic Processes in the Reproduction of Inequality: An Interactionist Analysis." *Social Forces* 79 (2): 419–452.

Seizer, Susan. 2005. *Stigmas of the Tamil Stage.* Durham, NC: Duke University Press.

Selwyn, Tom. 1980. "The Order of Men and the Order of Things: An Examination of Food Transactions in an Indian Village." *International Journal of the Sociology of Law* 8 (3): 297–317.

Sennett, Richard and Jonathan Cobb. 1972. *The Hidden Injuries of Class.* New York: Vintage.

Shah, Ghanshyam. 1987. "Middle-Class Politics: Case of Anti-Reservation Agitations in Gujarat." *Economic and Political Weekly* 22 (19–21): AN155–AN172.

Shah, Mihir, Rangu Rao, and P. S. Vijay Shankar. 2007. "Rural Credit in 20th Century India: Overview of History and Perspectives." *Economic and Political Weekly* 42 (15): 1351–1364.

Shenk, Mary K. 2005. "Kin Investment in Wage-Labor Economies: Effects on Child and Marriage Market Outcomes." *Human Nature* 16 (1): 81–114.

Shukla, Rajesh. 2010. *How India Earns, Spends, and Saves.* New Delhi: Sage.

Shulman, David Dean. 1980. "On South Indian Bandits and Kings." *Indian Economic and Social History Review* 17 (3): 283–306.

Skuse, Andrew. 2005. "Enlivened Objects: The Social Life, Death, and Rebirth of Radio as Commodity in Afghanistan." *Journal of Material Culture* 10 (2): 123–137.

Smart, Alan. 1993. "Gifts, Bribes, and *Guanxi*: Reconsideration of Bourdieu's Capital." *Cultural Anthropology* 8 (3): 388–408.

Smith, Adam. 1976 [1759]. *The Theory of Moral Sentiments.* Edited by D. D. Raphael and A. L. Macfie. Oxford: Clarendon.

Sridharan, E. 2004. "The Growth and Sectoral Composition of India's Middle Class: Its Impact on the Politics of Economic Liberalization." *India Review* 3 (4): 405–428.

———. 2008. "The Political Economy of the Middle Classes in Liberalising India." Working paper, Institute of South Asian Studies, National University of Singapore.

Srinivas, Lakshmi. 2010. "Cinema Halls, Locality, and Urban Life." *Ethnography* 11 (1): 189–205.

Srinivas, M. N. 1962. *Caste in Modern India and Other Essays.* Bombay: Asia.

———. 1976. *The Remembered Village*. New Delhi: Oxford University Press.

———. 1984. *Some Reflections on Dowry*. Delhi: Oxford University Press.

———. 1989. *The Cohesive Role of Sanskritisation and Other Essays*. Oxford: Oxford University Press.

Srinivas, Tulasi. 2002. "Flush with Success: Bathing, Defecation, Worship, and Social Change in South India." *Space and Culture* 5 (4): 368–386.

Srinivasan, Mytheli. 2003. "Emotion, Identity, and the Female Subject: Tamil Women's Magazines in Colonial India, 1890–1940." *Journal of Women's History* 14 (4): 59–82.

Srinivasan, Sharada. 2005. "Daughters or Dowries? The Changing Nature of Dowry Practices in South India." *World Development* 33 (4): 593–615.

Srivastava, Sanjay. 2011. "Urban Spaces, Disney-divinity and the Moral Middle Classes in Delhi." In *Elite and Everyman*, edited by Amita Baviskar and Raka Ray, 364–390. London: Routledge.

———. 2015. *Entangled Urbanism*. New Delhi: Oxford University Press.

Staples, James. 2003. "Disguise, Revelation, and Copyright: Disassembling the South Indian Leper." *Journal of the Royal Anthropological Institute*, n.s., 9 (2): 295–315.

Subrahmanyam, Sanjay. 1990. *The Political Economy of Commerce*. Cambridge: Cambridge University Press.

Taguchi, Yoko. 2013. "Civic Sense and Cleanliness: Pedagogy and Aesthetics in Middle-Class Mumbai Activism." *Contemporary South Asia* 21 (2): 89–101.

Tamil Nadu Government. 2003. "Prohibition of Charging Exorbitant Interest Act." *Tamil Nadu Government Gazette Extraordinary*, 171–172.

Taylor, Charles. 1994. "The Politics of Recognition." In *Multi-Culturalism*, edited by Amy Gutmann, 25–73. Princeton: Princeton University Press.

Tenhunen, Sirpa. 2014. "Mobile Telephony, Mediation, and Gender in Rural India." *Contemporary South Asia* 22 (2): 157–170.

Thiruchendran, Selvy. 1997. *Ideology, Caste, Class, and Gender*. New Delhi: Vikas.

Thompson, E. P. 1963. *The Making of the English Working Class*. London: Victor Gollancz.

Thorner, Alice. 1982. "Semi-Feudalism or Capitalism? Contemporary Debate on Classes and Modes of Production in India." *Economic and Political Weekly* 17 (49): 1961–1968; 17 (50): 1993–1998; 17 (51): 2061–2066.

Thornton, Sarah. 1996. *Club Cultures*. Middletown, CT: Wesleyan University Press.

Throop, C. Jason and Keith M. Murphy. 2002. "Bourdieu and Phenomenology: A Critical Assessment." *Anthropological Theory* 2 (2): 185–207.

Tilly, Charles. 1998. *Durable Inequality*. Berkeley: University of California Press.

———. 2001. "Relational Origins of Inequality." *Anthropological Theory* 1 (3): 355–372.

Tolen, Rachel. 2000. "Transfers of Knowledge and Privileged Spheres of Practice: Servants and Employers in a Madras Railway Colony." In *Home and Hegemony*, edited by Kathleen M. Adams and Sara Dickey, 63–86. Ann Arbor: University of Michigan Press.

TRAI (Telecom Regulatory Authority of India). 2015. "The Indian Telecom Services Performance Indicators January–March, 2015." Accessed 25 August 2015, http://trai .gov.in/WriteReadData/PIRReport/Documents/Indicator-Reports-Mar12082015.pdf.

Trautmann, Thomas R. 1981. *Dravidian Kinship*. Cambridge: Cambridge University Press.

Trawick, Margaret. 1990. *Notes on Love in a Tamil Family*. Berkeley: University of California Press.

Turner, Victor. 1984. "Liminality and the Performative Genres." In *Rite, Drama, Festival, Spectacle*, edited by John J. MacAloon, 19–41. Philadelphia: ISHI.

Uberoi, Patricia. 2006. *Freedom and Destiny*. New Delhi: Oxford University Press.

———. 2008. "Aspirational Weddings: The Bridal Magazine and the Canons of 'Decent Marriage.'" In *Patterns of Middle Class Consumption in India and China*, edited by Christophe Jaffrelot and Peter van der Veer, 230–262. New Delhi: Sage.

Upadhya, Carol Boyack. 1990. "Dowry and Women's Property in Coastal Andhra Pradesh." *Contributions to Indian Sociology*, n.s., 24 (1): 29–59.

———. 2011. "Software and the 'New' Middle Class in the 'New India.'" In *Elite and Everyman*, edited by Amita Baviskar and Raka Ray, 167–192. London: Routledge.

Vanaik, Achin. 2002. "Consumerism and New Classes in India." In *Thinking Social Science in India*, edited by Sujata Patel, Jasodhara Bagchi, and Krishna Raj, 227–234. New Delhi: Sage.

van Hollen, Cecilia. 2003. *Birth on the Threshold*. Berkeley: University of California Press.

van Wessel, Margit. 2004. "Talking about Consumption: How an Indian Middle Class Dissociates from Middle-Class Life." *Cultural Dynamics* 16 (1): 93–116.

Varshney, Ashutosh. 2000. "Is India Becoming More Democratic?" *Journal of Asian Studies* 59 (1): 3–25.

Venkatachalapathy, A. R. 2006. *In Those Days There Was No Coffee*. New Delhi: Yoda.

Vijayabaskar M., Padmini Swaminathan, Anandhi S., and Gayatri Balagopal. 2004. "Human Development in Tamil Nadu: Examining Linkages." *Economic and Political Weekly* 39 (8): 797–802.

Vivek, S. 2014. *Delivering Public Services Effectively: Tamil Nadu and Beyond*. New Delhi: Oxford University Press.

Wacquant, Loïc. 2008. "Pierre Bourdieu." In *Key Sociological Thinkers*, 2nd ed., edited by Rob Stones, 261–276. New York: Palgrave Macmillan.

Waheed, Abdul. 2009. "Dowry among Indian Muslims: Ideals and Practices." *Journal of Gender Studies* 16 (1): 47–75.

Waldrop, Anne. 2004. "Gating and Class Relations: The Case of a New Delhi 'Colony.'" *City & Society* 16 (2): 93–116.

———. 2012. "Grandmother, Mother, and Daughter: Changing Agency of Indian, Middle-Class Women, 1908–2008." *Modern Asian Studies* 46 (3): 601–638.

Warrell, Lindy. 1990. "Conflict and Hierarchy: Jealousy among the Sinhalese Buddhists." *South Asia* 13 (1): 19–41.

Washbrook, D. A. 1989. "Caste, Class, and Dominance in Modern Tamil Nadu: Non-Brahmanism, Dravidianism and Tamil Nationalism." In *Dominance and State Power in Modern India*, edited by Francine R. Frankel and M.S.A. Rao, 204–264. Delhi: Oxford University Press.

———. 2006. "Colonialism, Globalization, and the Economy of South-East India, c. 1700–1900." Working Papers of the Global Economic History Network (GEHN) 24–06.

———. 2010. "Merchants, Markets, and Commerce in Early Modern South India." *Journal of the Economic and Social History of the Orient* 53 (1/2): 266–289.

Wilson, Nicole A. 2013. "Confrontation and Compromise: Middle-Class Matchmaking in Twenty-First-Century South India." *Asian Ethnology* 72 (1): 33–53.

Wood, Geof. 2003. "Staying Secure, Staying Poor: The 'Faustian Bargain.'" *World Development* 31 (3): 455–471.

Woodward, Sophie. 2005. "Looking Good: Feeling Right—Aesthetics of the Self." In *Clothing as Material Culture*, edited by Susan Küchler and Daniel Miller, 21–40. Oxford: Berg.

World Bank. 2008a. "India at a Glance." Accessed October 19, 2008, http://devdata.worldbank.org/AAG/ind_aag.pdf.

———. 2008b. "India, Development Indicators." Accessed October 19, 2008, http://ddp-ext.worldbank.org/ext/ddpreports/ViewSharedReport?REPORT_ID=9147&REQUEST_TYPE=VIEWADVANCED&WSP=N&HF=N/CPProfile.asp.

Young, Stephen. 2010. "The 'Moral Hazards' of Microfinance: Restructuring Rural Credit in India." *Antipode* 42 (1): 201–223.

Index

About the Author

SARA DICKEY is a professor of anthropology at Bowdoin College. In addition to carrying out research on class identities and relations in urban South India, she has studied the production, consumption, and circulation of Tamil cinema, and the roles of cinema and fan clubs in state politics.

CPSIA information can be obtained
at www.ICGtesting.com
Printed in the USA
LVOW13s2334300718
585377LV00017B/270/P

9 780813 583914